FRANCIS

A POPE FOR OUR TIME

The Definitive Biography

FRANCIS

A POPE FOR OUR TIME

The Definitive Biography

by Luis Rosales and Daniel Olivera

Humanix Books
www.humanixbooks.com
Boca Raton, FL, USA

Francis: A Pope for Our Time
© 2013 Humanix Books

Humanix Books
P.O. Box 20989
West Palm Beach, FL 33416
USA
www.humanixbooks.com
email: info@humanixbooks.com

Humanix Books is a division of Humanix Publishing LLC. Its trademark, consisting of the words "Humanix Books" is registered in the U.S. Patent and Trademark Office and in other countries.

Photo credit: Dan Kirtwood/Getty Images.

Printed in the United States of America and the United Kingdom.

ISBN (Hardcover) 978-1-63006-002-2
ISBN (E-book) 978-1-63006-005-3

Library of Congress Control Number 2013941319

To my mother, who was with me until the end. To the memory of my father. To María de los Ángeles, Ariel, Ignacio, Marcos, and Martín. And to the Olivera, Miranda, López-Maurizzi, and Belloni families.

— *Daniel Olivera*

To my parents, my sister, and my nephews, for their constant support; to my Buenos Aires and Mendoza friends; to Marcelo Giugale, Javier Pose, and Nicolás Pasaman, for their invaluable contributions.

— *Luis Rosales*

Contents

Preface ix

Introduction xi

PART ONE: THE MAN

Chapter 1
The First Miracle of Pope Francis 3

Chapter 2
It Takes a Village 19

Chapter 3
Bearing Witness 29

Chapter 4
The Man of God 35

Chapter 5
A Church for the Poor 51

Chapter 6
Politics and Faith: Two Roads 67

Chapter 7
The Price of Power 85

PART TWO: DOCTRINE AND CHALLENGES

Chapter 8
Saint Francis of Assisi 107

Chapter 9
Poverty 123

Chapter 10
Ecumenism and Interfaith Dialogue 135

Chapter 11
The New Challenges 153

Chapter 12
Spotlight on Latin America 167

Chapter 13
A Pope from the End of the Earth 183

Endnotes 197

Bibliography 203

Index 209

Preface

FOR TWO ARGENTINE journalists, as are both authors of this book, to write and tell the world about Pope Francis is like describing a part of ourselves. We approached it in two parts. The first, by Daniel Olivera, describes the man and his life; the second, by Luis Rosales, focuses on his doctrine and the challenges that lie ahead.

Humanix Books called upon us precisely given these two conditions: our profession and our nationality. As social commentators, the "Pope mania" that broke out in Argentina as a consequence of his election is an especially interesting phenomenon for us to observe, and it will probably create an impact that will last a long time. The news coverage of Francis' almost surprise ascent to Peter's Throne, as well as the enormous amount of attention paid to his every action and gesture, are just a prelude to an influence that will become much more than just a passing fad. We belong to a global society, interconnected and instant — a world in crisis where ideologies are exhaustively discussed and yet where people's attention barely lasts as long as a TV segment, a few messages on a social network, or a few minutes on a website. That is why the possibility of the renewal and strengthening of a stable and permanent institution such as the Catholic Church is at the very least an interesting subject to analyze — even more so if the new leadership in Rome is willing to question, from its own standpoint, the practices, customs, and traditions of one of the world's most influential organizations.

Introduction

THE CATHOLIC CHURCH is going through a profound crisis. Beyond internal institutional and doctrinal struggles, it is also faced with the strong and growing tendency of people today to distance themselves from spirituality. Advancements in science and technology have embedded the idea of godlessness in society, without considering how these formidable achievements of modern life can help lead to a more transcendent objective. Hence, Pope Francis' arrival is deeply moving and emotional to a community in dire need of direction and spiritual renewal. His humility and simplicity, combined with his proven political prowess and his ability to communicate, create reason to hope that the Vatican will change its course after years of abandoning the essence of Christ's teachings and path.

Many hope Francis will be a dogmatic reformer and that he will "modernize" the institution over which he presides, following the pulse of public opinion. But these hopes are the antithesis of Francis' philosophy. He strongly believes, and has shown it throughout his pastoral life, that following the changing winds of public opinion is unnecessary in order to be influential or successful. He knows his role is more analogous to that of a lighthouse that must signal the presence of cliffs and dangers, especially during stormy nights, pointing out the boundaries where mankind seriously risks losing sight of its own meaning and reason for existence.

Conservative and strict when it comes to the dogmatic and an almost irreverent reformer when it comes to the symbolic, Francis promises to leave his mark.

His name choice — Francis — defines his path. Invoking the wisdom, discipline, and politics of the Jesuit order, it stands at the intersection where piety, dialogue, and Franciscan humility meet. Without altering the essence of faith's doctrines, his personal stamp and life example will cause a profound renaissance in the Church's practices and internal life, which have strayed considerably from Christ's original mandate to Peter. Ending the constant intrigue and destructive bureaucracy governing from the Vatican's palaces will be no easy task. It never has been easy, but during these last few years, the distortions have reached a point comparable to the worst of times, when the Pope was more akin to a ruler, with power, authority, and even armies. There will likely be much resistance, but choosing a man from the order created by Saint Ignatius of Loyola seems like the right path. It is perhaps a paradox of destiny that the so-called, first "Black Pope" (referring to the black garb of the Jesuit order) has been chosen to maintain the pristine, white vestment that symbolizes Peter's successor.

Francis will have to bring transparency to the Vatican's financial management, not only to push away doubts and suspicions, but also to clean up the coffers and be able to plan for future pastoral and charitable work. But that will only be the beginning, as his impact will be felt beyond the walls that surround Vatican City. The Catholic Church, with its 1.2 billion believers (almost 17 percent of humankind), constitutes the biggest religious organization in the world. In addition, it is the Christian family's core. Together with the eastern churches (divided in the schism of 1054) and the Protestant diaspora (a product of sixteenth-century reform), it represents the beliefs of more than a third of the people on the planet. Yet the divisions between the various branches of Christianity remain as entrenched as ever.

As a cardinal, Francis demonstrated in infinite instances that he is open to dialogue and meetings, and as the current Pope, unity and consensus remain key words in his lexicon and thoughts. His humble introduction to the world stage — emphasizing his role as Rome's bishop rather than highlighting the pomp of the Papacy — was not only a transcendent gesture, but almost an essential condition as he attempts to unify the Catholic Church, its followers, and fellow members of the Christian faith.

But his calling to unite goes even beyond this. While in Buenos Aires, he was in constant dialogue with representatives of other creeds, especially Judaism and Islam. A common enemy threatens all of them. The apparent triumph of Nietzsche's idea that "God is dead" is clearly manifest in the fact that millions of people live and die without even questioning who created them or why. That is why an interreligious dialogue will be an important issue for Francis, as it always has been.

Leading by example with his life, his gestures, and his thoughts, Francis' work with the poor demonstrates firsthand our collective obligation to help, genuinely and without assumption, those who are in need. His spiritual ancestors — Saint Francis of Assisi and the Piedmontese saints, Don Bosco, Don Cafasso, and Don Orione —illustrated a path he has always followed: to help in times of crisis and bestow the tools for betterment upon those in need, distributing fish to satisfy hunger, while also teaching how to fish.

As his fellow countrymen, Francis' election gives us a profound sense of joy and pride. It is a happiness shared with all Latin Americans and residents of other regions of the underdeveloped world, who regard him as a symbol of their struggle and triumph in the face of adversity. We look to his papacy as an opportunity — harnessing one of the most influential, spiritual positions in the history of humankind — to demonstrate our collective tenacity and resolve.

And yet, Western values subverted by perpetual crisis, suffering, and injustice represent a dichotomy that is especially evident in Argentina. Francis, as with all middle-class Argentines, has one foot in each world. By way of heritage, culture, and blood, he is the son of a cultured and abundant Europe. Yet through his pastoral work, he understands the poor and disenfranchised people of the earth as well as anyone. It is precisely this balance that is essential to extracting transcendental meaning from a world that may so often seem arbitrary and unjust.

The energy and passion we dedicate to everything in this region is already being felt from Saint Peter's Basilica—strength to denounce injustice but also strength to suggest solutions, and ingenuity to resolve situations that sometimes may appear to be hopeless. That is also why we are proud, due to the contribution we can make from the world's periphery, precisely now that the center is in trouble. We must take advantage of this opportunity for so many millions of silenced voices to be heard — those who simply dream of a better future for themselves and their children. In short, this is about collaborating from an exceptional place, with Francis' example and life, in the construction of a world that, in peace and harmony, manages to integrate and embrace all of its residents.

PART ONE

The Man

Chapter 1

The First Miracle of Pope Francis

Francis' first miracle occurred six years before he came into this world. This story, fraught with symbolism that only time could help reveal, began in 1928 in a small Piedmont town, in an Italy where its selfless and hardworking people fought to evolve from a quiet and humble rural life into a more complex world of modernization and industrialization. It took place, more precisely, in Portacomaro — a tiny village that by the 1920s was home to some 2700 residents.

Within this context and during that time, Rosa Margarita Vasallo de Bergoglio (known in Italy as Rosa Margherita Vasallo) became determined to fight for her lineage and her progeny in a changing world that she increasingly viewed as uncertain and dangerous.

News in Portacomaro, as in every Italian town, traveled quickly even a century prior to the Internet's existence. Everyone knew that Italy had dangerously veered toward totalitarianism. By 1919, a charismatic yet brutal character had started to gain notice when he created an armed political group, which he called the "Fasci Italiani di Combattimento." It was none other than Benito Mussolini, who, with notoriously violent methods, unceremoniously battled socialist, communist, and anarchist activists.

Backed by a formidable force of men who would not hesitate to beat or kill a political opponent, Mussolini managed to secure a position as a member of the Italian Parliament in 1921. A year later, with a praetorian guard of more than thirty thousand militia befittingly known as "Blackshirts" (Camicie Nere), he took Rome by storm — the capital of what had once been the most powerful empire of ancient times. In the face of such brute force, King Victor Emmanuel III, the last symbol of the Italian establishment that sought to become a democratic republic, was forced to surrender. From that day forward, the world would come to know Mussolini as "Il Duce" (the leader). And the fascist ideology he shaped by promising to fight communism to the death would later become the serpent's egg where Adolph Hitler's National Socialism nested.

Rosa felt a stabbing pain in her chest at the thought of what was to come, although her town had yet to receive news of the political tsunami that had hit the other side of the Alps in Germany and Austria. Rosa and her husband, Juan Bergoglio (known in Italy as Giovanni), were oblivious to the existence of a former corporal in the German Army, a veteran of World War I, who, in 1923, had organized a Mussolini-style coup d'état in Bavaria, but had failed and had hence been jailed for four years. They were also unaware that this paranoid and messianic man, who called himself "Führer" (or again, leader), used his time in Landsberg Prison to write the main outline to *Mein Kampf*, a treatise on his political philosophy. Within those first drafts was a summary of his demented scheme — one that ended the lives of more than sixty million human beings. It held Germany's plot for resurrection following the perceived injustices of the 1919 Treaty of Versailles, the plan to annihilate Marxism, the concept of the National Socialist state, the techniques of the Nazi Party's propaganda machine, and the vision of Germany's rise to the peak of world power.

While Hitler wrote his blueprint for nationalism and war in prison, and Il Duce began to plot the invasion of the Abyssinian African territories (present-day Ethiopia) in a wild attempt to restore the old Roman Empire, Rosa instinctively sensed it was time for her branch of the Bergoglios to flee to the Americas, the promised land for those who sought peace, bread, and work. Rosa's three brothers-in-law had done just that, establishing themselves in 1922 in the small Argentine province of Entre Ríos. They had most definitely achieved success in the New World by creating a business focused on paving the inhospitable roads of the remote towns of central Argentina, and with savings and determination, they had accumulated considerable wealth — so much so that they built a Belle Époque mansion known as the Bergoglio Palace. Given the time and place, the mansion was considered lavish. It had four floors and a heavy, noisy contraption called an elevator, which fascinated the neighbors, who observed in awe as it went up and down.

If her brothers-in-law had managed to establish their fate in such little time, reasoned Rosa, why couldn't she and her family do the same? So the Portacomaro Bergoglios, the ones who sold the best jams and beverages from their pastry shop in town, began to plan a course of action. America gave them, as it did many other Italians and Europeans of those times, hope for a future of honest work and freedom from the political turmoil engulfing Europe in the years between the wars.

With an extraordinary inner strength, Rosa designed a roadmap to the New World — a detailed course with many miles of road to conquer, questions to be answered, and fears to be overcome. But she was determined to make it to the land that promised a fortunate future, absent of wars and full of prosperity. The only dilemma — which the majority of her countrymen had also faced — was whether to choose the United States of America or the harbor at the end of the world in mysterious Buenos Aires.

Two out of three European immigrants chose North America. New York, Chicago, and Boston in particular had assimilated many of Rosa's countrymen. Since the end of the nineteenth century, Italians, most with humble backgrounds and lacking even basic English-language skills, congregated in what became known as "Little Italy" neighborhoods in the major cities of the United States. They also brought with them their Christian devotion, strengthening Catholicism in a Protestant land.

Why then did Rosa, one afternoon, decide to give her life savings to a prestigious New World travel agency in exchange for steamship tickets that granted the Bergoglio clan passage from Genoa to Buenos Aires? Why not head to New York?

That was the first existential dilemma that the Bergoglios had to resolve. And that conflict's resolution became the first miracle performed by Francis.

Ten years prior to his birth, toward the end of the 1920s, his grandmother Rosa had determined that the promised land would be Argentina. They would set sail for a harbor that had already received almost 6.5 million immigrants between 1870 and the Bergoglios' 1929 departure.

Cosmopolitan and feverish, in those days Buenos Aires was the South American city that most resembled New York. It had the first subway in Latin America, built in 1914, and the highest literacy rate on the continent — a multiethnic and multicultural hybrid as rich and varied as the Big Apple itself.

The transoceanic travel business for immigrants was booming. Over those sixty years, ocean liners that transported Italians, Spaniards, Swiss,

Germans, Bulgarians, Poles, Ukrainians — every and all European eth-
nicity — had reduced the voyage from an average of fifty days to Buenos
Aires down to thirteen, and even less with fair weather. The cleanliness and
security conditions of the ships were noticeably improved, and the ticket
cost was dramatically lower than in years' past. However, such opportunity
was still not within everyone's reach.

It was here that Rosa Bergoglio made a pivotal decision: she chose to
spend her last lira of savings to buy second-class tickets for her family.
Such an example would make a profound impression on the spirit of Mario
José Francisco (born Mario Giuseppe Francesco) — Francis' father, Rosa's
son, and the first of the Bergoglio family to be named after the patron saint
of Assisi. The Bergoglios' practical nature dictated that they spend only
as needed — no room for waste or frivolity. This time, however, the family acquired more expensive tickets that would secure a journey typically
reserved for well-off businessmen, small landowners, and clergy members.
The "common people" traveled in third class, but Rosa had no intention of
sharing that fate. For her, it wasn't a question of social belonging or boarding under false pretenses; it was a strategy.

On the legendary ocean liners of that era, social classes were so obvious that there was no need for introductions or rituals to understand
them. On the westward journey were the rich Argentines returning to
the nation of their birth, and along with wealthy French, Spaniard, and
Brazilian passengers, they enjoyed the comforts of luxury travel and
were the first to disembark the massive steamer that had shuttled them
from continent to continent. Also aboard were people of respectable but
more modest incomes, the doctors, the officers, and the priests traveling in second class. And then came the wrinkled clothing and familiar
shouts of the humble — those who left nothing behind because they no
longer had anything.

Everyone traveled on the same ship, but they experienced very different
journeys. They were on parallel paths that brushed each other by chance
but in reality were separated by an insurmountable social abyss. During
the voyage, first- and second-class passengers were rigorously "protected"
from third-class incursions, while they were allowed to invade the third-
class area with little risk and otherwise enjoy the comforts and privileges
of their more expensive accommodations.

Argentine law stated that an immigrant was a person who arrived by
steamboat or sailboat, in second or third class, who was less than sixty

years of age, and free from physical defects or illnesses. Fitting such a description as easily in second class as she would have in third, Rosa Bergoglio proudly embraced her new title in the world.

By October 1927, with tickets in hand, Rosa's determination and steely level-headedness had finally paid off. And that's when the miracle occurred.

The Bergoglio family was due to set sail on the infamous *Principessa Mafalda* — the most impressive ocean liner constructed in Italy to date, and the only vessel capable of connecting the Genoa harbor with Argentina in only fourteen days, an astonishing record for the maritime routes of the time. Built in 1908 and launched in Naples in April 1909, on October 25, 1927 the *Mafalda* was setting sail on its ninetieth voyage.

At 9,200 tons, 465 feet long, and 55 feet wide, the awe-inspiring *Mafalda* was destined to cover the Genoa-Barcelona-Rio de Janeiro-Montevideo-Buenos Aires itinerary. One of the fastest ships of its time, it was the first luxury steamship to connect the Rio de la Plata and Mediterranean coasts. After its inaugural voyage, it became the favorite vessel of wealthy Argentine, Uruguayan, and Brazilian families who traveled to Europe, and a consistent carrier of thousands of immigrants, such as the Bergoglios, on its return journeys.

Only one piece of Rosa's plan failed. The fear of fascism's expansion in Italy and the almost certain possibility of another world war struck deep in the heart of Portacomaro. For the first time in its history, the citizens of this Piedmontese town began a massive emigration, and more than 15 percent of the Portacomaresi rushed to sell their houses and lands. Such an exodus caused a setback in the small real estate market, dragging home prices down and crushing property values.

The difficulties were escalating, but so was Rosa's determination. She had decided to leave, and economic circumstances were not going to stop her. But Rosa and José's house had been on the market for a year, with no offers. They were also unable to find a buyer for their pastry shop, the place that for many years had afforded them a living. Without those thousands of liras, the Bergoglios would be unable to reach and set roots in Buenos Aires, New York, or any other place in the world.

She went over her calculations again and again. The more she added and subtracted, the more she confirmed the same thing: the financial situation was dire. All of their savings was invested in their tickets, but as the day of their departure approached, she knew she couldn't leave without selling her house.

Fate persisted; no buyers for their house emerged, and on the morning of October 11, 1927, their scheduled departure date, Rosa felt her hopes escape through a hole in her heart. Feeling helpless and resigned, she watched the *Principessa Mafalda* depart the Genoa harbor with no Bergoglios aboard.

Despite Rosa's fighting spirit and unbreakable will, the disappointment was immense. Yet the story does not end here — almost ninety years later, she would reside in the annals of history as the grandmother of Francis, the first Latin American Pope in the two-thousand-year existence of the Roman Catholic Church.

That day, Rosa considered giving up. All her strength faltered. With great effort, she only managed to get the travel agency to half-heartedly agree to rebook her tickets. She knew that her passport to the New World rested solely on the sale of her home. She couldn't allow the sea to swallow her savings with the same voracity that fate was determined to consume her dreams of prosperity.

The anguish of those "lost" hours and days would inevitably remain woven into the very fabric of the Bergoglios'. Each conversation, each family memory, would be redirected to that first failed journey. Rosa, Juan, and their family yearned for each and every one of those fifteen days of that idealized trip on the *Mafalda*.

None of them could have imagined, not even in their wildest dreams, what would come to be on the tragic night of October 25, 1927, in the Atlantic Ocean waters off the Brazilian coast, while Rosa, her husband, and her son slept in their warm and unsellable home in Portacomaro.

This story occurred at sea and it deserves to be told at length. If God's hand hadn't touched Rosa and prevented the sale of their home and pastry shop in Portacomaro, the Bergoglios' fate would have been cut short, and the Church's fate forever altered.

As always, God writes straight on crooked lines.

On the morning of October 11, 1927, the captain of the *Principessa Mafalda* was preparing for the journey, set to depart at noon, with some worry — the great ship's engines were misbehaving, and the arrangements for the planned itinerary were far from settled. At one point, the maritime company itself considered canceling the trip. They believed they could use the limited first-class ticket sales as a good excuse to kindly suggest that the luxury cabin passengers transfer to the *Giulio Cesare*, another enormous ship that was about to set sail to Buenos Aires.

The powerful Brazilian Da Cunha family did not hesitate: they canceled their *Mafalda* tickets and transferred to the other vessel. Other passengers did the same and proceeded to remove their huge leather suitcases from the ship.

Luis Felipe Mayol, an Argentine traveler, stubbornly refused to change his route. He had traveled many times on the *Mafalda*, felt very comfortable with its seaworthiness, and did not see any reason why he should change his mind, apart from the nervous chatter of some of his fellow travelers.

Whether due to the pressure mounted by that first-class passenger, or other reasons yet to be determined, the ship nonetheless prepared to depart. They took advantage of the opportunity to load a heavily guarded shipment of 250,000 gold liras, sent to Argentina by the Italian government. How important was the departure of this valuable cargo for the captain to ignore the unsettling nature of the morning's events? The answer to this question was lost with the *Mafalda* itself.

So, on the morning of their departure, sixty-two first-class passengers climbed the gangplank — five of them were going to Rio de Janeiro, sixteen were en route to the Brazilian harbor of Santos, close to Sao Paulo, and forty-one were disembarking in Buenos Aires. Eighty-three passengers occupied the second-class cabins — ten to Rio de Janeiro, twenty to Santos, and fifty-three to Buenos Aires. In addition, there were 828 restless and noisy third-class passengers, almost all immigrants, many with one-way tickets to Buenos Aires; others belonged to the *peones golondrina*, the "swallow" workers who arrived to earn some money harvesting crops (work that was starting to become scarce in Europe) and return home.

On top of these 973 passengers, there were 288 crewmembers, amounting to 1,261 people aboard the *Principessa Mafalda*.

The original noon departure time on October 11 came and went. Using various excuses, the officers calmed the passengers' impatience, while in the ship's innards an army of mechanics worked feverishly to finish prepping the engines, which seemed to resist all repair. The ship company decided that this would be *Mafalda's* last trip at sea. Its machinery, which at one point had been cutting edge, had simply become obsolete.

Finally, under a calm 6 p.m. sunset, after a six-hour delay, the steamer set sail. The *Mafalda* left Genoa behind, and proudly headed for Buenos Aires.

The captain had orders to sail at a regular cruise speed, despite the ship's poor condition. And, naturally, the journey went downhill as soon as they lost sight of the Ligurian coast. They were late arriving in Barcelona and were forced to remain there for twenty-four hours to fix a pump.

When it embarked from Spain, the *Mafalda* was displaying disconcerting symptoms. The ship's vibrations were abnormal and so intense that they constantly bothered the unlucky port-side passengers. The trip was on the verge of becoming a complete disaster.

Out into the Atlantic, two days away from Gibraltar, the port engine broke down. The captain ordered the ship to stop, and while they searched for a solution, the boat drifted for six hours, like a gigantic buoy lost at sea. The repairs did not succeed, and so the *Mafalda* continued its journey for one full day with just one engine, slightly keeled over to the port side.

The exasperating situation forced the captain to change the itinerary. Instead of heading to Dakar on the West African coast, he aimed the boat to the harbor at São Vicente, one of the islands of Cape Verde. The distressed passengers were told that the change of course was due to the need to load coal, but many understood that this was just an excuse and that something was terribly off in the heart of the *Mafalda*.

After temporary fixes were made on São Vicente, the ship finally began its main Atlantic crossing for the Brazilian coast. But the problems persisted. The vibrations sounded like pounding metal drums, producing an incessant and disturbing racket. Floors, ceilings, and partitions visibly shook, and passengers began to clearly display their unease. There was no way to hide the issue. The savvier travelers could see the problems in plain sight, while the novices sensed that what was happening could not be normal.

In first class, worry turned into rumor, and rumor spurred some passengers into action. In an improvised conclave at sea, they decided to formally request the captain interrupt the trip and head toward the nearest harbor due to the vessel's deteriorating condition. Two or three passengers began to collect signatures, but they were faced with resistance from others who believed they risked instigating an onboard riot, which would not help their cause. This group of opponents refused to sign their names, fearing that such an act of disobedience would likely create tension between passengers and crewmembers.

On October 24, 1927, the *Principessa Mafalda* reached the Brazilian coast off Porto Seguro. That same day, while the ship traveled at a reduced speed, a Dutch cargo ship with only a few passengers, the *Alhena*, sailed by heading in the same direction, from Rotterdam to Buenos Aires. It quickly passed the Italian ship and disappeared to the south.

A day later, the *Principessa Mafalda* navigated eight miles off Abrolhos, Brazil, at a perfectly safe distance from the coast. It was a magnificent day with a radiant sun, soft breeze, and calm sea. The captain, perhaps encouraged by the excellent conditions, ordered the ship to speed up. The *Alhena's* silhouette quickly became visible, and by mid-afternoon the *Mafalda* had left the Dutch ship behind.

The gorgeous day was waning into a luminous and warm sunset. From third class came gleeful folk music as passengers sang and danced to accordions and guitars, leaving behind the fears that had dogged them during the voyage. In the first-class halls, the orchestra played popular tunes and the young people enthusiastically danced the foxtrot. Other passengers read on deck, played cards, or sipped drinks at the bar while waiting for dinner to be served. The waiters had readied the tables in the dining rooms and the chefs were putting the last touches on their creations and preparing to announce the first call to dinner.

Suddenly, in a fatal instant, it happened.

A strange, unsettling noise jolted the ship, the structure shuddered, and the *Mafalda* came to a sharp standstill at sea. General astonishment silenced the third-class singing; above deck, the orchestra stopped playing mid-song and the dancing couples let go of each other in bewilderment.

The ship's chief officer visited the dining halls to provide some explanation. With a calm voice, he said that one of the engines had malfunctioned, which forced them to come to a halt. He informed the passengers that there was no immediate danger and urged them to continue with their festivities. He signaled the orchestra, and the musicians dutifully commenced with a whirlwind of cheerful and lively notes. The passengers followed suit and returned to what they had been doing. Many entered the dining hall, ready to dilute the delay with a decent dinner.

What had truly happened to the *Principessa Mafalda*, the transatlantic ocean liner that should have carried the Bergoglios on their maiden voyage to the New World? The left propeller shaft had split, which at the time was turning at ninety-three revolutions per minute. As it came apart, the enormous blades continued their rotation, crashing against the hull and causing a huge tear in the metal. A flood of seawater immediately began to pour into the vessel.

Struck with the sudden emergency, the captain ordered the crew to turn off the boilers and reduce the valve pressure. Despite the gravity of the breakdown, the captain believed his men could fix the problem within a few hours and they would be able to set off for Rio de Janeiro. However, as a precaution, he ordered the start of evacuation procedures and called for help via radiotelegraphy. Sirens dramatically began to sound, alerting the crew to prepare evacuation boats and life jackets.

Down below, crewmembers frantically worked to seal the tear in the hull. Iron sheets and cement were desperately applied to the opening, and for a moment it seemed the damage would be repaired and all danger avoided. But the seawater's enormous pressure was stronger than the seamen's efforts. One of the side sheets violently collapsed as if it were made of cardboard, and a deluge of water swept workers away, destroying what had taken hours to repair.

A whirlwind of fury and foam began to flood the engine room, and the doom of the *Principessa Mafalda* was sealed. The captain immediately realized what had happened — and what was still to come — and urged the rescue efforts to speed up. According to his calculations, the *Mafalda* would float for several hours — enough time, he thought, to safely evacuate all crew and passengers. With a commanding yet calm voice, he ordered all portholes and other openings closed.

Unfortunately, his authority was undermined by the terror and panic of the crewmembers. Some of them disobeyed or only partially obeyed their orders. Portholes were not closed properly, and many skylights remained open. As well, the ship's watertight compartment doors were defective and unable to be closed. Soon a torrent of water came pouring through these cracks, accelerating the sinking of the vessel.

Dusk. The air, at first a soft breeze, picked up within a few minutes to become a strong gust. The swell, until then calm, quickly turned rough. Wind, shouted orders, whistles, the grind of the lifeboat pulleys . . . all signs of the looming shipwreck confirmed the passengers' worst fears, which quickly give way to sheer panic. The *Mafalda* slowly sunk stern first, yet the port-side list rapidly became noticeable until all could feel it. Furniture, equipment, and other objects began to slide down the steeply tilted floor, adding to the rising pandemonium.

The final straw came from the third-class passengers. The 616 Italians (most from the province of Macerata), 118 Syrians, 50 Spaniards, 38 Yugoslavians, 2 Austrians, 1 Hungarian, 1 Swiss, 1 Argentine, and 1 Uruguayan, crowded like cattle in cramped quarters, erupted in a collective frenzy. Nothing could be heard above the din of panic and screams. Their homeland was far behind them, and now their destination, so close, became insignificant in the face of mere survival.

The evacuation strategies that had started in an orderly fashion crumbled in the blink of an eye. The terrified immigrants ignored orders, disregarded all safety measures, invaded other decks, and spread panic in their path. The company that owned the *Mafalda* had prohibited officers from carrying firearms on board, a measure that seemed absurd and unnecessary at the time. With absolutely no coercive power at their disposal, their orders unheeded, the officers were overwhelmed by the chaos.

The lifeboats were halfway down the side of the ship when the surge of immigrants arrived on the scene. They hastily threw themselves into the boats, tripping and shoving, plunging on top of one another, until the smaller vessels were loaded dangerously beyond their capacity. Consequently, when some of those boats hit the water, they were destroyed on impact. Clusters of humans fell into the ocean and quickly disappeared beneath the surface. Additionally, some of the lifeboats were not up to par for a rescue effort, something that was determined only at the height of the emergency. Some were hard to lower, others leaked, and some weren't even buoyant. To complete the deteriorating scenario, it was soon clear that there weren't enough boats to load the more than a thousand people traveling aboard the *Mafalda*.

The panic intensified, becoming as overwhelming and fierce as the sea itself. Third-class passengers had merged with second, and all were out of control. When the first-class, who until then had apparently remained calm, tried to seek the safety of the lifeboats, they found hundreds of frantic people from the other two classes blocking their route.

The captain, maintaining cast-iron composure, methodically led the rescue. From the bridge, using a megaphone, he gave orders in his firm and steady voice. But the unfolding drama was overcoming his efforts. His calculations were off and the *Mafalda* was sinking much faster than expected. The electrical system weakened and threatened to leave them in the dark. The radiotelegraphy equipment, the ship's link to outside help, was not working well. Water had already reached the boilers, and they were on the verge of causing an explosion that would destroy everything — ship, passengers, and the dwindling hopes of survival.

Locked up in his cabin, the *Principessa Mafalda's* radio operator did not give up: "Come all. Come soon!"

Two ships immediately received the *Mafalda's* first SOS. Both were visible, though far away: the *Alhena*, which had been sailing port side to the *Mafalda*, and the Empire Star, an English ship heading to London on the sinking ocean liner's starboard.

The first to arrive was the *Alhena*, which turned off its engines four hundred yards from the *Mafalda* and drifted until it was only a hundred yards away. The passengers on the Dutch ship had already taken their places to provide help and free up more crewmembers for the rescue. The water appeared to be full of desperate, thrashing people. Some swam with difficulty; others clung to pieces of wood. There were lifeboats jammed with people stacked atop each other and grasping the gunwales, those below faltering under the weight of those above. The Dutch officers lowered their boats and rowed as hard as they could toward the survivors; some even dove impatiently into the water, swimming hurriedly to aid the victims.

The Dutch ship's captain could not recall ever seeing such a horrendous scene. From the bridge, he observed as one of the shipwrecked passengers, almost depleted, managed to grab onto one of the lifeboats. Behind him, a fifteen-year-old boy struggled more than swam, and, reaching the limit of his endurance, clung to one of the man's legs. When the man felt he was being dragged under the surface, he firmed his grasp on the boat and, with his free leg, fiercely kicked the boy's face, who quickly disappeared underwater.

If what the sea's surface had to offer was horrific, the *Mafalda's* innards were even worse. The panic was reaching a hellish magnitude. Waiters, maids, and other crewmembers vied with passengers to reach safety and survival. The ship's chief engineer fired a shot into his temple. Four officers forgot their duties, grabbed some life jackets, and headed toward the deck to save themselves. They were blocked off by a sea of terrified passengers, who, when noticing what they were up to, savagely lunged at them and beat them to death for their life jackets. Meanwhile, many immigrants roved the ship's compartments in gangs, entering first-class cabins, halls, and storage areas, thoroughly ransacking each space and grabbing every valuable object they could find that was more or less portable.

In the end, the *Principessa Mafalda's* captain salvaged his honor. He remained on the bridge throughout the desperate ordeal, giving instructions in a heroic effort to save his passengers and crew. A witness who helped him until the last minute stated that when the tragic end was imminent, the commander told him to save himself, and he in turn asked, "What about you, captain?"

"No, thanks," the officer responded briefly. "My place is here."

As the *Principessa Mafalda* quickly sank, illuminated by the powerful spotlights of the other ships aiding the rescue, the Italian captain appeared at the prow dressed in his white uniform. He remained upright, undoubtedly tied to something so he wouldn't fall overboard. Someone shouted to him in Italian through a megaphone, "Throw yourself into the sea! We'll save you!" He refused and was swallowed by the ocean in less than three minutes.

Nine people were left to suffer the complete sinking of the ship, holding onto a sea ladder for dear life for a full half hour. They met a horrible death when sharks attacked and devoured them.

Although exact figures have never been known, of the 1,261 people on board, it is believed that 445, including passengers and crewmembers died in the sinking of the *Principessa Mafalda*. The hopes and dreams of courageous immigrants in search of a better life, now swallowed by those warm southern seas, proved a heart-wrenching tragedy all its own.

A mysterious blessing had befallen the Bergoglios of Portacomaro. Rosa, her husband, Juan, and the young Mario José Francisco had avoided death without even aiming to provoke it. Had it not been for the lucky circumstances that prevented them from selling their house and pastry shop in time, Francis would never have been born.

News of the *Principessa Mafalda's* sinking off the Brazilian coast reached the Bergoglios' household weeks after the event. As shock and mourning gave way to thanks for God's mercy, the three of them deciphered — each in their own way — the significance of this miraculous twist of fate

Fourteen months later, on a torrid and humid January morning, an elegant woman with lively dark eyes and a fashionable 1920s bob haircut descended the gangway of the *Giulio Cesare*. Perhaps what commanded the attention of the passengers and crewmembers, more than her beauty, was what she was wearing: a mink coat with a fox collar — magnificent to exhibit at a gala performance at Milan's La Scala, but inappropriate while disembarking a ship full of immigrants in the heat of summer in South America.

But as with everything in the Bergoglios' lives, nothing was without forethought. Rosa Margarita had chosen a good way to protect the thousands of liras that made up their entire fortune — by sewing it inside the fox collar's lining. This nest egg supported the family as they established a new life, and it carried them through the economic devastation of the 1930s — the shock waves of North America's Great Depression.

That was how Francis, not even a dream in the Bergoglio lineage, performed his first miracle long before he was born. Rosa Maragarita's fortitude and quiet clarity may have guarded her offspring from the capricious hand of fate, but her careful choices were undoubtedly a product of divine intervention.

They conquered the New World in their own way. She managed to encourage Mario José Francisco to earn a degree as a public accountant, introduced him to Regina María Sivori (another immigrant, the daughter of parents from Piedmont and Genoa) at a Buenos Aires neighborhood chapel in 1934, and supported his marriage to her the following year, the way God intended.

In 1936, from that simple story of courage, resolve, and, above all, love, Jorge Mario was born, a child of immigrants who the world is now discovering as Pope Francis.

Though Francis will be eternally grateful to his parents for having given him the gift of life and moral lessons, he can't help but feel a special connection to that daring, determined, and sensitive grandmother with a particular wisdom — a person who undeniably left an indelible mark on his life and faith.

How much of grandmother Rosa Margarita's Piedmont blood courses through the veins of Pope Francis? How much was Francis influenced by his *nonna's* stories about Piedmont when it was still an independent kingdom in an Italy that was not yet a sovereign state? Piedmont had been battered by Napoleon Bonaparte's wars of conquest. Misery, hunger, and despair were everyday realities that the Bergoglios' ancestors and neighbors endured at the start of the nineteenth century. How much of his passion for the impoverished and underprivileged injustices now to be tackled from the Chair of Saint Peter came from his dear grandmother's stories and their shared vision?

As it turns out, a lot. There is a long-standing and rich tradition of Christian devotion in Piedmont, and two modern Christian saints originated in that northern region of Italy.

The first was Giovanni Bosco, better known as Don Bosco, a priest, educator, and founder of the Salesian order, formerly known as the Society of St. Francis de Sales. Born in 1815 and hailing from the Piedmont hillside village of Becchi, he dedicated his life to the advancement and education of disadvantaged youth, and his philosophy and example of charity spread throughout the world.

The other dear son of Piedmont Catholics was Luigi Orione, born in Pontecurone in 1872. Don Orione, as he was known, dedicated his entire life to helping children and the poor and to bringing his hometown closer to the Pope and his Church through charitable work. He founded the Sons of Divine Providence, an order that eventually extended to Latin America with centers in Argentina, Chile, and Brazil. Driven by his great passion for the Church and the salvation of souls, Don Orione was actively interested in the emerging issues of the turn of the century, including modernism, socialism, the Church's ongoing liberty and unity, and the Christianization of the working class.

Francis absorbed his Grandmother Rosa's exemplary stories of Don Bosco and Don Orione, and those narratives permanently instilled in him a sense of charity, brotherhood, and compassion. This emotion was so strong that, over time, Francis became a fervent admirer of the work of the great master of nostalgia, the German poet Friedrich Hölderlin, who combined the aesthetics of Romanticism with Christian sentiment. Francis will forever hold dear one of the beautiful poems Hölderlin dedicated to his own grandmother when she turned seventy-two years old, as it exemplifies his love and respect for his own grandmother.

It opens with: "You lived through many things . . . Oh, great mother . . . you lived through many things."

Its closing: "Let man not fall short of what he promised you as a child."

Chapter 2

It Takes a Village

I F COINCIDENCE OR chance plays a role in people's lives, in the matrix of Francis' story, it seems more like divine intervention. At least that's what seemingly happened when his parents, Mario Giuseppe Francesco Bergoglio and Regina María Sívori, fell in love.

Back then, the encounter that would join them for life took place in none other than the Salesian Chapel of San Antonio de Padua. Where, if not a church, could the love that brought Francis into the world have bloomed? The chapel was the emblematic hub of Almagro, their Catholic, working-class neighborhood in Buenos Aires. The city itself was as magical and mysterious as New York at a time when the world sought to escape the misery of the Great Depression and the looming specter of a second and even more dreadful world war. Within this context, the church was a unifying element, providing charity, solace, and, most importantly, faith during times of great uncertainty.

As in the intertwined tales of the renowned Argentine writer Jorge Luis Borges, stories of the Bergoglio family impress themselves upon one another, and the same constant, predictable, and invisible thread connects them all. In the story of Pope Francis, that thread is faith.

This incredible account, the intimacy of which transcends the streets of Almagro, Buenos Aires, and Argentina to reveal the genesis of a Pope, begins not with a member of the Bergoglio family but with a local priest. Lorenzo Massa, like Francis, was a descendant an Italian family that arrived in Buenos Aires with the objective of escaping their impoverished homeland. Faithful servant of the Salesian church in his Almagro neighborhood, he graduated in 1925 with only one hope: to free underprivileged street children from a life of misery. Only one year later, he was named director of the Chapel of San Antonio de Padua.

Following Don Bosco's example, Father Massa accomplished several initiatives that would have great impact on his community, country, and beyond. He was responsible for establishing several schools throughout Argentina, as well as organizing the Don Bosco Explorers, a now international Salesian youth group and camp. But it was a chance encounter in his own parish that would have profound repercussions in the life of Pope Francis.

At the turn of the century, the Almagro district was inhabited mainly by European immigrants of little means. Most neighbors were humble Italians and Spaniards, possessing middle-class values but doomed to work long hours for lower-class wages. The children spent a good portion of their days on the dirt roads, without the protective presence of an adult, enjoying unencumbered freedom. Hours were passed carelessly and without pretense.

Similar to what it had accomplished in such colonies such as India, Kenya, and South Africa, the British Empire weaved Argentina together by funding the construction of an intricate railway system, the likes of which are impressive even by today's standards. But the English also introduced a game that soon became a sensation among the youth of Argentina. That game was football, known in the United States as soccer and in Spanish-speaking countries as *fútbol*, but to the low-income kids of Almagro, it was *fulbo*.

One afternoon during his daily neighborhood stroll, which enabled him to remain accessible and in touch with his community and its needs, Father Massa stopped to observe a group of children playing soccer on a street corner. He was captivated by the skill and graceful motion of those lanky legs covered in dirt and bruises. At one point in the game, one of the children ran after the ball and, without taking into account the consequences, lunged to grab it the same instant a streetcar was passing. (Buenos Aires, as with major US and European cities, had an extensive tram and subway system that connected its neighborhoods with the city center.) Father Massa's scream rang out above the stampede of children scrambling to save their friend. Thankfully, the boy managed to jump out of the way of the streetcar, escaping the incident with only a healthy fright and a few fresh scrapes to add to his collection.

At that moment, Father Massa came up with an idea that would ultimately transform into something enormous. He brought all the children together and proposed they continue to play, but in a more appropriate and safe place. The street, he knew, was never a safe place, and especially so when a ball was involved. As the young director of the San Antonio de Padua Chapel, he invited them to use its yard as an improvised soccer field. (In Argentina, such muddy playing fields are called *potreros*.)

Father Massa, raising his finger and looking down into the coterie's anxious, wide, brown eyes, put forth only one condition: "You must participate in religious services and learn catechism." To Massa, this idea was brilliant in two ways. First, it achieved one of Don Bosco's main objectives: to rescue children from the street and distance them from its dangerous conditions. Second, it brought them closer to the Church and instilled a sense of community and emotional support — two irrefutable evangelical tools.

Amenable to the arrangement, the boys formed pickup teams and continued their games in the chapel field. Excited by this achievement, the priest wrote about his encounters with these neighborhood children in his personal diary.

And so the seed was planted of what would become one of the most successful soccer clubs in the world, with one of the largest and most loyal fan bases in all of Latin America. Fan attendance grew to the point where the yard became too small to contain everyone, so they decided to create a formal club, with its headquarters based in none other than the San Antonio de Padua Chapel. From there, they would begin searching for an even larger venue.

However, something did not sit right with the priest: the budding club's name. Wanting to pay homage to the young priest's vision of community unification, that first group of boys who came together by chance called themselves Forzosos de Almagro, or "The Force of Almagro." But to Father Massa, "Force" had a hint of implicit violence that went against the club's values. He met with the founding group and proposed more humane alternatives that better reflected the cause that truly brought them together.

After some brainstorming, one of the young athletes suggested calling it Lorenzo Massa, in honor of the person who had opened the chapel's doors to them.

"No way," said the priest, who felt the mere idea was self-centered and improper. He insisted they look for other options, but most of the team passionately defended the idea of calling it Club Lorenzo Massa.

After hours of discussion, refusals, and pleas, they reached a compromise: the team would be called Lorenzo, not in honor of Massa but rather in honor of the Roman martyr San Lorenzo (the Holy Chalice's guardian, who was slowly burned to death atop a gridiron in the third century). To complete it, they added the neighborhood's name — the place that had witnessed their births and molded their identities. Massa found it to be a reasonable resolution and christened the brand new club San Lorenzo de Almagro.

The rest of the story is familiar to any Latin American soccer fan. San Lorenzo de Almagro went on to become one of the biggest clubs in Argentina, boasting a rich and respected sports history in South America and around the world. The 1954 Argentine film *El Cura Lorenzo*, or *The Priest Lorenzo*, was inspired by Father Massa and the founding of the soccer club.

In 1934, almost thirty years after Father Massa united the community he loved so dearly, Mario Bergoglio, a young, elegant, devout Catholic met a striking woman, the daughter of a Piedmontese father and a Genovese mother. They had baptized her Regina in honor of the popular Italian opera singer Regina Paccini. Mario and Regina's eyes first met during a traditional Sunday mass at the San Antonio Chapel. It was love at first sight, and they never lost the magic of that moment. Barely a year later they got married, and so began Mario and Regina Bergoglio's first chapter in Argentina.

The newlyweds moved to the nearby neighborhood of San José de Flores. They lived in a humble, railroad-style house, long and narrow, with one room leading to another. It was a typical twentieth-century construction, called *casa chorizo* in Argentina, which to this day still exist in certain traditional Argentine neighborhoods. The house had a patio with an arbor covered by colorful blooming flowers eight months of the year.

And it was on a warm December 17, in the year of our Lord 1936 that Jorge Mario Bergoglio was welcomed into that modest home. On that day, cradling their beloved infant son, could Mario and Regina have ever imagined that some seventy-six years later, their child would become known to the world as Francis, called upon to illuminate the path of 1.2 billion Catholics?

In the lives of such transcendent individuals, the trivialities and minutia of day-to-day living, when examined in retrospect, take on intimate and revealing connotations. What were the first ten years of Francis' life like in that tight-knit, working-class neighborhood? How much of his reserved personality and ascetic austerity — remarkably august qualities that shone through from the moment he prayed his first Angelus in Saint Peter's

Square — was shaped during those years and in that milieu? To what degree did his spirit of open dialogue develop among the ties and common codes established with the other kids of Flores?

To answer some of these questions, we must look once again to some important women in the future pope's early life. If Nonna Rosa Margarita was the first woman to pass her fortitude and wisdom along the Bergoglio bloodline, there were two others who were equally integral in shaping Francis' character.

Francis himself described his memories of the particular tie that joined him and his mother, Regina: "With my mother, we listened to the operas broadcast on Radio del Estado (now Radio Nacional) at two o'clock on Saturday afternoons. She'd sit us down around the radio and, before the opera got under way, she would explain what it was about . Listening to *Othello*, she'd say, 'Listen — he's going to sing a very beautiful song now.' The truth is that on Saturday afternoons at two o'clock with my mother and my siblings, enjoying music, was a wonderful time."

How did Mamá Regina manage to train three children under the age of ten to quietly and respectfully appreciate opera? Francis remembers all too well: "Sometimes we'd drift off halfway through, but she'd hold our attention, keeping up her explanations throughout the performance. In *Othello*, for example, she'd warn us, 'Listen up: now he kills her . . .'"

Mamá Regina was not the only female figure who decisively influenced his formative years. On a pedestal, practically next to his mother, are the dear memories of his first-grade teacher. Both women played a tremendous role in shaping young Jorge Mario's sensibilities — his unique cultural and intellectual inquisitiveness. But if Regina did so through music, Estela Quiroga did so through the written word. She was the legendary Escuela Número 8 first-grade teacher in the eleventh school district where Francis began his education.

First with the penmanship of a child, then with the thoughtful sentiment of an adult, Francis maintained a systematic epistolary correspondence with his teacher, forging a close bond that would last sixty-four years. He shared with her every one of his achievements and awaited her response as one bides for the most valuable treasures. When he was ordained a priest, Estela was in the first row, crying with sheer emotion and pride. In 2001, the year her best student was consecrated as Cardinal Primate of Argentina, an aged yet still lucid Estela Quiroga explained, "He's like another son to me . . . I'm very happy he is now the Cardinal of Argentina." When she passed away in 2006 at age ninety-six, she took along with her the unrequited hope of seeing her "little one" become Pope.

Estela took an instant liking to the thin little boy with the piercing gaze the moment she saw him. Shy and fearful as little ones naturally are on their first day of school, he entrusted himself to her. Ms. Quiroga took him by the hand and guided him from that moment on. She taught him how to add and subtract, how to read, how to spell, and later how to connect words to form sentences. She even imparted to him the foundations of his catechism. But above all, she was the woman responsible for instilling in him the love of knowledge.

Estela Quiroga knew how to channel Francis' romantic, adolescent spirit as well. She would hand him classic novels, suggesting that he immerse himself in such literature as Dante Alighieri's *Divine Comedy*. At twelve, she gave him an old, used copy of *The Betrothed* by Italian Romanticist Alessandro Manzoni. Francis was delighted with the story of Fermo and Lucia and reinterpreted passages in an attempt to adapt them to his own reality. In it he read:

> Good-bye mountains, fountains of the waters, and incomparable cliffs rising toward the sky, known to those who have grown among you, imprinted in their minds, not less than the appearance of the closest family members; streams, with a discernible loud rumble, like the sound of domestic voices; scattered white houses hanging on the edge, like a herd of grazing sheep; good-bye . . .

Young Francis, feeling the tug of his Italian ancestry, took Manzoni's beautiful words as a call to love. And that call came to him in the form of a young girl from the neighborhood named Amalia, who became his girlfriend when he was barely twelve years old in 1938.

But that innocent romance was cut short before it even had a chance to bloom. Amalia's parents considered the relationship to be inappropriate given their age, and their bond was nipped in the bud in a severe manner given the innocence of their youth — Amalia's father, typical of the times, instilled proper behavior by means of corporal punishment.

The day Francis was chosen as Pope, Amalia revealed the secret she had kept for more than sixty years. Tenderly smiling at the memory of what had merely been childish mischief, she recalled, "My dad beat me for daring to receive a letter from a boy."

What did Francis' first love letter say?

Amalia unveiled the mystery: "He had drawn a little house with a red roof and white walls. Above the drawing, he had written: 'This is the house I'm going to buy you when we get married.'"

When Amalia's father, confusing adolescent fantasy with reality, raised his hand to teach his daughter a lesson in propriety, Francis' frustration was overwhelming. Overcome by the pangs of young, unrequited love, his last words to the girl were, "If I don't marry you, I'm going to become a priest."[2]

How much did this episode influence his subsequent awakening for his priestly calling? The answer is impossible to decipher; it resides in the most intimate recesses of his soul.

In any case, this experience obviously left an indelible impression on Francis in his early adolescence, accentuating his shyness. After all, he had the typical dream of all first-generation immigrants: to marry a "good girl," buy a house, and start a family. But fate's intervention prevailed, and all he could do was refer to Manzoni's sage, poetic words: "Forbidden love is one of the best experiences a human being can feel. It's fascinating because, within it, all who can, lead, and in the end those who want to, obey."

But reality contradicted Manzoni. Francis might not have wanted to obey, but he had to. In those days, a grown-up's words — parents, uncles and aunts, teachers — were akin to that of a judge's sentence. An order was not to be refuted; it was obeyed.

And that observation leads us to another pivotal moment in the life of the future pope. This time it was instigated not by a woman but by a man: his father, Mario.

We begin with a question: What was the father-son relationship like in a matriarchal family such as the Bergoglios?

Their relationship could be defined as "good," within the social boundaries of the time. The man of the house worked and provided the family's daily sustenance. In addition, he was in charge of the direction and life decisions of each family member, at least as a formality. But in those days, a father was more of a remote authority figure, leaving the day-to-day raising of children to the women of the family.

Within such a rigid structure, the opportunities for communication between father and son were scarce. However, it is here where the divine inspiration of Father Lorenzo Massa impacted his community so intimately. Jorge and his father, usually just the two of them, enjoyed Sunday outings to the San Lorenzo de Almagro field to watch soccer. It afforded them not only recreation, but quality bonding time as well. They both were captivated by the mystique of the club's poignant history, sharing elation in times of victory and the downtrodden brooding that came with each defeat. Usually, father and son spoke about the week's most important events on their way home from the games.

That's why Francis was speechless the day his father called him to the drawing room. Comparable to a parlor or formal living room, it was where the Bergoglio family addressed important issues. Once his son was seated in front of him, Mario unexpectedly said, "Look, since you're about to start high school,[2] it's best you also start to work. Now that you are on vacation, I will get you a job."

Francis, all of thirteen years old, stared at his dad in bewilderment. Work? His father was an accountant and respected in his field; at home, his family led a comfortable life, with no financial difficulties. The Bergoglios certainly didn't have an excess of money, but they had enough to live a respectable life, with hard work and few pleasures, but with all needs met. Though they did not have a car or go on regular summer vacations, Francis and his siblings never heard anyone talk about financial hardship at home.

But what initially seemed a suggestion quickly became a demand. Mario believed that instilling a strong work ethic in young Jorge would guarantee him a future in a world that was becoming increasingly competitive. As custom dictated and his intellect advised, and true to his shy and submissive nature, Francis remained quiet, listened, and nodded.

And so, with no further discussion, only a few days later Francis began working at a neighborhood sock factory.

Jorge's employers were clients of the accounting firm where his father worked, and this was the only "benefit" he counted on when it came to being hired there. Once on the job, the boy was far from privileged simply because he was the son of the factory's accountant. On the contrary — *because* of his father's recommendation, he had to make a greater effort to carry out his tasks, whatever the cost, in order to meet his employers' especially high level of expectation and trust in him.

And so, for two years the teenaged Francis diligently performed his cleaning duties — mop, broom, squeegee, and rags in hand, every day, Monday through Friday, he got down to business. What began as a summer job turned into a permanent position due to his efficiency and strong sense of integrity.

When he turned fifteen and had earned his employers' trust, Jorge received his first promotion: as a reward for a job well done, he was transferred to the accounting department, where he began to perform administrative tasks. However, what was at first considered an achievement over time became dull and routine, with few incentives for a young man with his level of curiosity and drive, especially for one willing to attend high school in the morning and work in the afternoon.

Having been exposed to the working world thanks to his father's "urging," this time Francis decided that he would take the initiative and find a job that would better hold his interest and perhaps provide him with a stable future . . . or so he planned at the time, anyway.

He decided to study in an industrial school specializing in food chemistry; the goal would be to work in a laboratory. He tenaciously searched for a position, and almost to the day he was to begin his second-to-last year in high school, he was accepted as a junior employee in a lab in his hometown neighborhood. He worked from 7 a.m. to 1 p.m., had a one-hour lunch break, and then headed to school until 8 p.m.

This schedule may seem excessively demanding for someone who had barely reached his seventeenth birthday, especially compared to today's average high schooler, but looking back, Francis has a totally opposite point of view on the matter. Today, he says he is "very grateful" that his father insisted that he work at such an early age. "Work was one of the lessons that most helped me in life," he emphasized while recounting his story.

Those words also implicitly disclose an even deeper lesson gleaned from secular work. Francis remembers his second job fondly — the one in the lab, which he found on his own merit. To this day, he believes that his time in that lab taught him both the positive and negative aspects of all earthly work, important insights that would carry over to his pastoral work with the poor and downtrodden of Argentina.

What's more, the experience was an invaluable one because it brought yet another influential woman into his life: in this case, it was the lab chief, Esther Ballestrino de Careaga. A biochemistry technician born in Paraguay, Careaga was a supporter of the Communist Party. This last piece of information is not to be taken lightly. Her political affiliation, which was such a significant influence in shaping young Francis' own political positions, would also be the reason she was kidnapped and murdered in 1977 by members of a secret government security force during Argentina's last military dictatorship. Her violent death — one of an estimated thirty thousand that occurred during Argentina's greatest tragedy — was still twenty-five years away.

Chapter 3

Bearing Witness

FRANCIS WAS ONLY sixteen years old when he met Esther, and he would have never imagined that the name of the woman he so admired would end up on the list of "the disappeared" that would be published in North America and Europe a quarter century later.

Why was Esther Ballestrino de Careaga's case so internationally renowned? She was aligned with the Mothers of the Plaza de Mayo, a small group of women who had organized to search for their missing children, and were willing to speak out against the brutal injustices that occurred at the hand of a sinister dictatorship — the darkest and most grievous chapter in Argentine history. Among those who met the same, tragic end were two French nuns who were compassionate enough to offer a safe haven where the group could meet. Both nuns, Esther, and eleven others were kidnapped between December 8 and December 10, 1977, by a "task force," a term used to describe the military death squads who dedicated themselves to kidnapping and killing political, union, and social leaders in Argentina between 1976 and 1983.

Sister Leonie Duquet was taken from her Ramos Mejía home in the San Pablo parish, located on the outskirts of Buenos Aires, and transported to the Navy School of Mechanics (Escuela de Mecánica de la Armada, or ESMA), which was being used as an illegal detention center. There she encountered fellow nun, Alice Domon, as well as the twelve others who had been kidnapped from the Santa Cruz Church, right in the middle of Buenos Aires' bustling downtown area.

The kidnappers included a frigate lieutenant named Alfredo Astiz. Pretending to be the brother of one of the disappeared, Astiz had been responsible for infiltrating the Mothers of the Plaza de Mayo under the false identity of Gustavo Niño. He ingratiated himself within the group and attended their regular meetings in the Santa Cruz Church. On December 8, 1977, when leaving that fateful day, he "marked" twelve people by kissing them on the cheek while saying good-bye, disturbingly reminiscent of Judas' kiss of Jesus in the Garden of Gethsemane.

The task force only kept the group at ESMA for a few days. When faced with repercussions in France and other European countries due to the kidnapping of the French nuns, they photographed the women inside ESMA holding a copy of the Argentine newspaper La Nación with a Montonero[1] flag in the background to make it look as if that group, instead, was responsible for the kidnappings.

The kidnappers finally decided to get rid of their captives by throwing them all into the sea, an especially cruel form of execution that became known as the "death flights." However, the ocean tide returned seven bodies to the coast, and between December 20 and 30, 1977, the corpses washed up on the Atlantic Ocean beaches of the Santa Teresita resort, less than two hundred miles from Buenos Aires. The bodies were hastily buried in a nearby cemetery.

This revealing story of Argentina's "Dirty War" was beyond anyone's imagination back in 1952, when Esther taught Francis that dignity did not come from lineage, surname, or even one's education and training. Esther taught him that true dignity only came from hard work. Francis learned through Esther's example that a man or a woman supports a family through hard work and eats from the fruit of his or her own labor. Her point was that dignity lies there: in being proud of working, not of the money earned by doing the work. It would become Esther Ballestrino's invisible yet powerful legacy.

In July 2005, the Argentine Team of Forensic Anthropology confirmed that remains that had been excavated from the cemetery as part of an ongoing government investigation were of the disappeared women.[2] Almost immediately, the surviving son of Mary Bianco (one of those "marked" by Astiz at the Santa Cruz Church) asked for a meeting with Francis, then Cardinal Bergoglio.

"We want them to be laid to rest in the Santa Cruz Church," proposed the son. And so the two men, sitting side by side, burdened by the weight of such a cruel story, spoke about the mothers' fight, their time at ESMA, the role of Astiz, and that fatal flight. Francis did not even attempt to hold back his tears. Mary Bianco's son hugged Bergoglio as they shared in the agony of this atrocious ordeal. Emotions reached a peak when Bianco's son informed the priest that Esther's remains had also been identified in the investigation.

Francis thought of Esther's words and his adolescence, his stomach sinking, when he finally discovered his mentor's fate. He never imagined that this brave and honest woman would become one of the three founding Mothers of Plaza de Mayo — along with Mary Bianco and Azucena Villaflor — to be kidnapped, drugged, and thrown off navy planes alive. The only "sin" she had committed was requesting the return of her child, and helping others achieve the same.

Francis, without a doubt, knew what he was meant to do. He intervened so that Mary, Esther, and Azucena's remains could finally rest in peace in the Santa Cruz Church — the exact same church from which the group had disappeared. The circle was coming to a close, at last, in God's peace.

On the day when the urns reached their final resting place, a sign rose among the crowd with the words, "Esther, Mary, and Azucena — 30,000 detained and disappeared, present, now and forever."

At the height of the mass, breaking all ceremonial norms, hundreds of people burst into chant: "Mothers of the Plaza, the people embrace you!" The words, restorative and beatific, reverberated off the walls surrounding that historic mass.

After the ceremony, when the church had once again fallen silent, Bergoglio asked of Mary's son, "Please, pray for me."

And so, Francis bid farewell to Esther, the Paraguayan biochemist who willingly and unselfishly shared her wisdom and philosophies, who imparted her work ethic and principles of progress to a young man who was just starting on his path in life.

During Francis' formative years, Argentina's working class experienced a profound and historic transformation. Guided by the hand of a soldier named Juan Domingo Perón and his wife, María Eva Duarte de Perón (known to the people as Evita), Argentina experienced a true revolution that put power and decision-making into the hands of the working class. Perón's movement was unprecedented in Latin America and marked a pivotal point in Argentina's political and social life.

The defining event that transformed the country occurred on October 17, 1945, with the legendary Plaza de Mayo — the hub of political life in Buenos Aires — as its epicenter. Toward the east of the plaza, with its back facing the Río de la Plata, stands the Casa Rosada, the government's headquarters. Facing it is the colonial town hall, the Cabildo, where independence from Spain was declared in 1810. Toward the south stands the Metropolitan Cathedral, where Jorge Mario Bergoglio served as archbishop before being named Pope Francis.

When the events occurred in the Plaza de Mayo in 1945, Francis was nine years old — a third grader. Neither his parents nor any members of the Bergoglio family had any sort of political affiliation, although belonging to the working class, they could not ignore the advent of Peronism.

At the start of October 1945, Argentina was being governed by President General Edelmiro J. Farrell. As part of a group of young officials, together they had taken hold of the republic's reins in 1943, when they staged a classic coup d'état, much like the ones that devastated all of Latin America during those decades. By 1945, however, a key figure in his administration, Colonel Juan Domingo Perón, had risen to become the most important political figure in the country.

From a relatively low-level position within the Department of Labor and Social Security, Perón had managed to launch a series of forward-thinking social laws. His reforms for all registered workers included an eight-hour workday, paid vacation, a yearly bonus, and mandatory rest from Saturday at noon through the end of Sunday, as well as encouraging a massive amount of workers to affiliate with their corresponding unions. It was a very progressive agenda for that period in Latin America, and the entire package of benefits, which for the first time favored the working class, earned him unprecedented popularity among Argentina's citizenry.

The growth of Perón's popularity awoke distrust among most of his military colleagues, as well as the country's political and economic establishments. Hence, Perón was forced to quit his public position in an effort to dismantle his political agenda. He was then detained and transferred to Martín García Island on the Río de la Plata, approximately twelve miles from Buenos Aires.

When news of Perón's detention broke, the people's reaction was extreme. The Central Federal Commission of the General Labor Alliance (which brought together the most powerful unions in Argentina) declared a general strike starting at midnight on October 18 "as a defensive measure of the social conquests threatened by oligarchy and capitalism's reactions." However, the union initiative was taken over by the working class; laborers began to abandon their positions on the afternoon of October 16. By October 17, thousands of workers streaming from the industrial belt of Greater Buenos Aires made their way to the Plaza de Mayo to demand Perón's release.

The popular pressure was so great that the government finally had no choice but to give in. Perón was transferred to Buenos Aires, and in a political event unprecedented in Latin American history, the working class demanded their leader's presence at the Casa Rosada. That night, crowning a historic day, Perón appeared on a balcony to greet the crowd chanting his name, and with arms high and palms open, he premiered his signature wave to the roar of his beloved public.

October 17, 1945, is without a doubt the most widely covered political event in Argentine history, and the one that sparked the most interest worldwide. It was later immortalized with the debut of Andrew Lloyd Weber's musical *Evita* in 1976, and the major motion picture of the same name in 1996, starring Madonna and Antonio Banderas. Today, it is commemorated in Argentina as Loyalty Day.

Among the many accounts of that social and political phenomenon, Francis has always had an affinity for the frank and genuine nature of the first-hand memories of the workers directly responsible for the events of October 17. One of his favorite articles, entitled "La Gente Venia del Sur," or "The People Came from the South," was written by Argentine historian Felipe Pigna and is now considered a classic story of October 17. Pigna's source was Sebastián Borro, a laborer who participated in this historic incident. The article was first published in the Argentine newspaper *La Opinión* on October 15, 1972, nearing the event's twenty-seventh anniversary.

In the article, Borro provides a heartfelt eyewitness account of the call to action he and his fellow metalworkers received from other laborers, the mass of people descending on Plaza de Mayo, and the growing intensity of the crowd ("it became more and more passionate — full of joy and fervor," he remembered). Recalling the dramatic climax of that historic day, Borro told Pigna: "What I personally experienced were the people coming from the south: Berisso, Avellaneda, Lanús, Lomas de Zamora.[3]

As the crowd grew, banners appeared in the Plaza de Mayo. It was the first time I saw anything like it: I had never seen such an extraordinary gathering. When Colonel Perón appeared at the balcony, I felt the Plaza tremble. It was an amazing uproar, extremely emotional. Everything seemed to come down."

When these events took place, Francis hadn't even turned ten, so he was not yet mature enough to process their political impact. Over time, however, family discussions and self-education gave way to a broader understanding and deeper personal connection to the Peronist phenomenon.

By 1952, when he met Esther in the biochemistry lab, Francis already had a budding political position. He could identify with Peronism and the figures of Juan Domingo Perón and Evita. They had won democratically held elections a few months after October 17 and since then had driven a true social revolution, giving unprecedented rights (including the universal vote for women and a voluminous body of labor laws) to workers and the most deprived sectors of society.

Young Francis began to believe that if work opened the door to human reality and constituted the first and clearest mandate of God — to be fruitful, and to replenish the earth and subdue it (Genesis 1:28) — ideologically he felt comfortable with Peronism, although he clearly didn't blindly subscribe to all of the party's precepts. His commitment to Peronism cost him a few punishments in high school (presumably because he wore the Peronist emblem on his school uniform's lapel), but it also gained him insightful, almost daily discussions with his dear Esther.

She challenged his ideas with the rigid dogma of the Communist Party. And he refuted hers with a classic Peronist response: The only truth is reality. And the reality was that most of the Argentine working class was Peronist. The social and labor rights that Peronism bestowed upon the working class were an irrefutable reality for the young Francis, and it remained so throughout his life.

Chapter 4

The Man of God

THAT WHICH IS sacred often occurs without warning. The calendar signaled the start of spring on that September day in 1953; it would also note the dawn of Francis' faith. Far from the noise and bustle of Flores yet in its midst, on the Feast of Saint Matthew, a seventeen-year-old boy was drawn into his parish church seeking the Sacrament of Reconciliation.

In 1806, four years prior to Argentina's independence, the residents of Flores, armed with more will than resources, built themselves a church. The building was rickety, with a straw ceiling and palm crosspieces. Each mass was dedicated to the Virgin of Miracles in hopes the church would not collapse upon the parishioners. Maybe it was that story of simplicity and solidarity that inspired him, or maybe it was just meant to be, but the fact remains that young Francis first felt God's calling within that very parish, as a barely perceptible voice, summoning him to that dimly lit confessional and changing his life forever.

Francis has since recounted that warm spring afternoon a thousand times, and it is considered one of his life's most well-known milestones. Yet, that which only he will ever know — the sacred mystery of his call to faith — he could not yet reveal to anyone else. He hid it in the far recesses of his soul and treasured it in his memory, recalling it each night in the hopes of understanding this powerful and increasingly urgent impulse to serve God. Nearly seventeen, at an age full of uncertainty and change, his undeniable certitude would remain his own for still a while to come.

As he matured, that faint whisper would become a scream. Denying his true nature was like denying the sunrise. Francis knew he wanted to be a priest — to serve God. He wanted to surrender to that unassailable union of body, soul, mind, and spirit.

In prayer's impermeable silence, Francis felt at peace with God and with his conviction. Yet now he felt the need to share his feelings with someone. Years before he discussed his decision with his parents, Francis, spoke with his spiritual director, Father Enrique Pozzoli, from Almagro's Salesian community. Father Pozzoli had known young Francis since he was only eight days old. On Christmas of 1936, his consecrated hand baptized Francis in Almagro's San Carlos Borromeo and Maria Auxiliadora Basilica, in the heart of Buenos Aires. Francis' godparents were Francesco Sívori and Rosa Margarita, the grandmother who was so dear to him.

Father Pozzoli encouraged him to speak about discovering his faith and what that meant in life. He also suggested he travel to the Tandil Mountains in the Argentine Pampas region. Francis was eighteen and suffered from severe respiratory problems, and Father Pozzoli felt the fresh, mountain air would promote healing. Although Francis never publicly addressed this health issue (not even to deny later news reports claiming he has only one lung), during his late teens it came to light that the ailment was quite serious.

Unable to come up with a specific diagnosis, doctors had drained the affected area with catheters, an immensely painful procedure, and finally decided to extract the top part of his right lung. His family suffered by his side, and while he was still recovering, he recalls that a nun approached him and said, "With your pain, you are imitating Jesus."

Francis turned that phrase into a prayer. Now more than ever, he definitely knew he wanted to become a priest. Weak and convalescent, Francis took Father Pozzoli's advice and traveled to the mountains, roughly two hundred miles from Buenos Aires, to a valley famous for its mild weather and moderate, healing climate.

His time spent there was not only a physical retreat, but a spiritual one as well. He barely spoke to others, yet he was always good-natured with everyone he met. He encountered a priest, also Salesian, with whom he shared his desire to pursue his faith. His name was Roberto Musante, and he would play an important role in Francis' life in years to come, during Argentina's dark period, when both men had matured and been fully shaped in their Christian faith.

Musante believed in the existence of utopian societies. He mentioned this to Francis and eventually went out to seek them, moving to Angola, Africa, where poverty blanketed a country that was rich in oil below its sands, but arid and inhospitable above. He lived in the desolate Don Bosco complex there, barely surviving. In Luanda, Angola's capital city, the Salesian mission operated from the Lixiera neighborhood, which when translated from the Portuguese, truly does its name justice: "Trash." They lived with no electricity or water, in the filthiest of conditions. Musante pursued his spiritual calling by helping young children learn how to read and write so they might one day secure a job instead of being relegated to a life of sifting through garbage to survive.

Francis took another road, but with a similar direction. While Musante embraced the Salesian mission and was influenced by Don Bosco's legacy, Francis followed Saint Ignatius of Loyola's path.

The Society of Jesus, founded by Saint Ignatius in 1534, formalized as an order by Pope Paul III in 1540, and intimately tied to Argentina's history since 1585, is a group of men consecrated to God who must be ready to serve "anywhere in the world." Jesuits, as its members are known, take the three vows of priesthood imposed by the Catholic Church — poverty, chastity, and obedience — and a fourth, particular to their order: obedience to the Pope. This last one brought with it much opposition during the Catholic Counter-Reformation years. In fact, eighteenth-century Protestant governments sought to end the Society of Jesus because of how its members staunchly defended the papacy and its political, territorial, financial, and social power.

The Jesuits counted among their enemies some well-known and powerful figures, including philosophers Montesquieu and Voltaire and French emperor Napoleon Bonaparte, who in his memoir defined them as follows: "The Jesuits are a military organization, not a religious order. Their chief is an army general, not a mere monastery abbot. And this organization's objective is power, power in its most tyrannical form. Absolute and universal power, power to control the world under only one man's [the Jesuits' Superior General] will, Jesuitism is the epitome of despotism and, simultaneously, is the largest and most grandiose of abuses."

That military model of which Napoleon wrote was precisely what attracted young Francis to the Jesuits. The Argentine congregation's work in places like San Isidro, San Fernando, Zárate, and Luján; in the missions on the coast; in the Buenos Aires province and in the city itself, where the order founded the Universidad de El Salvador; on the farms (created as education centers) in the Córdoba province, where the Jesuits also founded the prestigious Universidad Nacional de Córdoba — all were living proof of what young Francis found so seductive. Obedience, discipline, and mission were three principles that Francis wanted to apply to his life.

By the time he was twenty-one years old, Francis had an unwavering conviction that left no room for doubt. Finally he summoned the courage to speak with his father and share his deepest emotions, praying that he would receive his support. The Lord complied. However, it was his grandmother who expressed the most joy at his news. "If God is beckoning you, bless him," said Rosa, yet with a soothing gesture, she added, "In any case, these doors are always open if you want to come back." Those comforting words were exactly what he needed to hear, and his beloved grandmother, as always, did not disappoint.

He did not have the same luck with his mother. When he told her he was considering becoming a priest, she tried to talk him out of it. "I don't know, I don't see you as . . . You should wait a bit . . . You're the eldest . . . Keep working . . . Finish university . . ." — these were among the various arguments she used in an attempt to dissuade him. "Truth is, my mother was extremely upset."

Since he had never mentioned anything of the sort before, his confession took the family by surprise — everyone except Nonna Rosa, that is. She always sensed that her bright and silent grandson had an iron will.

The day he spoke with his family about his calling, his mother instantly understood the message her son had given her a few years earlier. She hadn't been able to see it so clearly at the time. When Francis finished his chemistry studies, she asked him what he planned to study in college. "Medicine," responded Francis, according to what his younger sister María Elena recalls. In response, his mother emptied a storage room and designated it his study area. Every day, after his part-time job at the lab, Francis returned home and locked himself in that room. However, one morning, his mother was taken by surprise: she discovered not books on anatomy and medicine in the room, but rather books on theology and Catholicism. Disturbed, she decided to confront her eldest child.

"What's this?" she asked.

He responded, "It's medicine — medicine for the soul."

There were actually more than just theology books in the room. Although as a boy he was not formally affiliated with any political party,

Francis had certain political interests and he satisfied them by reading such publications as *Nuestra Palabra*, a magazine circulated by the Argentine Communist Party, and similar political polemics that Esther Ballestrino de Careage, his lab boss, quietly passed on to him.

The disparity between Jorge's social and political concerns and his desire to enter the priesthood bewildered his mother. But he had already made up his mind about attending seminary, and they both knew there was no turning back. And so, Francis enrolled in the Diocesan Seminary of Villa Devoto, a Jesuit institution named for the neighborhood in which it was located.

Francis started his novitiate in the Society of Jesus in March of 1958. At the seminary, he strengthened the foundation on which he would build his ministry and mission of faith. The novitiate lasts two years and within that time, the candidate's initial impressions of religious life are experienced through spiritual exercises, the study of the Society's constitutions, and the history of the order and of communal life. The teacher of novices guides and strengthens their faith, so that each novice freely and consciously chooses his life's path. The well-known vows of obedience, chastity, and poverty that rule a priestly life are taken at this time.

When this phase came to a close, Francis finished his studies at Casa Loyola, the Jesuit seminary outside Santiago, Chile. Casa Loyola was an exquisite estate built in the late 1930s in the town of Padre Hurtado (named for the Jesuit Saint Alberto Hurtado), surrounded by hundred-year-old apple, pear, plum, and walnut trees. This was the beginning of the second stage of formation of the Jesuit order for Francis, when the students are known as scholastics (or brothers if they choose a nonordained course of study). He lived in the seminary house at the rural commune for almost three years — the time it took to complete his juniorate, the Jesuit's humanist education. During the juniorate, the student learns languages and receives a basic introduction to humanism, guiding him toward the objective of living an apostolic life.

At this retreat, for the first time, Francis truly experienced the rigors of this educational path. He would wake at 6 a.m., and his first activity was to participate in Latin masses and learn Gregorian chants. Afterward, he attended classes in history, literature, Latin, and Greek.

Life at Casa Loyola was strict and unusually demanding for the young men in their early twenties, with much prayer and meditation and little recreation. They did not share classrooms or conversations. They could shower with hot water only twice a week. Food was frugal, and they ate in silence while pondering the Scriptures. They were not allowed to read the newspaper and could only listen to classical music. Their only recreational outlet was afternoon sports (soccer and swimming), where the young men could interact freely, although Francis, given his health condition, abstained from participating.

Returning to Buenos Aires in 1961, Franicis continued his coursework, earning a degree in psychology at the Colegio Maximo de San Jose in 1963. Francis then began teaching. He served as a literature and psychology professor at Colegio de la Inmaculada Concepción de Santa Fe and also taught at the Colegio del Salvador.

He was, by all reports, a strict professor, but everyone respected him. They called him "Professor Carucha" behind his back (*carucha* is a teasing way of describing someone with a long face). His students would occasionally try to challenge him, but they quickly learned that his good-natured character became harsh when anyone questioned his conviction — and his conviction was bound to religious dogma. It's difficult to believe, knowing the gentle-natured Francis of the present, that a former student would ever describe him as intolerant or tyrannical.

Francis shared with his students the renowned prose of Jorge Luis Borges and Fyodor Dostoevsky, and he regularly incorporated inspiring passages from great literary works into his lessons. "I was always impressed by what Ricardo Güiraldes [an Argentine writer of gaucho literature] mentions in *Don Segundo Sombra*, that his life was sealed by water," cited Francis. "As a boy, he resembled a lively stream among the stones; as a man, a boisterous river; and as an old man, backwater." He also asked his students to write short stories, and he even introduced them to Jorge Luis Borges when he traveled to Buenos Aires.

Though teaching didn't exactly come naturally to Francis, he rose to the occasion. Given his background, he thought he'd be assigned a scientific subject, so he was quite surprised when he was designated a literature and psychology professor. Nonetheless, he fulfilled his role with the greatest of passion in a Jesuit college that back then had an excellent reputation. He was a versatile teacher, open to students' opinions and encouraging them with his own earnest enthusiasm.

Father Leonardo Nardín, the current rector at Colegio de la Inmaculada Concepción de Santa Fe, had Francis as his spiritual guide at the time. "He was a maestro training students. He was the one who introduced Jorge

Luis Borges and other great writers to our school," recalls Nardín. "He kept a low profile, but was also courageous given that when he needed to open his mouth to speak his mind, he did it. He never looked out for himself, but was rather interested in social issues. He's very in tune with what people are going through. He knows how to place himself in another person's shoes — the one living through poverty and misery. He supported poor families or unemployed people. He always tended to them with an affection and a familiarity that was surprising. Very simple and straightforward."

At Santa Fe, everyone listened to Francis' sermons. He was brilliant at posing simple yet profound questions to his parishioners — ones that would elicit reflection and introspection. One time, the ten-year-old son of one of his former students from the Inmaculada Concepción School stood in front of him and asked, "Who created God?" Francis looked at him and responded, without a trace of doubt, "No one. He has always existed."

And that is how the mystery of eternity, faith, and immortality was re-solved — with those four words. The serenity and conviction of his answer left the child at ease.

His professorship came to an end, and 1967 to 1970 was followed by more theological study. Francis attended the School of Theology at Cole-gio Maximo de San Jose and, upon graduation, finally concluded his for-mal education. When he finished, he was ordained as deacon, the previous step to becoming a priest.

Ordained by Ramón José Castellano, the Argentinian Archbishop of Córdoba, Francis' priesthood began on December 13, 1969. Despite the passage of time, he still carries with him a gift he received on that memo-rable morning of his ordination — a letter his grandmother Rosa wrote to him, half in Italian Piedmontese dialect and half in Spanish. It says:

> On this beautiful day in which you are able to hold Christ the Sav-ior in your consecrated hands and a wide path opens before you to-ward the most profound apostleship, I give you this modest present with very little material value, but very high spiritual value.

His grandmother had taken the precaution to prepare the letter years prior to his ordination, in case she died and was unable to witness it, yet she finally had the chance to hand it to him in person. She went on to say:

> May my grandchildren, to whom I have given the best part of my heart, have a long and happy life; however, if one day pain, sickness,

or loss of a loved one should fill you with grief, remember that one sigh at the Tabernacle, where lies the largest most dignified martyr, and one glance at Maria at the foot of the cross can make a drop of comfort fall on the most profound and painful wounds.

Of all the wisdom, advice, and direction that life has offered Francis, he treasures his nonna's poignant and heartfelt message most of all. He keeps it inside his personal planner, and it traveled with him to the Vatican when he became Bishop of Rome.

Once ordained, Francis traveled to Spain to fulfill his tertianship — the third phase of the Jesuit formation. This stage strengthens the young priests' intellectual and spiritual knowledge of the Society and its tenets. Francis attended the Universidad Alcalá de Henares in Madrid, where he immersed himself in rigorous spiritual exercises and reflected on the rules of the Society, written by Saint Ignatius himself and known as the Constitutions.

On April 22, 1973, after a journey fifteen years in the making, Francis took his final Jesuit vows. Apart from the vows of chastity, poverty, and obedience that he had already taken, it was now time to take the final, fourth vow: obedience to the Pope. And so, with the circle finally closed, Francis returned to Argentina, feeling more like a priest and Jesuit than anything else that could define him.

Francis became a teacher of novices at the Seminary of Villa Barilari in San Miguel and served as a professor of theology there. In July 1973, he was named Provincial of Argentina's Society of Jesus, a position he held for six years.[1] Under his command were 15 houses, 166 priests, 32 brothers, and 20 students — a family that needed support and evangelization, relying on his example.

Francis completely dedicated himself to his pastoral task while the country entered its dark years and descended into the depths of violence. By 1980, he had become the rector of the Colegio Máximo de San Miguel. Simultaneously, he served as the parish priest of the San José Church in the same neighborhood.

Since Francis was named Pope, friends and colleagues that he'd grown to know over the years have delighted in telling anecdotes about him from the past. Gustavo Antico, now rector of the Santa Catalina Church in Siena but back then a student at Colegio Máximo, recalls that the first time he saw Francis, he said, "You — off to the pigs." Francis was referring to the farm he had created to feed disadvantaged children. People gave them sheep and pigs to raise, which were fed with leftovers donated by local supermarkets. The pigs had to be fed and their pens cleaned.

No one wanted that job. The young priest, feeling uneasy about the life he had chosen, looked down, unable to find the courage to show his displeasure. He soon realized that Francis would never have made him do a job he himself had never done before. "In fact, on more than one occasion, Francis came to the pigpen to work with us and helped lighten the load," remembers Antico. "How could I refuse to do the work? . . . Could I protest if I was a novice and he, twice our age, was the Provincial and did it with pleasure?"

Those were intense years for Francis. In practice, he devoted himself to two essential pillars in Jesuit training: education and mission. He worked and served in any capacity necessary, teaching classes and giving direction and blessings anywhere and anytime the opportunity presented itself. Years later, he explained his philosophy on the importance of evangelical work: "The Church needs to transform its structures and pastoral ways, guiding them [the clergy] to be missionaries. We must go where we are needed, where the people are, where those who desire it do not dare reach out to the [traditional] framework and old-fashioned ways because these do not reflect their expectations and feelings."

With the strong foundation of his Christian training and Jesuit roots, Francis extended himself to the furthest limits. He was young, his health was visibly improved (after his lung surgery, he was able to breath at 90 percent of normal capacity), and his life's purpose appeared unmistakably clear and laid out before him. Any inner, human torments were reserved for prayer.

In 1986, he traveled to Germany to study and cultivate the views he would use to finish his doctoral thesis. Francis was fascinated by the life and work of German theologian Romano Guardini,[2] and to find out all he could about him, he stayed at the Sankt Georgen (Saint George) Jesuit community in Frankfurt, where he further advanced his knowledge of philosophy and contemplative theology.

Francis had always been struck by the many things he and Guardini had in common, from their Italian origins to their degrees in chemistry and their pursuit of the priesthood. In 1939, Guardini was forced by the Nazis to resign from the Philosophy of Religion department at the University of Berlin because of an essay he wrote that criticized their mythological views on Jesus. That same year, the Nazis confiscated Rothenfels Castle, where he had established a youth retreat that promoted religion and the arts. Michael Sievernich, a theology professor, spoke to Francis about the parallels between those years in Guardini's life and the ones he lived through in Argentina in the 1970s. Like Guardini, Francis "also had to think about Catholicism and confronting violence," Sievernich explained.

Francis stayed in Germany for a few months, then returned to Argentina, overwhelmed by all he had learned during his short stay at Sankt Georgen. The Jesuits then sent him back to work at the Colegio del Salvador, a primary and secondary school from which the Universidad del Salvador grew in 1622. Five years earlier, the Universidad del Salvador had started a reorganization process guided by the Society of Jesus. It had nothing to do with structural changes, but rather was focused on rescuing the institution's original spirit. The school wanted to return to the inspirational and constructive mysticism of its founding fathers. "In those days, the 'founding mysticism' was alive," Francis himself said, twenty years after the reorganization effort. "So many memories! [. . .] Mysticism's validity is slowly and unknowingly lost in the consecutive circumstances with which life mistreats it: functionalism, diverse forms of corruption, internal political struggles, sadness of heart, and so on. On the other hand, all true mysticism is fundamentally aggressive: it prevails outside the Institution, not with tyrannical violence but rather with the docility that rises from wisdom."[3]

Francis always considered education and faith as part of the same body. In that same address, he warned of one of the most serious shifts in Argentina's higher education system:

> There is another reality to take into account: from 1975 until now, our university system has changed. Educational institutes and universities have multiplied and, painstakingly, we have noticed that some of them are based on a *priori* [presupposition] that does not coincide with the *universitas* [world/society], nor with people's dignities: for example, they speak of a private university's per capita profitability, refer to students as "clients," and it is all reduced to a business transaction, if not yet another expression of the seductive consumer hunger of our current culture. . . . Twenty years ago, when I wrote the Principles Letter, we had no idea the path history would take. We were faced with a scientific or utilitarian spirit, of clear and systematic ideologies and systems. However nowadays, Modernism's

powerful structures are inevitably falling apart and, with certain intellectual modesty, we call that shipwreck's remains (one we share) "postmodernism." The historic challenge contains the ambiguity of a crisis and today's man, through inertia, tends to reconstruct what happened "yesterday," when all he has left on his beach are the remains of a shattered voyage. Hence, let us not be surprised if, in the world's current gallery, we find a strange coexistence of racial or tribal hatred next to preachers of peace and harmony with the cosmos, cyber and computer worshipers together with modern "yogis" of transcendental meditation — the frantic search for a better quality of life while each day more people wane into misery and others faint of hunger. This entire panorama is encompassed by the tendency of the responsible powers and leaderships to standardize their decisions, avoiding great conflicts and, on the other hand, channeling the price and contradictions of great change toward communities, ethnic groups, and society's marginalized sectors.

Francis experienced the reorganization of the university from within until he was diverted to the Society of Jesus church in Córdoba, where he arrived as a spiritual guide. Reports picked up by some journalists, without citing sources, maintain that in fact he was "invited" to rest in Córdoba because he had started to express his disagreement with how his colleagues directed the Jesuit institutions, so the provincial who succeeded him, Victor Zorzín, decided to distance him from the conflict.

He arrived at the beautiful Company of Jesus Church, located on the corner of Obispo Trejo and Caseros, in the center of Córdoba's capital. The province was Jesuit from birth: when the capital city of Córdoba was founded, a site facing the Plaza Mayor was simultaneously assigned to the Jesuits without even having one member of the order present. When they arrived they were given the plot of land, where they built a shrine they used as a church. This building, finalized in 1671, consists of one floor in the form of a Latin cross, with stonewalls held together by lime and an austere stone façade. The old, original chapel is one of the country's oldest ecclesiastical constructions.

Córdoba became home to Francis, and there he took a vow of silence and became just another Jesuit. His functions were simple: conduct mass, hear confession, impart blessings to the people of Córdoba who came to pray, and finish his doctorate. "He was a profoundly poor man," says the current director of the Company of Jesus Chruch, Ángel Rossi, when describing him during those days.

Francis' "exile" ended abruptly less than two years later, when Cardinal Antonio Quarracino recommended him to his superiors in Rome as Auxiliary Bishop of Buenos Aires. An auxiliary bishop is appointed to a diocese to aid the current bishop when he is no longer fully able to carry out his duties effectively, or if the diocese is too large to be controlled by one bishop alone. Cardinal Quarracino wanted Francis as a "close collaborator," so Francis returned to the city, although he chose not to live in one of the archdiocese homes, requesting instead to move to a Jesuit residence.

On May 20, 1992, Pope John Paul II designated Francis Auxiliary Bishop of the Diocese of Buenos Aires. From then on, as established by religious law, Francis no longer owed his obedience to his superiors in the Society of Jesus, although he still considered himself (and always will) a Jesuit. For the past thirty-four years, he had lived among his brethren in the Society. To whom else would he remain faithful?

And true to his Jesuit roots of missionary work, Francis admitted in a radio interview, "The best moments as a priest were the ones I spent with the people. That will always remain in my heart, having walked with the people that search for Jesus." Once he was named bishop, however, those days seemed to have been left behind. Reality imposed pressing urgencies, and ecclesiastic and political issues consumed most of his life. He was closer to the Father, but the hand of God had chosen him as bishop. And so he accepted.

A little over a month later, on June 27, he received the Episcopal ordination of Titular Bishop of the Diocese of Auca in the Buenos Aires Cathedral from Cardinal Quarracino, the apostolic nuncio Ubaldo Calabresi, and the Mercedes-Luján bishop, monsignor Emilio Ogñénovich. What did being Bishop of Auca mean to Francis? In truth, Auca was an extinct Catholic diocese. Under its original name Oca, it had been the Episcopal headquarters of the Catholic Church in Hispania (the Roman term for the Iberian Peninsula until 400 AD) between the third and fourth centuries. Its headquarters was in the province of Burgos, in the Castilla y León community.

For six years, Francis was an "absent" bishop of this diocese. The Code of Canon Law establishes that each bishop must head a diocese, because "a diocese may not exist without a bishop." Since auxiliary bishops cannot hold more than one position in an active diocese, the Holy See gives them historic, titular appointments.[4]

The designation caused some degree of dismay, since Francis, accustomed to being extremely productive in his calling, did not have a fully active "career" within the ecclesial hierarchy. In 1998, however, when Cardinal Quarracino died, Francis replaced him as Archbishop Primate of Argentina — the first Jesuit ever to head the Buenos Aires curia. True to his Jesuit roots, however, he did not take advantage of all the benefits and luxuries afforded to this title. He kept traveling by bus and subway and stayed in his Buenos Aires Cathedral quarters, refusing to live in the archbishop's residence in the exclusive Olivos neighborhood of Buenos Aires.

As archbishop, Francis left an impression on his community that transcended titles and offices. He made it a priority to visit the city's slums — the absolute poorest sections of Buenos Aires. He publicly spoke out about the severe marginalization and poverty that he encountered, especially in the municipal villa of 1-11-14 in the Bajo Flores section.

No matter how high Francis climbed the ecclesiastic ladder, he felt and lived like a clergyman. He appointed a team of priests to live and work in the roughly twenty Buenos Aires slums. As he designated more and more positions to this calling, he continually increased their resources, maintaining the entire operation under his protection and direct supervision. He forged an especially close bond with priest José "Pepe" Di Paola, who continues to dedicate himself to improving life in these depressed barrios.

On February 21, 2001, bestowed upon him by Pope John Paul II, Francis embraced the divine office of Cardinal[5] with the same devotion he had over four decades earlier when he entered the Jesuit community. From that day forward, he would carry the highest-ranking ecclesiastic dignity of the Catholic Church. Since the cardinals are clergy to Rome's service, each one has a title, which can be a bishopric, presbytery, or a deaconry of a temple in Rome. Francis was named cardinal of the title San Roberto Belarmino and the church that invokes the saint's memory in the Piazza Ungheria, located in the upscale Parioli district in Rome.

Francis accepted the challenge that divine providence had laid before him. His main mission would be to choose the Pope, but he would also be the voice for ordinary people — to speak for those whom he had so devotedly served throughout his career. In fact, when many of the proud Argentine faithful considered visiting Rome to witness the formal ceremony (called a Public Consistory), Francis, ever-practical and never one for pomp, requested that rather than incur the cost of traveling to Italy, they donate to the Church instead.

On that February day, Francis received the classic scarlet garments of a cardinal in the Church of Rome, symbolizing not only his level of authority but his willingness to die for his faith. Accustomed to the color black characteristic of his Jesuit order, he found it hard to change his clothing and habits on the sole imposition of a new title. The inner workings of the Church and its hierarchy, both in Argentina and the Vatican, left him uninspired. He never had the expectation of privilege; rather, he longed for the days of working in the trenches, with his troop of priests, serving the poor. He yearned to hear their genuine, humble, and heartfelt stories. However, this innate sense of nonconformity and uniqueness only served to set him apart as a leader.

––––––––––––––

On April 2, 2005, Cardinal Camarlengo Eduardo Martínez Somalo entered Pope John Paul II's bedchamber. As tradition dictates, he held a lit candle to the nose and mouth of the Pontiff, but alas, the flame did not flicker. With a silver hammer in hand, he gently tapped the Pope's forehead, each time calling out his baptismal name, Karol. Receiving no response, the cardinal turned to the witnesses and ceremoniously said, "The Pope is truly dead." With these words, the same silver hammer was used to deface the Pope's fisherman ring, destroying his papal seal and signaling the end of his pontifical authority. The bells of Saint Peter's informed the public of his passing.

As these rituals continued, Francis received the news, overcome by sadness, but wholly prepared to assume his role in filling Peter's vacant chair. Dressed in scarlet vestment and with a sullen heart, on April 18, 2005, Francis took his place in Saint Peter's Basilica and participated in the Pro Eligendo Pontifice, the papal funerary mass, where he prayed for the wisdom and fortitude to undertake the difficult task ahead. Then, in the Sistine Chapel, under the magnificent frescos of Michelangelo, he sang, together with his peers, the Veni Creator Spiritus, the hymn that places their trust in the Holy Spirit, promising to maintain the secrecy of the conclave.

Francis felt his heart sink. He was in a place he had never dreamed of reaching, accompanied only by his prayers and reflections on his own journey — all that had culminated in this precise moment in time. He heard the famous order *extra omnes* (everyone out), at which time all of those not belonging to the College of Cardinals, or somehow mandated to participate, had to exit. The Sistine Chapel's doors closed and the Swiss Guard, true to their name, remained motionless effigies, protecting under lock and key the conclave's proceedings.[6]

And he never imagined he would find himself in that very place eight years later, attending the same proceedings that, this time, would yield an extraordinarily unexpected result.

Chapter 5

A Church for the Poor

L OYAL TO HIS habits, Francis handwrote in his personal planner that he had a "special" appointment on Wednesday, May 13, 1992. It wasn't every day that Argentina's apostolic nuncio summoned him for a conversation. For Monsignor Ubaldo Calabresi, the direct representative of Pope John Paul II, contacting him at the Jesuit residence in Córdoba was undoubtedly a major issue.

The strangest thing about their meeting was the location. "Please wait for me at the airport," said the nuncio. The only additional information he offered was that they had to speak about an urgent issue, and since the nuncio had a brief layover in Córdoba, it was the perfect opportunity to address this pressing concern. Francis, always careful not to speculate without sufficient information, arrived half an hour early for their meeting and sat at the airport bar. He read newspapers, drank *café con leche*, and patiently awaited the nuncio's arrival.

As the conversation took its course, Francis still did not understand the urgency of the meeting. The nuncio limited himself to questions about the Argentine Church's inside operation — subjects that could have been discussed over the phone. Obligingly, and true to his style, Francis did not show a hint of impatience.

After all, he was face-to-face with Nuncio Calabresi, highly influential and well versed in the Church's internal politics. Calabresi had been appointed apostolic nuncio to Argentina in 1981 by Pope John Paul II himself, and he served at the nunciature in Buenos Aires until his retirement in 2000. At the time of his appointment, Argentina's military dictatorship was of great concern to the Vatican, as were the accusations of conspiracy among the ecclesiastic hierarchy, represented by the previous Argentine nuncio, Pio Laghi.

Laghi was an instrumental figure in the Church. His friends included Golda Meir, Mother Theresa, and George H. W. Bush. In 1978, he was the man who convinced Jorge Rafael Videla, the army's commander in chief and de facto president of Argentina, to accept Pope John Paul's intervention as a last resort to avoid a war with Chile over the Beagle conflict.[1] However, his role during the dictatorship was severely questioned, in response to which he took full advantage of his greatest virtue: silence.

In January 2009, Laghi died of leukemia in Rome at age eighty-five. Buried with him were two important undertakings entrusted to him by Pope Paul VI upon his 1974 appointment in Buenos Aires as nuncio: to neutralize the influence of the Movement of Priests for the Third World[2] and to rejuvenate the Argentine bishopric, bringing it closer to the Second Vatican Council.

The Catholic Church's role during the dictatorship was, and continues to be, a subject of debate in secular, religious, political, legal, and social circles in Argentina. As the March 1976 coup d'état began to play out, more than sixty bishops throughout the country gathered to evaluate the disturbing turn of events. Within their bishoprics, all had received news of kidnappings, disappearances, and firings due to labor union activities. They deliberated on whether to declare themselves against or in support of the dictatorship. With a two-thirds majority vote, they decided not to publicly decry the situation, but rather to confront the problem quietly. This decision would require them to openly support the dictatorship, but they were careful to draw up a document stating that they privately took action in order to help those in danger. As was expected of them, a bishop or cardinal would continue to stand side by side with the dictator during all public functions, and the Church would continue the common practice of blessing the military.

As a boarding call rang out over the airport loudspeaker, Calabresi discreetly looked at his wristwatch. Francis naturally assumed that their meeting was about to adjourn, when the nuncio looked him in the eyes and, without even the slightest change in tone, said, "Oh, one more thing. You were just named auxiliary bishop of Buenos Aires, and the appointment will be made public on the twentieth." Francis, blindsided and stunned by the news, repeated the nuncio's words in his head. That's a mere week from today, he thought to himself.

With that, the nuncio wished him well, blessed him, and departed for his gate. As the noisy chaos of the bustling airport seemed to fade into the background, Francis struggled to comprehend the shocking news, barely able to find his way to the exit.

That emotional paralysis was nothing new; it was a personality trait of his. He endured it as a child, when his flat feet prevented him from being the soccer player all Argentine children dream of becoming; as an adolescent, when Amalia's parents cut their love short; and as a priest in the early 1960s, when he found himself helpless in the face of extreme poverty during his mission in Chile.

But Francis knew himself well; years of introspection had made him adept at quelling his existential anguish. Now more than ever, he had no choice but to collect himself and regain his footing — after all, the Buenos Aires Cathedral and the imminent title of bishop awaited him. By force of will, he coached himself through stifling fear and began dwelling, instead, in the intoxication of possibility. Overwhelmed, he knew there was only one way to gain control over such an emotional onslaught: he returned to the Society of Jesus quarters and began to pray.

On that May afternoon, perhaps more than ever, Francis was able to feel the warmth of God's gaze upon him. To reach this spiritual plane, he appealed to a ritual he believed infallible: he recited the Rosary and the Psalms aloud.

He could not even tell how long he remained praying, standing in front of the Society of Jesus tabernacle. At one point he even thought he had fallen asleep in front of the image of Jesus Christ, occupying a uniquely intimate and mystical space with the son of God. When this meditative prayer concluded, he felt that he was in the arms of the Lord, wrapped in the comfort of God's embrace.

Years after this event, Francis understood that, in philosophical and spiritual terms, he truly achieved an altered, transcendental state. Only then, after hours immersed in prayer, was he able to begin to accept his appointment as auxiliary bishop of the Buenos Aires Cathedral, less than fifty blocks from where he was born and raised, and where he had grown in his faith.

From a more tangible standpoint, this news not only put an end to his exile in Còrdoba, but now he was getting promoted to the second most important position in Argentina's ecclesiastical hierarchy. The Buenos Aires Cathedral was, without a doubt, the symbolic representation of the first step in Francis' rise to earthly power in the Church. It would prove his greatest challenge since his call to faith some fifty-five years prior.

The Buenos Aires Cathedral had such a distinct history of adversity that it seemed to be the perfect place for a man who had embraced patience as a supreme value. More than four hundred years earlier, Buenos Aires' founder, the Spanish conquistador Juan de Garay, drove the first cross into the high ground surrounding the Plaza de Mayo in 1580. Garay decided that a church would be built there, despite being surrounded by hostile natives who threatened to destroy any traces of Catholic faith. Ambushed by the local, indigenous tribe while asleep on the banks of the Rio de la Plata, Garay and his group were murdered.

Legend has it that the land on which the church was to be built was cursed by the Querandies tribe, and subsequent events seemed to bore this out. The first adobe and wood construction was so unstable that it was demolished in 1605 due to imminent threat of collapse. Another church was constructed in its place, which, in 1618, was also demolished due to faulty construction and substandard materials.

Then, on January 19, 1621, Pope Paul V decided Buenos Aires was to be elevated to diocese, which urgently required a new building to fulfill the needs of the bishopric. This would be considered the first proper cathedral, but by 1641, it, too, was in a grave state of disrepair. And so, in 1662, five thousand pesos were requested from the treasury of the Castile and Aragon Kingdom[3] to construct a new building — the fourth to be erected in less than a hundred years.

Finally completed in 1671, the new cathedral boasted a wooden ceiling, three naves, and a tower. Yet once more, low-quality materials were used, and by 1678, an additional 12,000 pesos for repairs were requested from His Majesty in Spain. In 1680, when repairs were underway, the heavy altarpiece caused the ceiling to cave and severely compromised the integrity of the tower. Demolition was inevitable.

The year 1725 would see another new construction, and the year 1752 would bear witness to yet another disaster — the fifth to date. That was the last and final collapse. In 1758, the current cathedral was consecrated, putting an end to two centuries of calamity.

The Buenos Aires Metropolitan Cathedral, with such a complex history of ruin and rebirth, would become the place where Francis spent the longest portion of his life. He lived there for twenty-one years, from the beginning of his bishopric in 1992 until he left for Rome to occupy the papacy.

The place where a man works and sleeps speaks volumes about him. And Francis' home at the Buenos Aires Cathedral certainly has a story to tell. One might be surprised to learn that Francis, as bishop or archbishop, never used his formal office, a sober yet spacious room located on the second floor of a building adjacent to the Cathedral. In his opinion, it could intimidate visitors; he feared they might interpret his power as excessive, making him seem arrogant. He was always careful not to send that type of message; he considered arrogance to be among the most serious of sins — even more damaging than hatred.

So Francis decided to set up an office in a smaller space located on the first floor. His secretary's office was actually larger than his own. And as for his secretary's duties, for that matter, they didn't include setting any of his appointments. From his scant, humble workspace, Francis preferred to personally manage his schedule.

Amidst his impeccably ordered office, a glance at his tiny desktop serves as a window into the soul of a man. Under its glass top, scattered holy cards picturing consecrated virgins and saints are situated among a smattering of photos from Francis' prolific pastoral life. One that stands out is that of Juan José Jaime, better known as "el Cuervo" (the Crow). His photo depicts an almost terminally impoverished soul, devastated by drugs and alcohol. Now forty-three years old, Juan lived most of his life battered by the scourge of addiction. His home was a dump truck in the slum called Villa 21-24, in the Barracas neighborhood. El Cuervo and Francis would cross paths there, and somehow, through compassion and faith, Francis managed to pull him from the jaws of addiction. He remained with Juan until he recovered, and he kept the photo as proof that even the most hopeless of situations can be overcome with the help of God's grace.

Francis' living quarters, devoid of luxury or superfluous decoration, exuded an aura of asceticism and austerity. Just one floor above was Francis' bedroom, and like his office, it was extremely humble and spartan in decor. There was only a simple wooden bed, a crucifix that had traveled across the sea with his grandparents, and an electric heater to soften the harsh cold in the throes of Buenos Aires' humid winters. In the hallway was a pedestal showcasing an image of Christ, seated and wearing a crown of thorns: the Christ of Patience.

Across from Francis' living quarters was a room that he used as a library. He was always known to say that he didn't want to leave work behind when he died. In fact, he ended up discarding much of the material he wrote during his pastoral years. He did become very attached to one particular piece, however, and for some forty-five years, he has literally and figuratively carried it close to his heart, all the way to Saint Peter's throne. It was written in a moment of great spiritual intensity, shortly before being ordained a priest, and has since served as his personal credo.

> I want to believe in God the Father, that he loves me like a son, and in Jesus, the Lord, who instilled his Spirit in my life to make me smile and so take me to the eternal kingdom of life.

> I believe in my story, which was moved by God's loving gaze on a Spring Day, September 21, when He came to greet and invite me to follow Him.

> I believe in my pain, barren from selfishness, where I take refuge.

> I believe in my soul's abjection, which seeks to swallow without giving . . . Without giving.

> I believe the rest are good, and that I must fearlessly love them, without ever betraying them for my own safety.

> I believe in religious life.

> I believe I want to love a lot.

> I believe in everyday death, burning, which I avoid, but it smiles at me, inviting me to accept it.

> I believe in God's patience, welcoming, as good as a summer night.

> I believe dad is in heaven with the Lord.

> I believe Father Duarte [the priest who heard his confession that September 21] is also there, interceding on behalf of my priesthood.

> I believe in Mary, my mother, who loves me and will never leave me alone.

> And I await each day's surprise where love, strength, betrayal, and sin will manifest themselves and will accompany me until the final encounter with that marvelous face, which I do not know, and I continuously escape, yet I want to get to know and love.

> Amen.

The text is surprisingly simple and without hidden meaning. On the other hand, its innocent candor is hardly indicative of the Francis who was always open to the study of various philosophers and thinkers, in spite of them being against Catholic tradition.

Francis kept this precious document tucked in another of his most dear possessions: his breviary.[4] Also among its pages is the letter from his Nonna Rosa, as well as a poem by Italian writer Nino Costa entitled "Rassa Nostrana," an ode to the Italian emigration phenomenon that his grandmother would emotionally recite to him as a child. Consisting of two volumes, his breviary always accompanies him whenever and wherever he travels.

Also in his library, on a shelf, was a bowl full of white roses and a Santa Teresita holy card. When he had a complicated problem, Francis turned to that saint — not for her to resolve it, but rather to help him assume the problem.

Is it possible for an ecclesiastical leader to administer his power effectively from a place of such modesty? Francis was proof that it was. Furthermore, not only was it possible, but Francis believed it was *necessary*.

It was this tendency toward simplicity that enabled him to efficiently balance the many demands of his position. His job required rigorous focus and almost round-the-clock attention; Francis routinely woke up each day at 5 a.m., and retired shortly before midnight. Invariably, his day began with a two-hour prayer and meditation session, followed by work. After his frugal lunch, he'd take a short, forty-five-minute nap. Throughout his day, he dedicated as much time as possible to everyone he encountered, from the nation's politicians and most powerful businessmen to the poorest of the poor, the shoeless, the declassed, the marginalized — those without health, or family, or hope.

As bishop, Francis' schedule remained virtually unchanged for six years, but his work was about to become even more demanding. On the morning of February 28, 1998, Nuncio Ubaldo Calabresi called him again, this time to invite him to dinner. Although Francis rarely ever went out to dinner (he preferred to cook his own meals and eat alone, in meditation and contemplation), he clearly could not refuse a superior's request.

On that day, as they sipped their post-dinner coffee — a typical time for Argentines to discuss important issues — Francis noticed with surprise that the nuncio called the waiter over and whispered in his ear to bring dessert and champagne. He quickly thought of possible causes for celebration but couldn't pinpoint any, and from what he remembered, Nuncio Calabresi's birthday was on January 2, still ten months away.

Intrigued and consumed with anxiety, Francis asked if there was a holiday that had somehow slipped his mind. "No," answered the nuncio, "it's not your birthday or mine. We are celebrating because you are the new Archbishop of Buenos Aires."

It didn't end there. The nuncio, following John Paul II's instruction, also appointed him primate of Argentina and consecrated cardinal through the Pope. And just as he had done six years earlier in the Còrdoba airport, he delivered the news, promptly concluded the conversation, and was on his way.

With this new title, Francis became the top official in the Argentine Church. From that moment, his responsibilities would become exponentially greater. His every action would now be scrutinized — for the next sixteen years — by Argentina's government, financial and union establishments, the high dignitaries of other religious communities, and, of course, by the Church authorities in Rome.

True to form, Francis' first mandate was to make Jesus' church a reality: in other words, to make it a church for the poor. Hence, his first initiative was to dispatch an army of *curas villaros* (slum priests) to the various impoverished settlements of Buenos Aires and its surrounding industrial belt. To lend force to that initial push, he created the office of the Vicaria Episcopal para la Pastoral en Villas de Emergencia (Episcopal Pastoral Vicar for Slums in Crisis). Francis was committed to choosing for this office those priests whom he believed would be inspiring examples of social justice. It was the face of a new church — one truly committed to the poor and their needs.

No one needed to tell Francis what life was like in the slums. Since his return to Buenos Aires in 1992, he had walked the intricate alleys of Villa 1-11-14, the most populated and dangerous of slums, which was predominately populated by Peruvians, Bolivians, and Paraguayans in the 1990s. It had the unfortunate distinction of housing more drug-trafficking-related criminals per square mile than in all of Latin America.

Nowadays, around twenty thousand piled-up families — some sixty thousand inhabitants — survive in Villa 1-11-14. Francis used to walk its narrow streets on Saturdays and Sundays at dawn. The typical landscape consisted of trash — everything from food scraps to industrial waste — as well as hundreds of signs advertising the locally famous "broaster chicken" and dozens of sneakers hanging from electric wires, pointing out the places that sold cocaine, cocaine-based paste, crack cocaine, heroin, marijuana, ecstasy pills, or methamphetamines.

Amidst the squalor and addiction, Francis saw something else in that devastated barrio. He was convinced that in Argentina's slums, like others worldwide, religious practice was very strong, and this faith ran deep. He always believed that all of society should rest its gaze on the slums, because they carried a message from which all should learn.

Francis called the inhabitants of this peripheral society the "new slaves," or the "modern slaves." He always told his slum priest staff that slaves no longer arrived in Argentina by boat as they did in the seventeenth century. Rather, undocumented Bolivian immigrants who crossed the border were taken to the Buenos Aires slums to work under inhumane conditions in clandestine knitting and sewing shops. These "workers" suffered a degree of degradation akin to those from the Dominican Republic, Eastern Europe, and even the rural provinces of Argentina, who were smuggled in by human traffickers and turned to prostitution.[5]

Francis' experiences with human trafficking victims left such an indelible impression on him that after his first month as Pope, in a special audience in Rome, he received Susana Trimarco, the mother of María de los Ángeles Verón. The young "Marita" had been kidnapped in 2002 by a human trafficking network consisting of criminals and corrupt police officers and simply disappeared. Her family or the authorities were never able to recover her body.[6]

In cases of such extreme impoverishment and degradation, the desire to find meaning in a world where all seems lost is tremendously strong. Francis explained to his slum priests the theological phenomenon of the disadvantaged to seek out the *kerygma* —apostolic preaching of salvation through Christ's example — in times of dire desperation and suffering. The Christian kerygma can be summed up as follows: Jesus Christ is God; he became man to save us; he lived in the world like one of us; he suffered, died, was buried, and then was resurrected.

That is Christ's message — that we, too, may overcome our own suffering if we put our trust in this mystery of faith. Some, like Mary Magdalene, believe instantly, at first sight. Others believe after having doubts. And still others, like the Apostle Thomas, need to physically see and touch the wound to believe it exists. Each person has his or her own way of arriving at faith. Francis explained faith as a meeting with Christ, and the most impoverished of souls is the first to seek and be in the presence of Christ.

That's why Francis ministered by example in the Buenos Aires slums. His commitment to the underprivileged of his community is best illustrated by his continual practice of the Holy Thursday ritual.[7] Each Holy

Thursday, he would travel by bus, just as the average citizen would, to the city slums and proceed to wash the feet of men, women, and children — twelve in total, as Jesus did with his twelve apostles. This sign of humility would be repeated even during his years as Archbishop of Buenos Aires. To widespread coverage in the media, Francis continued this practice during his first Holy Week in Rome, where he visited a youth prison and washed the feet of twelve inmates, two of which were female.

During his time spent in the villas, Francis couldn't help but notice the fervor and dedication with which Father José María "Pepe" Di Paola cared for the residents. Father Pepe — bearded, long haired, and almost forty years Francis' junior — spent most of his life in Villa 21-21.

Father Pepe openly admired Francis: "Since he became archbishop," Pepe recalled, "he got involved and chose the people in the slums. He not only assigned more priests for the work, but also gave us resources." When Father Pepe first arrived in Villa 21 in 1997, there were forty thousand people in the district, but only four priests. From those humble beginnings, Father Pepe went on to build a network of farms for the recovery of child addicts, a community dining hall, a radio station, a business school, and a residence for the elderly.

Father Pepe always said that Francis was not only a friend, but also a sort of spiritual father. "One of the lessons that has always stayed with me," Pepe remembered, "is that the center of Argentina is not the Plaza de Mayo. He taught us that the center is the periphery. The slums — the places where people are excluded." This example of humility had a profound influence on Pepe's life's work.

Just as important as his pastoral and community work was the battle Francis fought against the drug lords and their hit men. By 2009, the pressure put on the priests by drug traffickers who produced, and sold drugs in Villa 21-24 had dangerously escalated. The team of slum priests, led by Francis, composed and released a document claiming that drugs were essentially decriminalized in the forgotten settlements and slums of the City of Buenos Aires. In this statement, the priests stress that the legal system has turned a blind eye to these areas where the cycle of drug trade and crime is so outrageously rampant.

As the media and people of Argentina learned of the news, the full implications of such a claim became evident, as the lives of the young priests of the villas were in danger. And that danger was very real — these dealers and smugglers were as vicious as any other Latin American cartel. The threat of physical violence against the priests — including extortion, death threats, and even direct murder attempts — was not uncommon.

The risks were so grave that Francis took a public stance, using his religious and political power to its fullest extent, exposing the death threats that Pepe and other priests received from the Villa 21-24 drug lords. The main threat came from the dealers of a cocaine-based paste known as *paco*, a very low-cost drug — one dollar can buy you a hit that could be lethal. Paco, similar to crack cocaine, is made from cocaine residue, but that isn't its only hazard; it might also contain glass or ground steel sponges, and it is often processed with sulfuric acid and kerosene.

"This is not a priest issue," said Francis, "it's everyone's issue; it's my issue as Archbishop of Buenos Aires and all of the bishops we support. We have to defend the 'offspring.' Our only option is to guide the children along the path of light."

Francis' potent message resounded in the corridors of power. After his statement, the Argentine government ordered the City of Buenos Aires slums and the Greater Buenos Aires industrial belt to be patrolled by the National Gendarmerie, a military force that specialized in securing the borders but also combated organized crime related to the production and sale of illegal drugs. No one wanted to carry the weight of the death of one of those young priests on their conscious.

The priests who do Francis' work are considered the spiritual heirs of the Movement of Priests for the Third World, led by priest Carlos Mugica in Argentina in the 1970s. Today, almost forty years after Mugica's violent death at the hands of a paramilitary group in 1974, they feel their commitment to the poor does not demand political partisanship or right or left ideological alignment; their commitment is based in faith alone.

Mugica's memory was a light that guided Father Pepe. "I value him more each day," Pepe once said. "The love he had for the Church, the priestly vocation, amidst a strong political discussion, which never changed his love for the priesthood and the poor. Even during the hardest of times, he had the clarity to say, 'No guys, this is a democracy, let's continue as a democracy.' I believe Mugica is one of the best examples the Catholic Church has, and today, those who used to criticize him value him. Mugica turned the priesthood around; he didn't remain in the church, but injected himself into social life, work, universities, and communication. He tries to see reality from the Gospel and the Church's social doctrine."

Priest Gustavo Carrara, thirty-six years old, is Francis' bastion in Villa

1-11-14. As with the entire slum priest team, he does not avoid confronting the debate from an ideological standpoint. Clear and straightforward, Carrara says, "I do not follow Marx; I follow the Gospel and the figure of Jesus. That is how my choosing the poor is embodied. My commitment to poverty comes from a religious perspective, not a political one. Because I want to remind you that Saint John Chrysostom, who lived in the third century, has texts that are much more daring than Marx."

Francis leaves the theoretical debates for his thoughts. He likes "practical" religion — the religion that deals with everyday life. That's how Darío Giménez, a humble businessman with two daughters, remembers him. He met the Holy Father on a bus, a few stops before arriving at Villa 21-24 in Barracas. Fifteen years ago, Darío, inspired by Father Pepe, converted to Catholicism when he experienced firsthand the teachings of Christ in his own community. Since then, Darío has worked as a volunteer at Nuestra Señora de Caacupé Church. "He's so humble he made me feel good," says Darío when recalling how he met Francis before he became Pope. "The last time he came, we invited him and he stayed for dinner. We didn't have anything very elaborate, just some spaghetti with tomato sauce. I will never forget his words. Suddenly, he looked into my eyes and said, 'I like to sit at the table of the poor because they serve food and share their heart. Sometimes those who have the most only share their food.'"

Religion for the people — the Christian faith in its simplest and starkest form — is Francis' faith. Whether in the villas or the churches, the location didn't matter — the idea was to minister to those who desired and needed it most. Graciela Bottega lost her twenty-four-year-old daughter, Tatiana Portiroli, in a Buenos Aires rail disaster known as the Once Tragedy.[8] Bottega said, "No one cared about what I felt. I hadn't lost my purse on the train, I had lost my daughter." Her pain was immense. After the funeral, Graciela couldn't find the support she needed to start her life over. But one day, she checked her e-mail and found a message from Francis. "I will never forget it. Someone cared about my life. Someone took interest in my pain." That simple e-mail left her with a renewed sense of hope and enabled her to carry on. One year after the tragedy, on its anniversary, the woman went to the Cathedral and found the author of those words, standing tall and greeting every one of the survivors and family members. "He hugged us all. He kissed us all. He looked into all of our eyes and he listened. We expected the support of an important someone, and he was the only one to provide it."

Francis' greatest efforts have been low profile — acts of random and humble service, invisible to the media's eye, which have proven his most effective method of evangelization. Yet he has also been willing to speak out in support of his passionate beliefs, as he did when he confronted the drug lords in the barrios. Another cause of his is combating hypocrisy in the church, particularly exclusion based on "old world" beliefs. Openly voicing his disapproval, he reminded his fellow clergymen, "In our ecclesiastical region there are priests who don't baptize the children of single mothers because they weren't conceived in the sanctity of marriage. These are today's hypocrites — those who clericalize the Church; those who separate the people of God from salvation. And this poor girl who, rather than returning the child to sender, had the courage to carry it into the world, must wander from parish to parish so that it's baptized!"

———————

The Luján Virgin, a terracotta icon made in 1630, is one of many representations by which the Virgin Mary is venerated. Sanctified by Pope Pius XI, she's been the patron of Argentina, Uruguay, and Paraguay since 1930. On October 29, 1893, Father Federico Grote, founder of the Catholic Worker's Circle, was the first to organize a pilgrimage to her sanctuary at Luján, a city located on the outskirts of Buenos Aires. Accompanied by four hundred men carrying the Argentine flag, they arrived at the virgin's feet to ask for employment protection. Three years later, there were three thousand pilgrims, and since then it has become a biannual event. The largest gathering of Argentina's faithful, every May 8 (the feast day of Our Lady of Luján) and December 8 (for the Feast of the Immaculate Conception), throngs of believers converge on Luján.

Francis has had perfect attendance. He's attended as a priest, as a bishop, and later as archbishop, but always first and foremost, as a pilgrim, side by side with his community. "This is the house of faith of our nation," Francis would say upon arrival at the sanctuary as cardinal.

In 1982, the sanctuary opened its doors to receive Pope John Paul II, who had come to Argentina while it was still at war with Great Britain over the Falkland Islands. It was a pastoral trip. "My trip to Argentina's capital," he said in a missive he wrote himself, "is a journey of love, hope, and goodwill, of a Father who is off to meet his children who suffer."

At the sanctuary, the Holy Father prayed for peace before the patron saint, offering up the historic "Golden Rose" he had brought from Rome.[9] A likely record-breaking 700,000 people were present at the basilica and its surroundings that day, listening to the mass he celebrated together with cardinals, bishops, and priests. John Paul II gave a homily in which he urged his followers to live in the image of Christ, and he prayed for the lives lost in the war with Great Britain and for an end to the conflict.

Francis especially enjoyed those pilgrimages and masses at Luján because of the living history and symbolism within the basilica, but above all because of the proximity it gave him to the people, especially the youth, of Argentina. He spoke to them frankly, urging them to join together with their community. "Let us be taught where to look more openly and readily available, less selfishly or interested," he pleaded in one of his homilies. "Let us be taught not to do our own thing, not to have people say of each of us, 'He does his own thing,' but rather create a view, a great view that makes us brothers, so that we are always concerned about everyone else."

Francis was also known to routinely join pilgrims each August 7 at the Sanctuary of Saint Cayetano, located on the west side of Buenos Aires. The Feast of Saint Cayetano, similar to the pilgrimage to Luján, is a phenomena of religious culture in Argentina and other Latin American and Catholic countries, whereby the faithful honor effigies of saints in hopes that a particular worldly need will be fulfilled. Saint Cayetano is probably the most venerated saint of the working class.

Saint Cayetano is not from Argentina, but from Italy. San Gaetano di Tiene was born in Venice and lived in Naples during the Renaissance. Before being sainted, he constructed hospitals for the terminally ill and founded a bank (which eventually became the Bank of Naples) so that the poor could avoid borrowing money at astronomical interest rates from usurers. He is best known as the patron saint of the unemployed or, as it's also put, of *pan y trabajo* (bread and work). To Argentines he's a *santo porteño* (a Buenos Aires saint), who left his eternal imprint, particularly in Liniers, a working-class and commercial neighborhood in Buenos Aires.

In Francis' homily from August, 7, 2012, we glean the true essence of the spirit of Saint Cayetano:

> Justice is that which gladdens the heart: when there is something for everyone; when one sees that there is equality, fairness; and when each has his own. When one sees that there is enough for

all, one feels a special joy in the heart. Each one's heart swells and merges with the others and makes us feel the Fatherland. The country flourishes when we see "noble equality on the throne," as our national anthem says. Injustice, by contrast, casts a shadow over everything. How sad it is when one sees that the resources could be perfectly adequate for everyone and it turns out to be not enough. [. . .] To say "all the boys and girls" is to say the entire future; to say "all the retirees" is to say all our history. Our people know that the whole is greater than the parts and that is why we ask for "bread and work for all." How despicable, then, is the one who treasures up belongings only for today, who has a tiny, selfish heart and only thinks about swiping that slice that he will not even take with him when he dies. Because nobody takes anything with them. I have never seen a moving van behind a funeral procession. My grandmother used to tell us, "The shroud has no pockets."

Charity, brotherhood, love of one's neighbor — Francis' powerful words that August day represent the very cornerstone of his pastoral doctrine.

Chapter 6

Politics and Faith, Two Roads

A FEW HOURS AFTER the papal conclave concluded and Francis was named the Roman Catholic Church's 266th pope, the digital edition of the Spanish newspaper *El Mundo* unearthed the controversies that surrounded Francis' political involvement in Argentina, especially with respect to the progressive policies of Néstor Kirchner (president of Argentina, 2003–2007), his wife, Cristina Fernández de Kirchner (Argentina's current president), and the military dictatorship of 1976–1983. The headline read: "Hard on the Kirchners, Soft on the Dictatorship."

Those eight words represent the embodiment of Francis' political challenges throughout his rise through the ranks of the Argentine Church. The article caused a media sensation, as it revisited Francis' and the Church's role in the greatest tragedy in Argentine history: the Dirty War. But in order to fully understand Francis' political ideals as they relate to his ecclesiastical philosophy, as well as how he navigated the turbulent events in Argentina in the mid-twentieth century, one must first understand the nature of the political climate in which Jorge Bergoglio was brought up.

Peronism, the political ideology of military officer and former Argentine president Juan Domingo Perón, has a seventy-year history. It grew out of a working-class movement of the masses, establishing a middle path between communism and capitalism during its initial stage, Juan Perón's first presidency, from 1946 to 1955. Though the Peronist reign ended with the 1976 ousting of Isabel Perón (third wife of Juan Perón) by military coup, Peronism's impact was still felt during the ensuing dictatorship, when the

Movement of Priests for the Third World turned their focus toward the disadvantaged despite the dangers involved. It loomed in the background when the neoliberal and conservative right were in power from 1989 to 1999, as evidenced by President Carlos Menem's promise of salary increases for the working class. In all, Peronism, a political movement consistently endorsed by the working class's majority vote, has officially governed Argentina for thirty-three of the last sixty-eight years, yet it continued to have a significant influence on Argentine politics even during years of conservative rule.

For all its popularity and endurance, Peronism has still been unable to deliver economic stability to its bedrock constituents. Julio María Sanguinetti, twice president of neighboring Uruguay, used a refined sense of irony to explain the dichotomy of Argentina's economy and politics. To understand the space that Argentina occupies in the world's economic landscape, Sanguinetti explained, "Countries could be classified into four categories: first, the developed countries; next, the underdeveloped countries; third, Japan, whose development cannot be explained; and finally Argentina, whose underdevelopment cannot be explained." This thought-provoking observation brings into question: Why, in a country so rich in natural resources, should such a large population of Argentines be unemployed, living in substandard conditions, and starving?

Like the Argentine economy, Peronism itself is not without its contradictions. In 2010, during an assembly of Latin American countries, Brazilian president Luiz Inácio Lula da Silva was asked what his political ideology might be if, instead of being born in northeast Brazil, he would have been born in one of Argentina's provinces. "I would've probably been a Peronist because everyone was or is one. But, in truth, I find it hard to comprehend. I don't really understand Peronism, but I do understand the significance and phenomenon of Perón's time in Argentina, just like the Getulio Vargas phenomenon in Brazil.[1] They defined the history of our countries. Getulio didn't manage to create in Brazil the type of movement founded by Perón in Argentina. We didn't have such a strong working-class party as Peronism. However, when I say I don't quite understand it, it's because it's almost like a religion. I've seen people on the right who are Peronist and I've seen people on the left who are Peronist. That is unheard of in any other place in the world. It's a miracle created only by Argentines."

Francis was not even eighteen years old when he was introduced to politics by his lab boss, Esther Ballestrino de Careaga. As previously discussed, she was a steadfast Communist. She knew Francis not only had religious thoughts but was also interested in politics. Esther advised him to read, among other books, *Nuestra Palabra y Propósitos* (*Our Word and Purposes*), an Argentine Communist Party publication that was quite popular during the 1940s and 1950s. Always stimulated by cultural and intellectual ideas, he was intrigued by the philosophy of Argentine Communist theorist Leónidas Barletta. But he was far from being a Communist; he was a true Peronist.

In 1954, when Argentina's Peronist Party had won the midterm elections with 62 percent of the vote, Jorge was only a few months shy of the legal voting age. Unfortunately, his first opportunity to exercise this right of citizenship would be delayed; when he finally turned eighteen and could legally vote, the 1955 coup d'état to depose Juan Perón occurred.

At this point in history, being both a Peronist and a practicing Catholic divided one's loyalties. Prior to the coup, Perón had accused Argentina's ecclesiastic hierarchy of conspiring with the military that wanted to overthrow him. He responded to this threat with extremely radical laws that directly contradicted religious doctrine: he enacted a law legalizing divorce, recognized the rights of so-called "illegitimate children," gave prostitution a legal framework, and prohibited public religious events. By the end of his first presidency, masses could not be celebrated outside of church, religious education was abolished in public schools (a blow to the Church, since its pastoral mission was firmly rooted in the school system), and ecclesiastic property tax extensions were cancelled.

In that climate of extreme confrontation, the traditional Catholic Corpus Christi procession[2] of June 11, 1955, became an anti-Peronist manifestation of more than one hundred thousand protestors. Argentine flags were burned that afternoon, and Perón's government reacted by deporting two bishops to Rome. The Vatican launched a counterattack, and those responsible for the bishops' expulsion were excommunicated from the Church, including Perón himself.

Then, on the fateful morning of June 16, sectors of Argentina's army, air force, and navy initiated a putsch[3] against Perón. They bombed the Plaza de Mayo, killing at least 350 innocent civilians and injuring more than 600. Perón survived the attack and, blaming the ecclesiastic hierarchy for providing the coup attempt with logistic support, initiated a harsh retaliation against the churches of Buenos Aires that very afternoon. As many as sixteen churches were burned, including the historic Cathedral — the same one that would house Francis as archbishop almost forty years later. In many cases, the churches were looted of liturgical vessels and other sacred objects.

How did this savage confrontation between government and church affect Francis both politically and religiously? He had always rejected all extreme and totalitarian ideology — which he believed included Communism, Fascism, Nazism, and Liberalism — but now, along with all Argentine citizens, he was immersed in the antagonism between Peronism and the Church.

The fact is, he tried to reconcile both positions. He attended the Corpus Christi procession, but not to rally against Perón. He was harshly critical of the burning of churches as revenge, but he was still a Peronist at heart. It was the first time Francis personally experienced what he always defined as his country's pathology — the Argentine tendency to point out what divides rather than what unites, which reinforces conflict rather than promoting compromise.

From that experience, Francis salvaged the concept of the "meeting culture," a philosophy based in communication, understanding, and acceptance, without prejudice, and without rejecting contrary ideas, whether religious or political. However, as in many cases, reality would supersede reason. Following Perón's ouster, a merciless eighteen-year persecution of Peronism began. Thousands of Peronists were forced into exile, including their leader. Counterrevolutionaries were executed. Plans were made to assassinate union leaders, mainly of the Justicialist[4] movement. Artists, intellectuals, and athletes were "purged" just for having sympathized with the doctrine. An absurd measure was even implemented banning the mention of Perón's name in public.

Argentina's harsh institutional changes fueled Francis' political inclination and his commitment to defend the rights of the disenfranchised. And he was not alone. In the years that followed, the Peronist resistance that emerged at the beginning of the 1960s gave birth to guerrilla youth movements that demanded Perón's return and a turn toward socialism. By the early 1970s, these guerilla groups became more hostile and violent, which prompted a profound division of Peronism into a right and left wing.

This split in the Peronist ranks ultimately led to bloodshed. On June 20, 1973, as more than two million supporters awaited Perón's return to Argentina at Buenos Aires' Ezeiza Airport, snipers affiliated with the right wing of Peronism opened fire on the crowd, killing 13 people and injuring 365. The deepening of the violence between the two camps unleashed an undeclared civil war, and Perón's death in 1974 would leave a power vacuum that could not possibly be filled, even by his widow, Isabel, who subsequently served as president for two years. The struggle finally culminated in the military coup of 1976 and the beginning of the brutal dictatorship years.

During this time, Francis was acting Provincial Superior in the Society of Jesus, submerged in Jesuit life. Though the country was shrouded in obscurity where the atrocities of the Dirty War were concerned, Francis and the Society were not exempt from the violent hand of the dictatorship. Carrying out the dictates of the Second Vatican Council and remaining eternally loyal to the Society of Jesus, though not always in accord with one another, were both paramount and challenging to Francis.

Alarmed by a growing liberal mind-set within the Catholic Church, Pope Pius IX convened the First Vatican Council in 1869. Of the two major dogmas set forth, *Pastor Aeternus*, or Papal Infallibility, was the most controversial. The second doctrine of the council, *Dei Filius* (Son of God), elucidating the Church's teachings and the mysteries of the Catholic faith, urged followers to reject reason in favor of faith. In 1870, the council was ended abruptly due to the outbreak of the Franco-Prussian War.

Following the First Vatican Council, Pope Pius X displayed a certain consistency in his decisions and declarations, which did not require the summoning of another council. Popes Pius XI and XII, on the other hand, were interested in reforming the work of the First Council. In 1923, Pius XI, hoping to finally salve the ravages of World War I that still plagued Europe, envisioned a new council that would revive spiritual values. But when he tried to review the original First Council documents, he was met with opposition. Pius XII had the same desire, but failing health prevented him from pursuing his agenda. With the passing of Pius XII in late 1958, Pope John XXIII was elected to the papacy at a time when the idea of a new Vatican Council had long since been shelved. Therefore, the call for "an ecumenical council for the universal Church," made by John XXIII on January 25, 1959, surprised the world and concerned the Roman curia.

Seventy-eight-year-old John XXIII had been elected pope only three months earlier, during a brief conclave (October 25–28, 1958). He was considered a temporary, compromise candidate for the papacy during a time when there were frequent tensions between conservatives and progressives within the Church. The post-war era in which he assumed office was a time of dizzying social and cultural change. It encompassed the end of colonialism and the growing and active presence of the Third World in global affairs; the continued industrialization of countries in the Northern Hemisphere; the decline of rural communities and the rise of huge urban centers; the birth of a consumer society; and finally, the advent of television, with its powerful impact on cultural and behavioral standards.

In the face of this mass social upheaval, Pope John XXIII saw a pressing need for a religious turnaround. He wanted to refocus the world's attention on such humanitarian issues as ongoing hunger in a large part of the world, the lack of human rights in countless countries, and the US-Soviet nuclear arms race that threatened to destroy humankind.

The Second Vatican Council, contrary to other councils (of which there were twenty-one throughout Christianity's history), was not summoned to reject heresy or bestow more power upon the papacy. Its first purpose, per John XXIII, was very clear: the *aggiornamento* (updating) of the Church, a term that replaced the word "reform." It was about renewal, adaptation, dialogue, and openness.

However, one of the three great objectives of the Council was the one that made the deepest impression on Francis, as it did on most of the bishops of Latin America who witnessed daily the pains of underdevelopment in their home countries. "The Church presents itself," John XXIII stated, "as it is and how it wants to be, as the Church for everyone, especially as the Church for the poor."

Years later, while speaking with some six thousand journalists, Pope Francis recalled how this dictum of John XXIII resurfaced during his own unlikely ascension to the papacy. During the conclave within the Sistine Chapel that consecrated him as pope, Brazilian Cardinal Claudio Hummes, Archbishop Emeritus of São Paulo, was by his side. As the voting took place and Francis emerged as a leading candidate, Hummes comforted him. In the end, when he had received two thirds of the votes, the chapel broke into applause. Hummes hugged and kissed him, and whispered in his ear, "Don't forget about the poor!"

"And that word went here," confessed Francis, touching his temple. "'The poor, the poor,' drummed inside my head. That relationship with the humblest ones made me think of Saint Francis of Assisi. I immediately thought of the wars in the world. And that also brought me to Francis, the man of peace. And so came about my name, from the heart. I was supposed to be called Francis because he is the man of poverty, the name of peace. Only the poor can provide peace. That is why my biggest wish is to be the pope of a poor Church for the poor."

In line with John XXIII's explicit call to shepherd the disadvantaged and downtrodden, a significant detail of the Second Vatican Council was the diverse representation in attendance. At the First Vatican Council, only 744 bishops attended, most of which were Italians. At the "Council of the poor," some 2,500 bishops were present, including more than 500 from Latin America, around 350 from Africa, and another 400 from Asia, Oceania, and the Arab world. In other words, almost half the bishops at the Council represented the positions and demands of millions of poor Catholics from underdeveloped countries.

The Second Vatican Council convened over four sessions corresponding to the autumns of 1962, 1963, 1964, and 1965, each one lasting two to three months. Pope John XXIII only lived to see the first session. When he died in June 1963, Giovanni Montini, named Pope Paul VI, was quickly elected to replace him.

What defines a council, in short, is its message. The Second Vatican Council tried to revive the Christian mandate through a renewal of God's words and liturgy. Its three objectives were to ensure the Mass would involve more personal interaction between clergy and congregation (resulting in the suspension of Latin in favor of each country's native language); strongly encourage unity among Catholics and fellow Christians; and initiate a world dialogue with a special emphasis on an "option for the poor."[6]

While the Council of Trent and Vatican I, the two previous councils, created theology from an abstract mode, concerned with precise, clear, and universal definitions, the Second Vatican Council used a biblical, patristic, and symbolic language; in other words, pastoral vernacular. It was a historic shift — a profound effort to return to it's roots and to engage the Church more directly with its flock and the modern world in which they lived.

During the Council sessions of the early to mid-1960s, the Cold War between the United States and the Soviet Union was reaching its height. Amidst the ideological battle between capitalism and communism that underpinned the actual fighting between the two superpowers and their proxies, a modernist mind-set emerged, scientifically focused and consumer driven. The Justice and Peace Commission was born out of the Second Vatican Council to counteract this societal drift, focusing on promoting world peace through the spirit of the Gospel. The Vatican also spoke of the Church's "social doctrine," involving issues such as human and civil rights, racial discrimination, and all levels of political and social corruption.

This philosophical precept, the first of its kind from Rome, served as a call to action, especially to Latin American bishops. And the most noteworthy aspect of the Second Vatican Council for Francis and thousands of Latin American pastors was, again, this talk of a preferential option for the poor.

How did the Latin American Church interpret the Council's mandate to work for the poor? The most prominent answer came from a homogenous movement of bishops that set out to spread so-called "liberation theology." For the liberation theologians, the poor were victims of a "social sin," or a societal framework that maintains oppression, injustice, and exploitation. In conceptual terms, the liberation theology doctrinarians considered the plight of the poor to be a sin that went beyond individual faults and became a collective sin.

The roots of this dedication to the impoverished of Latin America can be traced to Brazil, the country with the largest number of poor in the entire region. The trend began in the 1950s, when Brazil's Catholic Church organized the so-called "Base Communities" (called CEBs, per their Portuguese name). These were largely autonomous worship groups organized in poor rural and urban areas that bypassed the hierarchical authority of the Catholic Church. By 1965, when the results of the Second Vatican Council were known, Base Communities were widespread throughout Latin America. Around the same time, Paulo Freire, a teacher from northeastern Brazil — the most impoverished part of the country — developed a new method of teaching reading and writing to the poor through a revolutionary "process of understanding." As well, students and workers in Brazil became committed to social justice and formed teams under the banner of the Catholic Action movement, as did important Catholic intellectuals. Some Christians also began to use Marxist concepts to analyze Latin American society.

In this revolutionary environment within the Latin American church, a Peruvian priest named Gustavo Gutiérrez developed liberation theology in 1972. His 1973 book, *A Theology of Liberation: History, Politics, and Salvation*, outlined the philosophy in detail. Among several of its propositions, *A Theology of Liberation* attempted to address how to maintain Christian faith in an environment of oppression, and how people could make faith liberating rather than alienating.

Some of the notable priests who became unwavering proponents of Gutiérrez' liberation theology were Leonardo Boff of Brazil, Camilo Torres Restrepo of Colombia, Manuel Perez Martinez of Spain, Oscar Romero of El Salvador, and Juan Luis Segundo of Uruguay. Restrepo eventually embraced the idea of taking up arms to defend liberation theology and became a member of the guerrilla movement National Liberation Army. He was killed in 1966 during his first combat operation against the national army.

Among the most active proponents of this political/religious philosophy were members of the Movement of Priests for the Third World, or simply the Third World Priests, the name by which they were recognized in each *villa miseria* or underdeveloped town in Argentina. The group had been inspired by the fight for African-American civil rights led by Martin Luther King, Jr. in the United States, by events in South Africa, where a vigorous form of liberation theology developed in the fight against apartheid, as well as in Asia with the *Minjung* theology (which in Korean means "of the popular mass") and the peasant theology that developed in the Philippines. Liberation theology, with its fusing of political and religious avenues to address social injustice, was a natural fit for many of the Third World Priests, who, day after day, confronted the misery of some of the most impoverished places in the world.

It is important to note that for centuries, Latin America did not have its own theological doctrine; its religious principles were imported from the papacy, which was the very epitome of old-world, European thought. As well, Latin America was majorly dependent on Europe both politically and financially. For a movement to arise within the deeply traditional social order of Latin America that directly confronted the established authority of the Roman Catholic Church was truly a revolutionary development.

How did the young Francis interpret this secular insurgency? Could he consider himself a part of the Movement of Priests for the Third World, with its inclination toward liberation theology to minister to the poor? The reality is that he couldn't have even if he had wanted to because he had not yet been ordained as a priest. But even more accurately, he never found it easy to fit in with a particular political ideology. To Francis, the only valid ideology was the pure and simple theology of the Gospel, which was precisely the philosophy of Francis of Assisi.

Francis of Assisi carefully observed the practical teachings of Jesus, which inspired him to adopt pastoral methods to instill happiness in the poor. He couldn't bear their pain for them, and he didn't expect them to offer it to God to gain access to Heaven. According to the sacred texts, Jesus cured all: He resurrected the dead, turned water into wine to prolong joyous festivity, and did not impose fasts and penances on his disciples.

Jesus' response to oppression, unlike the Marxist reaction to "unjust structures," was neither theoretical, nor did it incite class struggle. It was a practical call to ease mankind's suffering. To cure a leper, whose sores were seen as divine punishment, was the biggest slap in the face to both the civil and religious powers of the time. So was washing the apostles' feet, or defending the adulteress against the Pharisees that demanded her being stoned to death in the name of Judaic law.

Francis' theology, and likely Saint Francis' before him, harkens back through Jesus' teachings to that of the Old Testament prophet Amos, the former shepherd who didn't even belong to the prophet class and who made it his calling to attack the mechanisms of peasant exploitation and oppression carried out by tyrannical kings. Amos, however, attacked both social injustice and the sin of idolism — the worship of anything other than God. To him, as to Jesus eight centuries later, God was the true protector and liberator of the oppressed.

That is why Amos was called the "prophet of the poor." And that is why the option for the poor that emerged as a priority from the Second Vatican Council could certainly have brought young Francis closer to so-called liberation theology. But that was not the case. Francis distanced himself from it precisely due to the Marxist instruments that the Movement of Priests for Third World took hold of to fight against social injustice. To Francis, religion, as seen and practiced in line with the prophet Amos, was not the "opiate of the masses" as Marxists claimed, but rather their guarantee of redemption. By the mid-1960s and throughout the 1970s, when thousands of young Argentine Catholics around the country began to believe that the greatest source of power was that which came from the barrel of a gun, Francis knew his true path.

In 1960, Francis was only twenty-four, with his whole life ahead of him. He was immersed in his work at the Jesuit Seminary of Santiago de Chile, in the Padre Hurtado retreat. But his experience there left a profound impression on him beyond his studies. In Chile, he personally "felt" poverty's severe denigration. "When you sit at the table, many only have a piece of bread as a meal," wrote a stunned Francis to his sister María Elena in May 1960 from San Alberto Hurtado. "When it rains and it's cold, many live in tin caves and sometimes have nothing to cover themselves with."

The scene was the same in Chile as it was around all of Latin America. Christian democracy — the most popular political movement at the time, situated in the middle of the ideological spectrum — governed Chile, and yet the official statistics showed that during the first five years of the 1960s, almost 40 percent of Chileans were homeless or poor. What especially attracted Francis' attention was the income inequality in the Andean valley communities.[6] The richest 20 percent received around seventeen times more income than the remaining 80 percent of the population — outrageous figures when compared with the United States, where the richest 20 percent earned just under nine times more than the poorest 20 percent.

Francis returned to Argentina in 1961 with that intellectual, theological, and practical foundation. What country awaited him? It was no different than the one he had left. Politically, Peronism continued to be banned and Perón was still in exile. (After the coup, he had taken refuge in Paraguay, Panama, Nicaragua, Venezuela, and the Dominican Republic, in that order, before going into exile in Madrid until his final return to Argentina in 1973.) Francis returned to an Argentina whose most powerful political party couldn't even participate in elections.

Beyond the country's political circumstances, Francis was still firmly resolute in his desire to reach the priesthood. That would finally come to pass in 1969, but in the interim, studying and teaching put him face-to-face with the youth movements of the 1960s, hungry for social and political change.

Within the Universidad del Salvador downtown Buenos Aires campus, Francis began to influence the intellect of a multitude of Catholic youths strongly attracted to the forbidden Peronism. (Apart from being a professor, he was also one of the university's spiritual directors.) Those young people, mostly from middle-class families, decided to become politically active after the June 28, 1966, coup led by General Juan Carlos Onganía, who installed a new government — a period known as the Argentinian Revolution.

Among his first goals, Onganía wanted to overturn the educational reform that had previously given universities autonomy. On the night of July 29, he ordered more than a thousand police officers from the so-called General Management of "Urban Order" of the Argentine Federal Police to forcibly evacuate five of the Universidad de Buenos Aires campuses occupied by students, professors, and alumni in opposition to the government's decision to intervene in the universities and annul their autonomous system. The police evicted the protestors at dawn, beating them with batons. The savage attack became known as La Noche de los Bastones Largos (the Night of the Long Batons) and marked the start of increasing violence in Argentina that lasted another eighteen years.

The young Catholics were stunned by the violent repression, and the reaction was immediate. Thousands of middle- and upper-class university students from Buenos Aires and other major cities became politically active, many of them challenging their own parents' political positions. If their parents had been anti-Peronists, then the students were going to be Peronists. If the parents had never laid hands on a weapon in the name of democracy, the students were willing to grab a gun, like Ernesto "Che" Guevara had done in Bolivia's jungle.

To channel that surge of youthful involvement was an arduous and complex task for professor Francis, who was only steps away from becoming a consecrated priest. The militant activity emanating from the university, both from the left and right, became a phenomenon of the masses. In the Universidad del Salvador's classrooms, a group of young people created a Catholic youth organization that hoped to become the "third position" between the increasingly radical and violent left of the Montoneros and the fascist right of the Concentración Nacional Universitaria. They called themselves the Guardia de Hierro, the Iron Guard (after the Romanian group of the same name, the Garda de Fier, a Fascist organization founded in 1927 by the ultra-Catholic Cornelieu Codrenau), and became a part of Argentina's political history in spite the group's short life — it dissolved in 1974. They also played a key role in Francis' story.

The seven years between 1966 and 1973 are crucial in finally tying together Francis' history, the politically active Catholic Church, and a Peronist Party in constant turmoil. In truth, Argentina was the hub of Latin America's social and political change, which, be it good or bad, defined the life (and death) of several generations.

Francis was ordained a priest on December 13, 1969, within the Society of Jesus' militarized and strict framework. He traveled to Spain to finish his theology studies and returned to Argentina in 1973, less than six months before Juan Perón's final return to his country to begin his third term as president after having been in exile for eighteen years.

Francis went from being a modest literature and philosophy professor to accumulating a huge share of power in the Jesuit order, and outside the Universidad del Salvador, he was confessor, spiritual director, and friend to the members of the Iron Guard. This particular bond between Francis and the youth of his community was a unique relationship that somehow bridged faith and social policy.

It's been said that Francis was known to meet with members of the Iron Guard at Los 36 Billares, a traditional café on Avenida de Mayo, frequented by the young leaders of the group. At thirty-seven, Francis was a figure of interest among any political group: he was a teacher of novices, theology professor, director of Colegio Máximo, and a Jesuit parochial consultant. He was the very picture of the Society of Jesus, an order of the Church that always defined itself through its obedience, intellectual rigor, and almost military-like, ascetic discipline — a facet also found in the Iron Guard and one that surely appealed to Francis.

During their meetings, the Iron Guard read the works of Lenin, the mystical Mircea Eliade, the sixteenth-century Jesuit Mateo Ricci, as well as *La Comunidad Organizada* (*An Organized Community*) by Juan Domingo Perón. That varied pastiche of philosophical influences made the Iron Guard an atypical group within the Peronism of the 1970s. At their peak, they were fifteen thousand strong.

Led by their charismatic leader, Alejandro "Gallego" Álvarez, the Iron Guard brandished its equidistance from the "Red Front" (the Montoneros) of the left and the "Black Front" (the Organization Command and the University National Concentration) of the right. In short, it was the third position, which Perón was championing at the time, in its purest state. And Francis felt very comfortable in that balanced position.

Franics' career in the Society of Jesus quickly accelerated in 1973, when in April of that year he swore his vote of perpetual profession to the Order and in July was named, from Spain, as Provincial of the Jesuits the highest postiton possible in Argentina. By 1974, he was given a very special task. The world's top leader of the Company of Jesus, Pedro Arrupe, ordered him to transfer the Universidad del Salvador to secular hands.

And so, Francis put his trust in two militant colleagues from the Iron Guard: Francisco Piñón, aka "Cacho," who became the university's director, and his friend Walter Romero, one of Álvarez' apostles, who became its chief operating officer. However, on July 1 of that same year, General Perón died, and Peronism entered a state of general dissolution that would facilitate the 1976 military coup. In that context, little by little, Álvarez disbanded the Iron Guard — an untimely decision that affected thousands of young political activists, as well as Francis.

Álvarez had spent twelve years of his life building an organization with hopes of offering a political position beyond the extremes of the left and right. What message was he trying to deliver by dissolving the Iron Guard? He never gave a public explanation; however, common sense and the development of events in Argentina show that there was no room for "balanced" positions. On the left, youth groups came together to demand a leap from Peronism to socialism. On the right, the quasi-militarized system of the unions joined forces with the Peronist orthodoxy.

The breakdown of the Iron Guard seemed to have severed many of Francis' political ties — specifically his Peronist ties. In response, he once again secluded himself in the Jesuit cloisters and focused on a more hands-on approach to the betterment of the disadvantaged within Argentina's political and social reality.

From 1974 onward, Francis' "official story" does not include any association with the tumultuous political events of his time: Perón's death; the wave of murders of politically active members of the right and left; Isabel Perón's weakness as president and the rise to power of her personal secretary, "El Brujo," José López Rega; the evolution of the Montoneros as a political-military organization looking to seize power through the use of force; Argentina's financial decline after the worldwide oil pricing crisis; and an institutional emptiness that strengthened the fires of the 1976 civil-military coup.

But Argentina's history is concentric, and the past is always determined to come back, with different faces, managing to reestablish itself in the present. Francis' story is proof of this. With each step up the ecclesiastical ladder — when he was named the archbishop of Buenos Aires; when John Paul II made him cardinal in 2001; four years later, when he was almost elected pope but lost the vote to Joseph Ratzinger, who became Benedict XVI — his past was reinvestigated and his associations and actions scrutinized. Eventually, Francis concluded that this familiar chorus of media "claims" would adversely affect his chances of ever being elected to the papacy.

Just hours before being named Pope, a file circulated in the halls of the Vatican containing snippets from an investigative journalism piece published in 1999 in the Argentine newspaper *Página 12*. The article maintained that Francis had been the "deliverer" to the government of two priests from his Jesuit congregation, who, after being detained for five months (from May to September 1976) in the illegal military detention center at ESMA, were found naked and drugged in a vacant lot on the outskirts of Buenos Aires. The priests, Orlando Yorio and Francisco Jalics, were carrying out intense social work in Villa 1-11-14 in Bajo Flores. Both were politically active in a movement called Christianity and Revolution, which was inspired by liberation theology and had strong ties to the Montoneros, the ferocious dictatorship's favorite target.

Historical records reflect that Yorio and Jalics were kidnapped by a task force while they were attending mass. The group that took part in the kidnapping of the two priests and eight missionaries was said to have been comprised of more than two hundred officers, who occupied the slum until the mass was over.

Reports linking Francis to the kidnapping began in 1986 with Emilio Fermín Mignone, an Argentine Catholic lawyer and president of an entity linked to the defense of human rights called the Center for Legal and Social Studies (CELS). He was the first to expose the kidnapping case in a book he wrote that year titled *Iglesia y Dictadura* (*Church and Dictatorship*). The allegations resurfaced in the 1999 *Página 12* article, while Francis was archbishop of Buenos Aires, by way of the prestigious Argentine journalist and human rights advocate Horacio Verbitsky. Since then, the claims have been revived every time there has been a new development in Yorio and Jalics' open case. The last update prior to the conclave that made Francis pope came in 2010, when several witness — among them Francis himself, the catechist María Elena Funes, and the journalist Verbitsky — were called to testify before the Argentine justice system during the ongoing mega-case, simply and appropriately known as ESMA, in Buenos Aires's Tribunal Oral Criminal Federal Número 5 (Federal Criminal Oral Court Number 5).

The sudden dissemination of details from the *Página 12* story in March of 2013 was seemingly intended to tarnish Francis' reputation, thus preventing his election as pope. At first, there was speculation that the file had been leaked by anticlerical sectors with close ties to people in the government of Argentina's current president, Cristina Fernández de Kirchner. Hours later, Francis' own spokespeople suggested that the masterminds behind the muckraking were secular Argentines with strong ties to an ultraconservative sector whose public face was Cardinal Leonardo Sandri. Current prefect of the Congregation for the Oriental Churches, Sandri was advisor to the Pontifical Commission for Latin America, and an individual with papal ambitions of his own. Although the negative coverage did not interfere with Francis' triumph, it did manage to reopen the devastatingly painful wounds of the Dirty War, many of which had never closed to begin with.

And it didn't end there. On March 17, 2013, five days after Francis was elected the 266th pope, *Página 12* published yet another chronicle of the events of almost four decades earlier, again written by Horacio Verbitsky. In it, Verbitsky quotes Jalics as saying an individual within the church — whom the priest would not name — had "told the officials who kidnapped us that we had worked on the scene of terrorist activity," essentially sanctioning their detention by the military. In a November 1977 letter to the general assistant of the Society of Jesus, Orlando Yorio corroborated his colleague's account, but he identifies the church official as Jorge Bergoglio.

Verbitsky goes on to state that he discovered documentation in the archives of the Department of Foreign Affairs that further implicated Francis in the affair. In 1979, when Jalics, then living in Germany, asked to have his expired passport renewed without having to return to Argentina (for fear he might be arrested again), Bergoglio reportedly told the embassy to honor the request but, behind the scenes, lobbied to have it rejected because Jalics had "obedience issues" and had been held at ESMA along with Yorio for "suspicious guerrilla contact."

Francis' version of the events surrounding the Yorio and Jalics case was provided in an interview he gave to journalist Sergio Rubin (Argentine) and Francesca Ambrogetti (Italian) for the book *Pope Francis: His Life in His Own Words*, originally published in 2010 in Spanish under the title *El Jesuita*. In it, Francis provides a frank picture of the complexity of the times in Argentina and the church's tangled relationship with the dictatorship. With regards to the two priests, he said he recognized the danger they were in due to their work in the barrios and that he offered them sanctuary in the Jesuit's provincial house. He continued: "I had never believed they were involved in 'subversive activities,' as their pursuers maintained, and they truly weren't. But because of their proximity to some priests in the slums, they were too exposed to the witch-hunt paranoia. Since they stayed in that neighborhood, Yorio and Jalics were kidnapped when the area was combed." When pressed by the interviewer that the priests "thought that you also considered them subversive, at least a little, and that you harassed them somewhat because of their progressive ideas," suggesting that he tacitly approved their kidnapping by withdrawing his protection, Francis responded forcefully: "I repeat: I did not throw them out of the congregation, nor did I want them to be left unprotected."

In the same interview published in Rubin and Ambrogetti's book, Francis paints a different picture regarding the documentation dug up by Verbitsky that seemingly confirmed his betrayal of Yorio and Jalics. When he received the request from Jalics to have his passport renewed from abroad, Francis said he personally delivered his approval by hand to the appropriate office. When the person behind the desk there asked why Jalics had left the country, he says he responded, "He and his friend were accused of being guerrilla fighters, but they had nothing to do with any such thing." Francis continued: "The author of the accusation against me [Verbitsky] went through the file of the secretary of worship, yet all he mentioned was that he found a scrap of paper on which that civil servant had noted that he had spoken to me and I had told him they were accused of being guerrilla fighters. In short, he had made a note of that part of the conversation but not the other part, where I said that the priests were not involved in anything of the sort."

The story of Francis' moral, intellectual, and practical behavior during three turbulent decades of political and social life in his country is as controversial, intricate, and inexplicable as Argentina itself. It opens with the emergence of Peronism in 1945 and threads through the still open debate regarding his responsibility in the kidnapping and torture of two Jesuit priests that were under his direct supervision in 1976.

A hectic life unfurled in the middle of it all, like an action film, with military coups, democracy shams, the revolutionary Second Vatican Council, the rise of liberation theology and the Third World priests, and the activities of armed guerrillas over most of a continent seething in the turmoil that characterized the 1960s and 1970s. This extraordinary plot gradually shaped the temperament and tempered the spirit of Jorge Bergoglio. And, at seventy-six, it was the path to his arrival at the gates of his "earthly heaven": the tabernacle of Saint Peter's Chapel, where, as Pope Francis, he is closer to the image of the consecrated Jesus Christ than any other human on Earth.

Chapter 7

The Price of Power

ALMOST THIRTY CENTURIES ago, a pastor named Amos lived in the Judean Desert, located between Israel and the West Bank. Apart from pasturing his livestock, Amos dedicated his time to pricking sycamore figs in order to speed the ripening process and increase their size and sweetness. Aside from their delicious flavor, the figs were a staple in the diet of the pastoral, desert tribes.

As with David, whom Yahweh called to carry out his public service, God convinced Amos that he should abandon his flock and become a prophet to the wayward people of Israel. From the solitary Judean Desert, he sent him to the Northern Kingdom of Israel, a territory with ten tribes, which had its capital in Samaria.

Amos' prophecy lasted twenty-five years — between 829 and 804 BC. He was named as the third of the Twelve Prophets, called "Minor Prophets"[1] given the brevity, but not the quality, of their books, and his proselytizing reached such magnitude that Zechariah, eleventh of the twelve Minor Prophets, mentioned him some three hundred years later.

In Amos' time, the Northern Kingdom of Israel, also known as the Kingdom of Samaria (the Southern Kingdom being Judah), was experiencing a period of great prosperity, growing in both size and culture. The religious cult of the kingdom enjoyed great splendor, in marked contrast to the living conditions of the lower classes. The luxury of the "great ones" was an insult to the thousands of poor people within the territories.

Amos, with a rudimentary and direct pastoral style, inspired by his loyalty to Yahweh, condemned the elites' corruption and social injustice and announced the end of Israel. Accused by Amaziah, priest of Bethel,[2] for conspiring against the king, Amos was expelled from the temple of Bethel and later received a blow to the head by one of Amaziah's sons, from which he died when he returned to his homeland.

Francis pulled the entire essence of his spiritual mission on Earth from the Book of Amos. In short, Amos and his book emulate a humble pastor who served only God, a true master of faith. His criticism of inequality and oppression came from a most sublime and genuine place — one free from all partisan, dogmatic, or monetary interest. Francis' own belief that opposition to social inequities could not remain silenced within him can be underscored by Amos' words, spoken some three thousand years ago: "The Lord, God, has spoken, who is not to prophecy?" Openly generous with the poorest and most in need, relentless critic of power and the powerful — be they governing officials, wealthy businesspeople, or church authorities — Francis followed the prophet Amos' lead with his denouncement of social injustice at all levels of society.

Contrary to Amos' experience, arriving in the Northern Kingdom of Israel during a period of great financial prosperity, when Francis was named archbishop of Buenos Aires in 1998, Argentina had entered a state of economic decline. This was the product of right-wing Peronist Carlos Saúl Menem's experiment with neoliberalism, characterized by a spate of privatizations and an unemployment rate constantly on the rise.

A few months after being named archbishop, Francis celebrated the Te Deum hymn of praise in the Metropolitan Cathedral. Argentina's most traditional religious service, it takes place on May 25, the national public holiday celebrating the May Revolution. In the first pew sat President Menem and City of Buenos Aires mayor Fernando de la Rúa. It was no coincidence that Francis chose a homily focused on reunion and hope. That day he said:

> As in the Passion of Christ, our story is full of crossroads, tensions, and conflicts. However, these people of faith knew how to carry their fate each time solidarity and work created a political friendship of racial and social coexistence that marked our lifestyle. As Argentines, we knew how to be and feel "part of" something, we knew how to accompany each other and get together. From its individual and collective creative ability and from its momentum

of spontaneous popular organization, our country has seen nascent moments of civil, political, and social change; cultural and scientific achievements that have removed us from isolation and exposed our values. Moments that, in short, have given us a sense of identity beyond our complex ethnic and historic composition. Moments where a conscience of brotherly labor has prevailed, although sometimes not thoroughly elaborated, but has been felt and even experienced as heroism. That's why the request is to set aside the sterile historicism manipulated by interests and ideologies or by mere destructive criticism. History bets on the superior truth, on recalling what unites and builds us, on the achievements more than the failures. And, looking toward pain and failure, may our memory be used to bet on peace and rights . . . and if we look at the hatred and violent fratricides, let our memory guide us so that the common interest prevails. The last few years, slowly and cruelly, have shaken us, and the silent voices of so many deceased cry out from Heaven pleading we do not repeat the same mistakes. Only this will give meaning to their tragic fates. Like the walking and frightened disciples, today we are asked to realize that carrying such a cross cannot be in vain.

The call to our historic memory also asks us to deepen our deepest achievements, those that cannot be seen in a quick and superficial glance. The effort of these past times was none other than to assert the democratic system, overcoming political divisions, which seemed an almost insurmountable social hiatus: today we look to respect the rules and accept dialogue as a means of civic coexistence. Leave nostalgia and pessimism and, like the Emmaus disciples, give way to our need to meet: "Stay with us because it is late and the day is over." The Gospel shows us the way: let us sit at the table and permit ourselves to be brought together by Christ's profound gesture. The blessed bread must be shared. The same one that is the fruit of sacrifice and labor, the image of eternal life, but that must be fulfilled now.

Similar to the Great Depression of 1929 and the current financial crisis crippling Greece, Cypress, Portugal, Spain, and, on a smaller scale, Italy, Argentina faced a devastating recession from 1998 to 2002. During that disastrous period, the gross domestic product (GDP) fell 18 percent and official unemployment rates went up 25 percent within the economically active population.

Argentina's crisis began with an artificial system called convertibility, where one dollar was equal to one Argentine peso, with no logical monetary backing. Investors lost faith in the government's ability to pay its accumulated debt, which set off a chain reaction that caused banks to close and businesses to go bankrupt.

As the financial crisis spread, the recession deepened. The loss of trust from foreign investors created a collapse of planned investments, which in turn caused the GDP to drop drastically. The direct consequences were an abrupt stop on investments and a sharp decline in consumption. In that crippling environment, Argentina suffered forty-five consecutive months of recession, with unemployment rates that climbed to 25.5 percent in 2002.

The human dimension of those macroeconomic numbers translated into abject poverty in the slums of Buenos Aires and the populous industrial belt. It also devastated the modest holdings of retirees, young adults, and middle-class families who had their savings confiscated by the banks in the so-called financial *corralito* (which in English would mean "little corral," an Argentine euphemism to illustrate the loss of deposits when the banks were unable to return their clients' savings). Within this context of extreme impoverishment of at least a third of Argentina's population, Francis spoke out like the prophet Amos had done three thousand years before him against the elite of Israel's kingdom.

The scapegoat was Carlos Menem's successor, Fernando de la Rúa, from the Unión Cívica Radical Party — the oldest in Argentina following a centrist ideology.[3] In 2001, nationwide protests over the economic crisis resulted in the deaths of thirty-nine people. After two days of rioting, de la Rúa escaped via helicopter from the terrace of the Casa Rosada (Argentina's White House) after announcing he was abandoning the presidency.

From his pulpit within the Argentine Church, Francis had led a very critical campaign against the neoliberalism that prevailed in the country and the rest of Latin America during the 1990s and which continued with de la Rúa's government. He adamantly objected to paying illegitimate external debt at the cost of the country's poorest sectors, and he was especially critical of the International Monetary Fund's prescriptions to "ease" the crisis.

Francis detected the symptoms of a "sick Argentina" prior to its collapse in 2001 and continuously proclaimed his concern over what he thought would be a ruinous outcome. His Te Deum message in 2000, similar to that of 1999 when Menem was present in the cathedral, thereupon became a civic plea — an outcry that reflected the mood of a society headed toward a financial and social disaster.

May 25, 2000, will be forever etched in the memories of all Argentines. President de la Rúa had been in office for barely five months, following Carlos Menem's decade-long term (1989–1999). That morning, with the nation's president (a practicing Catholic) standing only a few feet away, Francis poignantly took a stance in defense of the country's most deprived:

> Sometimes I ask myself if we are not marching, in certain life cir-
> cumstances of our society, like a sad cortège, and if we do not insist
> in placing a tombstone on our search as if we walked toward an in-
> evitable fate, an interweaving of the impossible, and we reluctantly
> accept small illusions devoid of hope. We must humbly recognize
> that the System [clearly alluding to democracy] has fallen into a
> wide umbra, the umbra of distrust, and that some promises and
> statements sound like a funeral procession, where everyone con-
> soles the relatives, but no one picks up the deceased.

Solemn words coming from Francis, who by then counted on his well-earned stature not only in the Buenos Aires clergy, but within Argentina itself. As Francis ascended the Argentine ecclesiastic structure, he modeled a new Church that was more distant from its other-worldly and far-removed tradition, to one that instead displayed a pronounced concern for the disadvantaged. Yet the values he displayed — his affable closeness to the people, his simplicity, and his selfless advice — had earned him an influential spiritual position that reverberated in the political, financial, and even judicial arenas of the country.

Francis began to use his influence to address the problems of a society immersed in a phenomenal financial and moral crisis. In 2000, he set up a direct line for the *curas villeros* in Buenos Aires to call him at any time in case of an emergency. He would continue to spend the night in parishes in humble neighborhoods or help a sick priest if need be. He continued traveling by bus or subway, setting aside the car and driver the church had assigned to him.

Loyal to the prophet Amos' mandate, he avoided all social events that would connect him with the financial establishment. He refused to live in the elegant archbishop's palace in Olivos, twelve miles away from Buenos Aires' center, just as he now has decided not to live in Vatican City's monumental and regal Apostolic Palace, which has housed all popes since 1903. Francis was so aware of Argentina's imminent financial demise, that when he was elevated to cardinal in February 2001 — ten months before the country's economy and fragile social equilibrium would collapse, forcing de la Rúa to resign — he refused to buy the clothing for his new position, but rather tailored his predecessor's outfit.

As the popular spokesperson for a nation in crisis, Francis felt his prestige rise among the people during this turbulent period. One of his more well-known gestures occurred amidst the social outburst of December 2001. From his office window in the Cathedral, Francis observed an officer raging at a woman who was simply asking the bank to return her life savings. Francis quickly phoned the secretary of the interior, vociferously requesting that the police differentiate between those stirring up trouble and ordinary citizens who were demanding their money, which was being held hostage by the banks.

Francis finally relented in his persistent criticism of political power during the Te Deum of May 25, 2003, after Argentina had begun to recover from the worst of its financial and social hardships. That morning, with the brand new president, Nestor Kirchner, among the congregation — he had taken office less than three hours earlier — Francis made a general call to all Argentines to "shoulder the nation," as if to offer an olive branch of alliance to the country's new leader.

The peace between Francis and President Kirchner would only last a year. The following year's homily would distance them forever. On that day, Francis first spoke in general terms about "the Argentines," whom he accused of being "open to intolerance," but he later made veiled charges against Kirchner and his government, singling out "those who feel so included that they exclude the rest, so clairvoyant that they are now blind." Harsher than Amos himself, Francis' criticism seemingly addressed Kirchner directly when he said, "Copying the tyrant and murderer's hate and violence is the best way to become his heir."

Francis' words were so severe that the next day his spokesperson had to explain that he was addressing Argentina's society as a whole, including the government and the Catholic Church itself. But Nestor Kirchner, with an even more indomitable temperament than Francis, was very bothered by the public episode and did not hide it. Kirchner made a decision that would mark the end of the relationship between the top Church representative and the president with more working-class support since Juan

Domingo Perón: he never again attended a Te Deum officiated by Francis. And in an unprecedented move in Argentina's two-hundred-year history, he moved the national celebration to different province capitals.

The distance between the two deepened when Nestor refused to attend the 2005 homily, which caused the Te Deum to be canceled. ("There's no relationship between the Church and the government," was Francis' spokesperson's response a few months later.) An exception was made for the 2006 tribute to the five Pallottines[4] massacred in the San Patricio Church in Buenos Aires during the military dictatorship. Regarding that moment — the last time they shared a ceremony — Francis always made sure to clarify that he had sent President Kirchner a letter inviting him to the tribute. "Furthermore," noted Francis, "since there was no Mass, I asked Kirchner to preside over the ceremony. Because, during his time in office, I always treated him for what he was: the nation's president."

The relationship between Francis and the Kirchners (Nestor and his wife, Cristina, who succeeded him as president) was as visceral as the main characters themselves. None of the three were known to mince words, and from that passionate and committed standpoint, they had insurmountable confrontations. They disagreed, and publicly acknowledged it, on such societal issues as poverty, same-sex marriage, and abortion — so much so that Nestor said the cardinal "had been sent by the opposition" to harry his administration. At the height of their rivalry, the Argentine president declared, "Our God is everyone's God, but careful; the devil also reaches everyone, those of us who use pants, and those who wear robes."

When President Cristina Fernandez de Kirchner took office in 2007, the bishopric met with her in order to slowly bridge the gap created by the ongoing dispute with her husband. Unfortunately, the peace did not last long. In 2008, amidst the first political crisis of Cristina's administration, which involved a confrontation between the government and farmers, Francis appealed to the president for a "grand gesture" to unblock the situation, but it was in vain. Despite an attempt at détente when Cristina attended a mass in Luján on the invitation of Francis, more confrontations arose the following year. Francis stated, "The worst risk is to homogenize thought," and called for the end of "social tension" or *crispación social*. In response, Kirchneristas used a play on words in Spanish — replacing the word *crispación* (tension) with "*cris-pasión*" (Christ Passion) — to ridicule him. And like a never-ending game, Francis angered them even more when he baldly stated, "The country hasn't taken care of the people for years."

The Te Deum of every May 25 became, in a way, a manifestation of the distancing between the Kirchners and the Church. In 2010, amidst the country's bicentennial celebrations, Cristina opted to attend the ceremony at the Luján Basilica together with Nestor. In 2011, she attended Archbishop Fabriciano Sigampa's homily in Resistencia. From the Buenos Aires Cathedral, Francis criticized the leaders' "delusions of grandeur."

The passing of the same-sex marriage law in 2010 was probably one of the tensest moments in their relationship. In fact, the official acceptance of these minority rights caused more than one department of power to distance itself from Francis. His "favorite" political figure, for years, was the deputy mayor of the City of Buenos Aires, Gabriela Michetti. She repeatedly stated that her confessor and spiritual guide was Francis, with whom she held meetings of faith for years. But the connection dissolved when Michetti did not fervently oppose gay marriage. While the issue was being debated, Michetti confined herself to a spiritual retreat in Córdoba, unable to define her position — she either supported her party and defended homosexual rights, or she defended her spiritual father's staunch conservative position. That indecisiveness did not help her relationship with Francis. Since then, he only received her on a limited number of occasions and out of pure politeness.

Contrary to Michetti's indecisiveness, Francis led every demonstration against gay marriage and sent a letter to all priests, in which he asked that they speak of the "unalterable good of marriage and family" in all their masses.

"I'm worried about the tone the discourse has acquired," was Cristina's answer to his uncompromising stance. "It's set up as a question of religious morals and an undermining of the natural order, when in truth what is being done is observing a reality that already exists."

Perhaps surprisingly, the abortion debate didn't worsen the confrontation between church and state because Cristina banned the dissemination of controversial literature that promoted pregnancy termination, which was taken as a concession to the Church. Nevertheless, Francis had to become pope for Cristina to finally approach him peacefully and begin to mend the years-old rift between them.

———————

Being named (often termed "made") cardinal is the highest dignity a consecrated man in the Catholic Church can achieve, with the exception of reaching the papacy itself. Hence, cardinals are known as the "Princes of the Church." When John Paul II made Francis a cardinal-priest (one of three orders of cardinal in the Catholic Church), he assigned him to the Church of San Roberto in Rome's diocese, located in the elegant Piazza Hungary. Saint Robert, a Doctor of the Church born in 1542, also a Jesuit like Francis, had a prominent role in the Counter-Reformation, which was aimed at halting the divisions that were occurring in the Church as a consequence of Martin Luther and John Calvin's ideas. It was a true paradox that the cardinal of the poor in Buenos Aires and Latin America would be linked to a chapel nestled in one of the most ritzy neighborhoods of the Italian capital.

Contrary to the prophet Amos, who was thrown out of the Bethel temple for confronting the powerful leaders in the Northern Kingdom territories of Israel, including the king, and was later stoned and ended his days in the Judean Desert, Francis forged his career as a Prince of the Church like a silversmith. And the first chance he got to put his patience and political talent to the test was April 2, 2005, the day Pope John Paul II's death was confirmed with a silver hammer. Francis, by dint of history and hierarchy, had gained access to the highest level of responsibility that a consecrated man could experience in his life: participation in the papal conclave.

After nine days of mourning, which included, per tradition, ceremonies celebrated in several churches in Rome following different rituals as a way of ratifying the Catholic Church's universality, and after the parade of believers who wanted to pay their final respects was over, the conclave date was finally set: April 18, 2005.

However, beyond the College of Cardinals' picturesque rituals, how did Francis come to mediate John Paul II's succession? What was in play was the very renewal of the Church, with Latin America being a "strategic" region. Francis was in a relatively low-level position among his brother cardinals — a "new" cardinal (he'd been made cardinal in 2001) from a country with a long Catholic tradition but with a population that barely hit 40 million people. And yet, the cardinal from "the end of the world" emerged from obscurity to become a serious contender as the next pope. The question is, why did his brethren not choose a candidate from Brazil or Mexico — the two countries with the largest Catholic populations on the planet?

The privilege of having foreseen the future of Francis falls upon a prestigious journalist specializing in the Vatican's inner workings, Sandro

Magister, who by 2002 had already written in *L'Espresso*, an Italian weekly newspaper, that if there were to be a papal conclave right then and there (John Paul II's weakened health at the time indicated an imminent end to his life), Francis would reap the benefits of "an avalanche of votes" that would make him the pope. What qualities did Magister see in Francis? "Shy, reserved, of few words, he doesn't move a finger to campaign, but that is exactly what is considered one of his greatest assets" he wrote based on information he received regarding how a block of important cardinals thought. Magister's profile of Francis and his possible future as Bishop of Rome — "His austerity and frugality, along with his intense spiritual life, are the personal qualities that increasingly elevate him to be 'popeworthy'"— would become more than accurate in light of the 2005 and 2013 votes.

A meticulous reconstruction of the process that led to the election of Benedict XVI in April 2005 gave way to the conclusion that the cardinals had grouped into three lines of thought: the conservatives, the centrists, and the progressives. The almost thirty years of John Paul II's papacy had strengthened the conservative's position, solidified by the enormous number of similar-minded priests who were made cardinals during his tenure.

In the first round of votes, during the afternoon of April 18, 2005, Cardinal Joseph Aloisius Ratzinger obtained forty-seven votes, a much closer call than expected, while Francis surprisingly appeared on the scene with ten votes. In third place came Italian progressive Carlo Maria Martini with nine votes.

The progressives launched Martini's candidacy simply as a strategy to calculate approximately how much support the conservatives aligned behind Ratzinger would obtain. Unexpectedly, Francis was now seen as a possibility to thwart, until then, the most popular candidate, given his more centrist sensibilities and low profile — practically the same virtues Vatican journalist Magister had highlighted three years earlier.

The next day, on April 19, at 9:30 a.m., there was another vote. Ratzinger received sixty-five votes, only twelve short of the seventy-seven needed to become the new pope, while Francis received thirty-five, which made him the second option. Two hours later, the procedure was repeated and in this third vote, Ratzinger reached seventy-two votes while Francis made it to forty, an unprecedented showing for a Latin American cardinal.

That same afternoon, at 5:30 p.m., the last voting round was conducted, the one that consecrated Ratzinger with eighty-four votes, seven more than required, as history's 265th pope with the name Benedict XVI. Though Francis came in second, a more in-depth analysis of the conclave shows that his standing among his cardinal peers had remained superlative throughout the weighty process.

Qualified Vatican observers, such as Catholic journalist and writer Vittorio Messori (the most translated "Vatican" author of the last few decades, with books including *Crossing the Threshold of Hope*, a long conversation with John Paul II, and *The Ratzinger Report*, a series of interviews with Cardinal Joseph Ratzinger), confirmed that "everyone agreed that during the first rounds of Conclave votes, cardinals Ratzinger and Bergoglio were practically neck and neck." Messori also revealed that "all comments coincide in affirming that 'the Argentine' had asked his colleagues to lean their votes toward Ratzinger, the strongest candidate, almost obligatory for having been the true theological mind of John Paul II, and hence best represented the idea of continuity."

Andrea Tornielli, another highly informed journalist who works for the Roman newspaper *Il Giornale*, went a step further and explained that Francis seemed overwhelmed by the increasing number of votes he began to receive in the second and third rounds, so he stepped aside and asked that his votes go to Ratzinger. The reason for such a decision? To Francis, Ratzinger represented the continuity of an ecclesiastic policy John Paul II had established for the 1.2 billion Catholics worldwide.

Francis' decision to step back was also a result of his concern for the Church's image. He did not want his surprise candidacy to delay the new pope's prompt election. Such stagnation in the vote could be interpreted as a symptom of disunity among the cardinals to the rest of the world observing in great expectation. This perception played a key role in the conclave as its members considered that if Ratzinger did not win in the first rounds, they risked entering a voting marathon, and in 2005, Francis did not want to carry such a huge responsibility.

There is no question that such a mature and sensitive gesture afforded Francis a tremendous amount of respect, which would be evident eight years later when the papal conclave anointed him "the pope of the poor" almost by acclamation. However, although the 2005 conclave helps explain the admiration many of his colleagues hold for Francis, the history of their regard for him has deeper roots. We must go back to the start of the twenty-first century, to 2001, when Francis was not yet even a cardinal, completely unknown to most international, high ecclesiastic dignitaries.

In October 2001, one month after the fateful 9/11 tragedy, New York archbishop Cardinal Edward Egan was at the Vatican taking part in a synod of bishops from around the world. Having been called back to New York to attend a tribute to the victims of the World Trade Center terrorist attack, his place as the assembly's general narrator, a key role, fell upon the almost unknown figure of Francis. His execution was excellent and he made a memorable impression. All Vatican observers agree that this was the starting point of his international recognition.

Thanks to his work at the synod, Francis had the privilege of being the most voted among the 252 priests from 118 countries in attendance to join the post-synod assembly representing all of Latin America. At the Fifth General Conference of the Bishops of Latin America and the Caribbean, celebrated in Aparecida, a city in the heart of Brazil, Francis would have still another opportunity to gain prestige and the notice of his peers. Aparecida is located about a hundred miles northeast of São Paulo (the most populated city in South America, with twenty-two million residents), midway to Rio de Janeiro. Based on historical accounts, in 1717 the governor representing Portugal's crown announced a trip to Minas Gerais, the second most populated of Brazil's twenty-six states. Three local fishermen from Aparecida — at the time just a town one passed through — decided to honor him with the fruit of their labor. They threw their nets into the river Paraiba, but instead of catching fish, they caught a headless, fifteen-inch-tall terracotta image of Our Lady's Immaculate Conception. It was later determined that the statue must have been made in 1650 by a monk in São Paulo, but there's no explanation as to how it ended up at the bottom of that particular river. The fishermen persisted and cast their net again. But, again, they failed to catch fish — all they found was the top part of the Virgin. After this surprising discovery, the fishermen caught an exceptional number of fish, and with this bounty they were able to tend to the visiting governor with all requisite honors.

Instantly, the Virgin was venerated at one of the fishermen's homes and its reputation spread among the local people. Shortly thereafter, the statue was transferred to a chapel, visited more and more frequently by the faithful from nearby towns, until in 1745, a church was constructed to house her.

The dedication expanded to such a degree that in 1930 Pope Pius XI consecrated the Virgin as Brazil's patron saint, and in 1955 the Our Lady of Aparecida Basilica Church was inaugurated — the second largest in the world after Saint Peter's in Rome. It is now visited by more than fifty million people a year. The pilgrimage to Aparecida reaches its zenith every October 12, the feast day of the patron saint.

It was in Aparecida, within that mystical context, that Francis drew up the final summary of the events of the Fifth General Conference of the Bishops of Latin America and the Caribbean, inaugurated by Pope Benedict XVI himself on July 13, 2007. Through a seemingly predestined chain of events, together with his work and evangelizing example, Francis emerged as the new leader of Latin America's Church. In the content and substance of the Aparecida Document, his intellectual and doctrinal authority, combined with his enduring commitment to the poor — a potent and necessary attribute in Latin America — was reaffirmed. Although the region had suffered great tension between the Liberation theologians and the more conservative sectors of the Church in the past, it would no longer be necessary to renounce Catholicism's basic mission of charity and service to the poor for fear of encouraging the arrival of authoritarian and atheist regimes. It was also demonstrated that it was perfectly possible to tend to the needy while respecting the traditional doctrines and authority of the Roman Church, as he had done in the poorest areas of Buenos Aires. This important doctrinal shift would be recorded in the Aparecida Document, which today allows us to better predict Pope Francis' reforms from the highest position within the Vatican.

The Aparecida Document outlines an equidistant position between the different points of view that pulsed through positions of power and influence in Latin America during the last years of the first decade of this century.

On one hand, it takes a harshly critical stance when speaking of "fragile democracies," "authoritarian diversions," and "an advance of authoritarian regression, which at times derives from regimens with a neo-populist[5] angle." A first take on this position could conclude that it was directed at the regimes of the Castro brothers in Cuba and former president Hugo Chávez in Venezuela, perhaps inspired by communication with the US State Department. But a closer look reveals that the Latin American bishops simultaneously distance themselves from American involvement by pointing out harsh aspects of free trade treaties inspired by the United States. They noted that the processes of regional economic integration should not be based only on government treaties or commercial relationships between countries, but rather they should become rooted in the lives and participation of the people. They made sure to clarify that in economic terms, they favored the integrity of honest production over the rapacious nature of financial speculation. Once again, by denouncing "wild and uncontrolled" pursuit of profits, social injustice, and excessive misuse of power, prophet Amos' inspiration shines through.

In the Aparecida Document, the Latin American bishops declare themselves "at the service of unity and brotherhood of our people," and when they say they desire "a united Latin America and Caribbean, reconciled and integrated," it mirrors what had already been mentioned in the Puebla and Santo Domingo documents.[6] This idea is underscored by the words the "Great Latin American Nation," which "is our big nation, but will really be big when it is so for everyone." The bishops maintained with conviction that "delaying integration would affect the most needy and vulnerable by deepening poverty and inequality." This position seemed to coincide with the so-called Bolivarian Revolution[7] championed by Chávez and other regional groups. But once again the bishops distanced themselves from such an extreme when they pointed out that the path toward such longed-for unity "will only be obtained through the search of a common identity and not just by way of confronting shared enemies."

The bishops specifically reiterated the preferential option for the poor (echoes of the Second Vatican Council), widening the concept and reach of this category to include the unemployed, migrants, the abandoned, the sick, and others. Additionally, they made sure to highlight the defense of the rights of indigenous people, and in accordance with contemporary realities, they insisted on the need to protect the environment of the continent with the most biodiversity on the planet.

The Church leaders also emphasized the importance of intensifying the ecumenical gathering of all Christian sects, and maintaining an interreligious dialogue with those of non-Christian beliefs. Francis' influence was particularly seen here, as he worked endlessly to unite all religious faiths so that "the vicious cycles that degrade the human condition can be broken," as Rabbi Abraham Skorka so eloquently defines this mission.

The Aparecida Document did not abandon the ecclesiastical foundation from which its authors derived their authority. When it came to controversial and difficult issues, the Latin American bishops assembled in Aparecida completely aligned themselves with the conservative sector that had reigned in Rome since John Paul II's time when they showed their support for the Church's moral agenda, including opposition to abortion, same-sex marriage, euthanasia, and the use of birth control methods.

"This will somewhat help you understand what the priests of Latin America are thinking," said Francis upon presenting a copy of the

Aparecida Document to president of Argentina, Cristina Fernandez de Kirchner, when she had the honor of being the first government official to be received by the new pope. The document served to confirm that, within the Latin American Church, under Francis' spiritual and doctrinal tutelage, a balance between opposing poles had finally been achieved, and a long chapter of discord would be closed.

It was not the only acknowledgment for Francis to come out of Aparecida. The day he officiated Mass, his homily caused a thunderous applause. No other celebrant was applauded under the same circumstances throughout the three-week long conference. Eyewitnesses recall that many participants took advantage of the breaks as an opportunity to talk with him and even take some pictures, as if he were a celebrity.

Six years had to pass after that historic conference for Francis' long journey to reach its final, extraordinary destination. It began on February 11, 2013, when Pope Benedict XVI suddenly announced to the world that he would resign from his position as leader of the Holy Roman Catholic Church.

It was a shocking decision. The head office hadn't been vacated in such a way since Gregory XII resigned in 1415. Benedict XVI was the first in almost six hundred years to willingly abandon the papacy.

Benedict XVI's resignation and the controversy surrounding it could well have been a component of the fictional Da Vinci Code saga. Officially, it was said that the reason was connected to Benedict's exhaustion and "loss of strength," which impeded him from assuming such high responsibility. Even his own brother, Georg, confirmed this reason from Regensburg, Germany, bluntly saying, "It was exhaustion caused by age."

Nevertheless, a wave of rumors quickly surfaced. Immediately after his resignation, at least four lines of interpretation emerged, all generated from the Vatican's own palaces.

The first line of thought, confirming the pope's official statement, pointed out that he had made the decision after a fall he suffered during his last trip to Mexico, which proved his exhaustion and deteriorating physical condition.

The second interpretation maintained that it was actually a premeditated move by a leader who many considered the "Machiavelli" of the

Church. Knowing the end of his life was near, Benedict wanted to influence the designation of his own successor, hence guaranteeing the continuity of certain policies and tendencies connected to the more conservative sectors.

Another hypothesis was that the ferocious internal divide within the Roman curia had become unbearable to Benedict — a divide that was exposed in an internal Vatican report detailing the so-called "Vatileaks," which included such serious matters as the denunciation of his own personal secretary, Paolo Gabrielle.

Lastly, some conspiracy theorists maintained that the pope had received pressure bordering on blackmail, which forced him to resign or run the risk of being poisoned.

When the rumor mill became unstoppable, Benedict XVI himself had to publicly explain his resignation: "I've decided to resign from the ministry God entrusted me with on April 19, 2005. I've decided this of my own free will, for the good of the Church, after having prayed for a long time and examined my conscience before God." He later added, "I'm deeply aware of the seriousness of such act, but I also know I no longer have the ability to work in the ministry with the vigor it requires."

Regardless of the reasons for Benedict's resignation, the Vatican followed the appropriate procedure stipulated by the current regulations. The Camarlengo[8] of the Holy Roman Church declared the *Sede Vacante* (Vacant Seat) on February 28, 2013, once Benedict XVI boarded a helicopter that removed him from the Vatican and flew him to the Apostolic Palace of Castel Gandolfo, the papal summer home. Catholics from around the world supported their former leader's decision, who humbly greeted his collaborators and cardinals and, like a type of modern monarch, set out on his journey of self-imposed exile and spiritual reflection.

According to the Apostolic Constitution approved by John Paul II in 1996, the start of the conclave to elect a successor had to be scheduled fifteen to twenty days after a resignation or death. However, given the presence of numerous cardinals in Rome, who had flown in especially to bid farewell to the resigning pope, such strict requirements were unnecessary. The timing could be expedited, and expedited it was.

The conclave began on March 4, 2013 and its members took a week to discuss different aspects of the Church's life and the management of Vatican state issues. Francis' participation was prominent in those meetings, reaffirming his position as leader of the Latin American Church.

Intrigue and inside issues once again took center stage, as is usual when choosing a new pope. The voting Princes of the Church grouped themselves into opposing ecclesiastical teams, somewhat like political parties. In recent years, Vatican secretary of state Tarcisio Bertone's influence had grown. His followers constituted the "Bertonians," an allusion to the Salesian that Benedict had entrusted with such an important government function. Then came the "Diplomats," distinguishing themselves with this name in acknowledgment of Bertone's perceived lack of experience in international issues. They, in turn, counted on the support of the so-called "Pastoralists."

These three camps (in addition to the eternal distinction between conservatives and reformists within the Church) created a great divide among the Italian cardinals in particular. This naturally distanced the possibility of the papacy returning to a candidate with close ties to the Roman curia, as had been the tradition throughout the centuries until the ascension of the Polish pope, John Paul II, and his successor, Benedict XVI of Germany.

A week later, on March 12, 2013, Francis, dressed in scarlet, entered the Sistine Chapel together with the other 114 electors to choose Peter's successor. From the start, the geographic makeup of the cardinal electors suggested that an important change was underway. Twenty-eight were Italian, thirty-two from other parts of Europe, twenty from the United States, thirteen from Latin America, eleven from Africa, and eleven from Asia and Oceania. The presence of so many cardinals from outside the Old World pointed toward the potential for a dramatic break with the past.

There is an old saying with regard to the papal election: He who goes into conclave a pope, comes out a cardinal. This adage refers to the premature predictions surrounding the likely candidate. Francis' election confirmed this saying, as the favorites going in were Cardinal Odilo Scherer, Archbishop of São Paulo, Brazil, and Angelo Scola of Milan.

However, the Holy Spirit's action, in addition to the irreconcilable division among the Italian cardinals, would be a determining factor in this conclave. As well, the decisive proselytizing of Cardinal Rafaello Martino and the archbishop of New York, Timothy Dolan, finished what had been cut short in 2005: the possibility that for the first time in two thousand years of Church history, the pope would be Latin American, and, additionally, for the first time since the reign of Syrian Gregory III in 731–741, he would not be European.

And so, after five rounds of voting, on March 13, Francis, the unglamorous, almost antimedia figure, without dramatic qualities or outstanding eloquence, obtained 90 of the 114 votes from the College of Cardinals.

It had been an extraordinary journey for Rosa Margarita's grandson, the shy young man who lost part of his right lung, the obedient Jesuit, the secret admirer of Juan Domingo Perón's legacy, the archbishop who always backed his "slum priests," the hermit who traveled by subway and bus and disregarded the luxuries of a consumerist society, the spiritual heir of the prophet Amos who lived in constant "war" against the abuse of power and the powerful. That man, Francis, humbly bowed within the solitude of the Room of Tears, and became the first member of the Order of the Society of Jesus in history to be named the Vicar of Christ on Earth.

As if he were following the dictation of a divine plan, with his actions, Francis immediately let the world know that something had changed in the Vatican. At the Vatican dinner on the night of his election, he captivated his audience of cardinals by saying, jokingly, "May God forgive you for choosing me." This tongue-in-cheek comment was mainly directed toward his mentor, American cardinal Timothy Dolan, who was vital in rounding up the votes that made him pope. When Francis made that remark, he was wearing the same shoes he had had on earlier in the day instead of the traditional red leather shoes of his new office. He had already refused to wear the magnificent golden cross of the papacy, instead retaining the iron-plated cross from his years as archbishop. Rather than ride in the papal limousine immediately after his election, he joined his fellow cardinals on the bus that they all had arrived in together. And prior to imparting his first blessing, Urbi et Orbi (to the City and the World), he asked to be blessed by the people gathered in the piazza below. Some might have interpreted this as the gesture of a demagogue. Clearly it was not, because hours later he surprised his peers, within the privacy of the cloisters, when he clarified that he did not want them to kiss his ring but simply give him a brotherly hug.

Francis' show of his desire for humble unity with his community continued as he jumped over the protective barriers in Saint Peter's Square to immerse himself within the crowd. There was a particularly poignant episode when, for the first time in Vatican history, he stopped the "popemobile," got out, and greeted a profoundly religious quadriplegic man named Cesare Cicconi, who lay prostrate on a stretcher. He personally showed up to pay the bill at his former living quarters, a church-run boardinghouse, from his own pocket. And a week later, from Rome, he called the man from whom he used to buy his Buenos Aires newspaper to tell him that he had unfortunately lost a client.

An amusing incident during his first month in office epitomizes his equally humble connection with the Vatican staff who tend to his comfort and safety. One morning at dawn, he encountered a Swiss Guard stationed at the entrance to Saint Martha's House[9] and brought him a chair so he could sit and rest. The guard, who had been standing all night fulfilling his service, thanked Francis for the kind gesture but said, "The rules do not allow me to sit."

"The rules?" asked Francis.

"Orders from my captain, Your Holiness," responded the guard, surprised.

"Well," replied Francis, "I'm the pope and I order you to sit down." Then he immediately returned to his apartment and came back with a sandwich of bread and jam for the guard. Before leaving, Francis politely added, "Buon appetito, my friend."

With similar good-natured humor, Francis was capable of receiving the president of Brazil, Dilma Rousseff, and look her straight in the eye while she said, "the pope is Argentine, but God is Brazilian," as he confirmed that he would travel to Rio de Janeiro to attend World Youth Day that July and extend his trip to the mythical Aparecida. And he was also capable of showing his desire for reconciliation when he received Argentine president Cristina Fernandez de Kirchner with a white rose — Saint Teresa's favorite.

During his first sixty days in the chair of Saint Peter, Francis continued to break all molds and protocols. He accepted jerseys from two of the best soccer players in the world: fellow Argentines Lionel Messi and Inter Milan's captain, Javier "Pupi" Zanetti, one of the soccer world's most public advocates for the poor. He made certain to send his condolences upon learning of the death of Great Britain's former prime minister Margaret Thatcher, despite knowing that in Argentina, the so-called "Iron Lady" is a despised political figure due to her role in Argentina's defeat in the Falkland Islands War.

A full-time politician, Francis sows seeds with each step he takes. He has a word or a compassionate gesture for those on the political left and the right, for believers and atheists, Jews and Muslims, Roman Catholics and Protestants, kings and beggars, reprobates and the virtuous. He's capable of creating a reconciliatory bridge, as he did between the two top human rights figures in Argentina, Hebe de Bonafini (head of the Mothers of Plaza de Mayo) and Estela de Carlotto (president of the Grandmothers of Plaza de Mayo), just as he is able to anticipate the changes to come in the strategic and controversial Institute for the Works of Religion, better known as the Vatican Bank. His plan — not unlike that of a political party newly swept into office — is to transform the Church into one of spartan austerity and rigor. Appropriate to Jesuit law, he wants the Church to evangelize the four cardinal points of the Earth, to open its arms so it spreads its faith to the existential periphery, to avoid the danger of self-reverence, and to rigorously fight against the danger of the spiritually mundane.

With his eyes set on God our Father, Francis defined himself when he recalled the prophet Jeremiah by saying, "I'm the rod of an almond tree." Since the dawn of creation, the almond tree's flower has been the first one to bloom in spring. And as Francis learned from his grandmother Rosa Margarita, "God loves us first; that's what love is about." From those words, he was born into faith the same day the calendar marked the beginning of spring.

PART TWO

Doctrine and Challenges

Chapter 8

Saint Francis of Assisi

"Annuntio vobis gaudium magnum;
Habemus Papam:
Eminentissimum ac reverendissimum Dominum,
Dominum Giorgium Marium,
Sanctæ Romanæ Ecclesiæ Cardinalem Bergoglio,
Qui sibi nomen imposuit Franciscum."

"I hereby announce to you a great joy. We have a pope: The most eminent and most reverend Lord Don Jorge Mario, the Holy Roman Church's Cardinal Bergoglio, who has taken on the name of Francis.**"**

O**N MARCH 13,** 2013, the Cardinal Protodeacon Jean Louis Tauran, from the balcony of Saint Peter's Basilica, announced the joyful news to a frenzied crowd — that same eager crowd that earlier had witnessed a white cloud of smoke billowing from the Sistine Chapel's chimney, indicating the grand occurrence.

As we now know, Cardinal Bergoglio chose to take on the name of Francis, paying homage to Saint Francis of Assisi, due to their shared dedication to the poor. Initially, however, many thought that His Holiness chose this name to honor Saint Francis Xavier, collaborator to Saint Ignatius of Loyola, founder of the Jesuit order to which the Argentine cardinal belonged. Due to Francis Xavier's Jesuit missionary activity in the Far East in the sixteenth century, aligning himself with the saint could have been an indication of Bergoglio's intention to expand the Church in Asia. Clearly, if there is one place where Catholicism can increase its influence, it is in Asia, and most especially in China. (That is, of course, if the country ends up turning toward democracy, where individual freedom prevails and its massive population is allowed to exercise its religious beliefs free of the oppressive control of the state.)

Others pointed out that perhaps he named himself after Saint Francis Solano, the Spanish monk who, in the sixteenth century and for more than twenty years tried to spread the Gospel among the indigenous population in South America. The saint was known for performing miracles in Cardinal Bergoglio's very homeland, and many thought that his new appointment to Saint Peter's Throne was just one more of Saint Francis Solano's miracles.

Some of his colleagues jokingly suggested he should choose the name Clement XV as a form of revenge against Clement XIV, the pope who, in 1773, published the brief *Dominus ac Redemptor* whereby the Company of Jesus was dissolved at the request of the Bourbon monarchies that ruled France and Spain. Kings in that family feared the enormous political and economic influence that Jesuits had acquired in their domains, especially in their South American colonies. Thus, they convinced the Holy Father to eliminate a dangerous counterweight to their absolute power. This completed a series of expulsions decreed initially by Portugal, later France, and finally Spain. In return for the action against the Jesuits, these countries would restitute valuable territories in southern France and Naples to the papacy. With Clement XIV's decision, the Jesuit Order was suppressed for forty years.

Francis himself put the debate to rest soon after his election, when he hosted six thousand accredited journalists from around the globe in the Vatican's impressive Paul VI Audience Hall. His Holiness' decision to honor the name and work of Saint Francis of Assisi underscores his commitment to renouncing, as much as possible from Saint Peter's Chair, earthly possessions in favor of service to humanity and to God, setting an example for the world. This commitment will forever color his reign, as it promises to constitute a real turning point — a before and after in the history of the Holy Catholic Church.

Giovanni di Bernardone was born to a well-off family in the city of Assisi, in what is now the province of Perugia in the Italian region of Umbria. He was born in either 1181 or 1182, according to the work *St. Francis of Assisi, A Biography*, by Omer Englebert, and corroborated by other historians. Giovanni's father, a fabric merchant, was part of an emerging bourgeois class that was becoming more affluent through commerce, following the paradigmatic shift of the time from a typically feudal economy to a more proto-capitalistic one. This trend was beginning to inspire a social mobility that would enable those with no inherited land or noble title to no longer be in thrall to the lords who had for so long monopolized wealth and social control.

Back then, the Holy Roman Empire encompassed much of the territories of modern-day Germany, Switzerland, northern Italy, and parts of France, Austria, and the Czech Republic, among others. Such countries as France, Great Britain, Russia, and the Scandinavian Nordic kingdoms barely resembled the nation-states they would become. The same was true for the Iberian Peninsula, where the Spanish kingdoms and Portugal occupied small portions of the north, their remaining traditional territories in the hands of Muslim caliphs. Central Italy was under the sovereignty of the pope, who, acting as any other ruler, governed, collected taxes, and even participated in wars.

Within that setting, Giovanni was instructed in such classical disciplines as Latin while he lived a comfortable existence in central Italy. But the wider world was one of chronic war, where the powerful disputed and distributed territories among themselves as though they were entitled by birthright to the land and the lives of the young men who fought for it in their names. Like most men his age, Giovanni, whom his family affectionately called Francesco or Francesito (given his predilection for the French language and culture), was constantly summoned to join the armies fielded by the rival rulers of the day.

The city of Assisi had managed to free itself from Germanic rule in 1197, and a few years later was faced with a war against neighboring Perugia. It was in this conflict, in 1202, during the Battle of Ponte de San Giovanni, that, according to Englebert's account, this young man would fall prisoner and remain so for over a year, an experience that apparently had a considerable influence on him. Based on eyewitness accounts, in 1205, as part of the papal troops mustered against the Holy Roman Empire and under the command of Gualterio de Brienne, young Francesco heard a voice that demanded his return to Assisi. He obeyed, and in a gesture misinterpreted by many, he displayed a profound shift in attitude. He began to show a marked disregard for earthly possessions, and a state of peace and contemplation that made his friends and acquaintances wonder if perhaps the young man had fallen in love. When asked about it, the future saint admitted to the possibility, but pointed out that the object of his affection was "the most noble, rich, and good" he had ever seen. Francesco's cryptic words were not referring to a woman, however, but to poverty, his faithful companion from that moment through the rest of his days.

There are many other accounts of Francesco answering the call of an ethereal voice, often manifesting itself in dialogue with animals and inanimate objects. Perhaps the most famous incident occurred at Saint Damian Chapel, where, according to accounts, Jesus allegedly called down to him from the crucifix , imploring that he sell everything to rebuild the chapel that was practically in ruins. Again he obeyed, selling his horse and all his belongings in an effort to hand over whatever he could produce to the parish priest. All these acts of charity were signs of detachment and conversion toward a life of austerity that would, from then on, deeply impact the way in which a good portion of the Church would begin to interpret Jesus' teachings.

According to Englebert's work, we now find a resolute young man who dared to rebel against paternal authority, which he challenged on several occasions by rejecting that which was most important to his family: business and wealth. Francesco defied the mainstream so much so, that on several occasions, his father decided to literally chain him up, a customary discipline at the time for unruly sons. Taking advantage of his mother's sympathy and his father's repeated absences on business trips, he managed to set himself free and continue his evolving life of contemplation and total detachment from earthly possessions, repeatedly rejecting his very own family fortune. His father, fed up and feeling helpless, decided to turn to civil authorities to bring some order to his house, but Francesco refused to be subordinated to earthly power, already considering himself a soldier of God.

From then on, his father left him in the hands of ecclesiastical authorities, who accepted the challenge and required his submission and respect for authority. Still, he outright rejected their dictates, arguing that he was not the son of Pedro di Bernardone but that he only recognized divine paternity. In a scene that would be immortalized as one of the most representative in the lives of saints, Francesco not only publicly returned to his father the cloth wares that he was to sell, but also returned the very clothes that he was wearing, completely disrobing in front of an astonished crowd. Torn between admiration and pity, the local bishop took him in, covering him with his cloak.

Meanwhile, he continued his retired life of contemplation, attending to lepers (something considered absolutely irrational at the time), rebuilding churches, and helping poor farmers and the needy. Together with his budding following, he lived through charity and was an extreme example of modesty, a lifestyle completely foreign to many of the Church's dignitaries who carried out their ministry amidst luxury and earthly powers. But, as always, his preaching was that of love and confraternity, not of confrontation and division, trying to unite and respect all points of view. He and his followers were never considered heretics, as was the case with sects such as the Cathars, which was an enormous advantage since at the time the Church began combating heresy by means of Inquisition, which would have surely destroyed any flowering of Francesco and his followers' work.

As Franciscan preaching started to take form, it gained respect within the clergy, thanks largely to the favor bestowed on the movement by Assisi's local bishop. It was precisely this prelate who arranged, sometime in 1209, a hearing of these humble brothers with Pope Innocent III, for which they embarked on a key trip to Rome. In that meeting, Francis obtained verbal approval from the pope on the first rule of operation of the order. This decision was made despite strong controversy between several cardinals about the practicality of proceeding with this authorization. One group had in mind the Church's stance against the disorganized proliferation of religious organizations, while the other noted the favorable effect the Franciscan model could have, given their extreme modesty and constant preaching of virtue characteristic of Christianity in its early years. Finally, the latter viewpoint prevailed, and so was born the Franciscan Order, whose members qualified as brothers, or minor friars. Back from Rome, they settled in the zone of Rivo Torto, within the municipality of Assisi, where they reaffirmed their vow of poverty and predilection for the dispossessed and the sick, including lepers.

Slowly but surely, the movement gained more followers, until it transformed into a notable congregation of friars that expanded throughout northern Italy, southern France, and Spain. Its example and virtue began to gain more influence and recognition within the Church, and the order was given legal status at the Fourth Lateran Council in 1215. Franciscans, along with Dominicans, were even allowed the authority to elect cardinals within their own cloisters, but Francis, true to his firm, uncompromising style, begged that his followers not be perverted with honors and ostentation. While always bearing in mind their obedience to the Church, he wanted them to always respect the power for spiritual change that the order possessed.

The order's work gained Francis so much prestige and recognition that in 1216, Pope Honorius III promulgated plenary indulgence[2] to anyone who travelled to the Franciscan's central sanctuary to take part in a yearly pilgrimage. This decision elicited its share of controversy due to the fact that there were few pilgrimages in place at that time.

A whole new phase in Francis' life began when he decided to embark on a series of evangelizing trips to the Middle East, land of Christianity's birth, now occupied by "unfaithful" Muslims. He traveled to the Nile Delta, where he encountered men of the Fifth Crusade, whom he advised to replace war with dialogue. In response, he was mocked by combatants who, days later, would be resoundingly defeated by Muslim troops. But Francis' efforts were not in vain — his views were so original at the time that they slowly sparked interest among nobility and crusaders, leading many of them to abandon arms and become friars and lesser brothers.

He continued preaching in the area, and after encountering Saracen[3] troops, he managed to gain an audience before the Sultan of Egypt, whom, through various rituals and ministry, he tried to convert to the Christian faith. He even offered to walk through fire if, should he emerge unharmed, the vizier would get baptized and encourage his people's conversion. The proposal was rejected outright, but it earned him the official's sympathy. The vizier got his brother, the Sultan of Damascus, who had jurisdiction over the Holy Land, to allow Francis to travel through the area, the territory we know today as Syria. These travels gained Francis notoriety as an innovator, endeavoring to carry out the same task the Christian monarchs of Europe had embarked upon when organizing the Crusades. The main objective of both was to liberate the Holy Land, but Francis' aim was to do so via the peaceful methods of conviction, discussion, and prayer.

When he returned from the East, he got to work restructuring his order, which had become somewhat disorganized in his absence. He managed to get the pope to issue new rules that instituted structured norms of conduct and procedures for members to follow. One such rule emphasized the need for candidates to manifest religious vocation with certainty so that only the most dedicated individuals would enter into the order; another prohibited deceptive practices at odds with the organization's precepts.

Once this reorganization phase was over, and before retreating into asceticism even further, Francis helped establish a Christian custom that is still practiced today. On Christmas Eve of 1223, in Greccio, he convinced a noble-man named Giovanni to re-create, on a hill on his property, the precise mo-ment when Jesus was born. They built a manger with live animals and hay and they summoned a large number of friars and other believers, to whom Francis offered a sermon. In so doing, he instated the Christmas tradition of the Nativity scene (crèche) to celebrate the arrival of God's son on Earth.

A few months later, he shut himself away even more and began living an extremely spartan and secluded existence in isolated areas of the moun-tains near Assisi. It was there that, toward the end of his life, historical testimony shows that a series of supernatural events elevated him to a level of divinity that brought him irreversibly closer to holiness.

Secluded in his remote, mountainous refuge and fasting for weeks at a time, the future saint was paid a series of extraordinary visits by balls of fire that announced great events linked to the passion of Christ. According to Saint Bonaventure, on September 14, 1224, Francis allegedly was in the presence of the Son of God himself, who transmitted the stigmata of his crucifixion onto him. From then on, he received wounds on his hands and feet where nails had held Jesus to the cross, and a wound on his side as if from the Roman soldier's spear that pierced Christ — these spontaneous wounds were evidence of Francis' holiness.

Back from his seclusion, and after a long pilgrimage to different locali-ties in which he was adored by faithful followers, Francis' health began de-teriorating daily. His sacred wounds would not stop bleeding and, despite being under the care of the best doctors of the time, his life came to an end at the early age of forty-four, on October 3, 1226. Giovanni di Bernardone was canonized Saint Francis of Assisi less than two years after his death by Pope Gregory IX.

This is how Saint Bonaventure described the image of the deceased and his stigmata in his biography of Saint Francis, Legenda Major, chapter XV, 2, 3:

> 2. You could see in those blessed limbs nails of his own flesh, mar-velously fabricated by divine power and so inherent to it that, if they were pressed on one side they would immediately emerge on the other, as if solid nerves in one piece. He very visibly bore on his body the wound on his side — not inflicted or produced by human hand — similar to the one on the Savior's wounded side that made the sacrament of redemption and regeneration of man blatantly clear in our Redeemer himself.

The appearance of the nails was black, similar to iron; yet the wound on the side was reddish and it formed, due to the contraction of the flesh, a kind of circle, appearing to the naked eye as a beautiful rose. The rest of his body — before, due to his sickness and his natural complexion, he was dark-skinned — now shone with an extraordinary whiteness, as if representing the beauty of his glorious dress.

3. His limbs presented themselves so soft and flexible to touch, that they seemed to have returned to their childhood tenderness and appeared decorated with some evident signs of innocence.

His extremely white skin was [in] stark contrast to the blackness of the nails, while the wound on the side appeared rubicund like a rose in spring. It is not unusual that such beautiful and prodigious variety elicited among those who contemplated [its] sentiments of joy and admiration.

The sons mourned the loss of such [a] polite Father, yet at the same time they experienced no less happiness when kissing the signs of the sovereign King on that body. The novelty of the miracle turned tears to jubilation, and understanding was filled with stupor when looking into the incident. It was, in fact, such an unheard of and surprising spectacle that, for those who contemplated it, it constituted a consolation of faith and an incentive for love; and for those who merely heard people talk about him, he turned into an object of admiration that awakened a vivid desire to see him.

Cardinal Bergoglio's decision to be named Francis will have several powerful meanings for his papacy, for the future of the Catholic Church, and for his influence on the world in which we live today.

The first, most clear and transcendent impact is the direct reference to poverty: a pope of the poor and for the poor. When the new pontiff refers to this subject, he not only refers to the unhealthy pursuit of material wealth but confirms what his predecessor Benedict XVI pointed out when he talked about the lack of spirituality in opulent and developed societies. Thanks to a nearly universal extension of capitalism as a form of social and economic organization adapted to different cultures, more and more people are escaping the lowest levels of poverty and entering a growing, global middle class. This shift, however, has also led toward increased materialism, which in turn has led to a form of spiritual and moral poverty typical of our times.

By the beginning of the twentieth century, the United States had made great socioeconomic strides when it managed to become a nation where the middle class constituted an ample majority. So was the case in Western Europe after World War II, and so it is today in so-called "emerging countries." This success, however, brings about an unintended consequence, which is the rise of a kind of deep, existential vacuum. With basic needs met, there springs a desire for a connection to the transcendental meaning of our journey in this world. It is with respect to this yearning that the presence of a charismatic and exemplary leader can be decidedly useful — a leader from precisely those corners of the Earth that are in the middle of a process of change, under the leadership of an institution of great authority and influence such as the Church of Rome.

The counterbalance to this spiritual and moral poverty will be analyzed in depth in upcoming chapters. We will revisit how the then archbishop of Buenos Aires preached daily with his example and dedication to those forgotten individuals barely surviving in the slums — modern slaves suffering the scourge of hunger, substance abuse, unemployment, prostitution, and exploitation in the workplace. We will examine the phenomenon of war as a natural form of human conflict resolution, at least with respect to the more troubled regions of the planet. With technological advances and cumulative experience, if humanity pools its collective resources, in a short time, extreme poverty, hunger, and misery can become a thing of the past. A pope who has dedicated his whole life to bearing witness to this constant struggle, taking advantage of the availability of these new tools, can decidedly contribute to its global implementation.

There are other important areas in which the pope's chosen name can have great impact. Saint Francis was also, through his life and work, the patron saint of animals. Almost nine centuries ago, he proclaimed the harmonious coexistence of different species and the necessary respect that we, the dominating one, had to show toward the rest of God's creation. One does not have to be an advocate for extreme measures — such as returning to a pure state of nature and rejecting any type of progress and advancement — to recognize that our planet, this tiny blue sphere that floats in immense space, will not tolerate the rhythm of irrational consumption of resources much longer.

Paradoxically, there exists a true contradiction between opposing values. While we all wish for a world free of poverty, at the same time we are aware that, if we don't establish basic criteria of respect for our planetary ecosystem, the whole model will collapse. It is estimated that if the entire populations of India and China, for example, managed to reach the level of consumption per capita of residents of the city of New York alone, we would need five times that of Earth's current resources to satisfy all their needs.

We are not hereby appealing to failed, extreme leftist movements, especially in the developed world, that have attacked the model of capitalism, which has proved to be an impressive tool to generate and distribute wealth across the planet. Now that the unrealistic realizations of a communist utopia, with its self-professed omnipotence and omniscience, have been demolished, proponents of the new left put forth environmentally centered arguments that are more modern and attractive to new generations. What we are saying is that we as a species have to find compatibility between economic growth to alleviate poverty and respect for the environment in order to make this a viable and sustainable journey.

Another impact of choosing the name Francis can be connected to the phase in the saint's life when he embarked on his pilgrimages to the East. There, without renouncing his faith or his commitment, he advised crusaders to drop their weapons and join his mission of evangelism, endeavoring to engage rather than fight Muslims and those of other faiths. This attitude eventually provided his order with the privilege of guarding Christianity's most sacred sites in the Holy Land, and it could yet bear interesting fruit when today we are faced with the enormous challenge of buffering the clash of the world's two majority monotheistic religions: Christianity and Islam. When there is faith in one God that is considered unique and true, any alternative is naturally excluded, thus extinguishing any possibility of coexistence and harmony. With 1.2 billion Catholics, among 2.2 billion Christians worldwide, confronted with more than 1.5 billion Muslims, we are threatened with a kind of apocalyptic Third World War that we must try to avoid at all costs.

A generalized confrontation between these two civilizations would make the confrontations of the last few years pale in comparison. If there is any hope for diplomatic dialogue to eliminate the possibility of a global conflict of this nature, then much can be achieved in the spiritual realm when one of the most influential religious leaders of the world is truly dedicated to this goal. By engaging the Muslim faithful, as he has always done, in a peaceful, nonconfrontational manner, he will be following the path set forth by his namesake some eight hundred years before.

Francis' dedication to interreligious understanding and cooperation throughout his career inspired great faith in his fellow Argentines. His country of origin is a kaleidoscope of races and cultures from all over the world. In many cases, while escaping persecution and racial or religious intolerance, these people found a place to develop in peace and harmony at the end of the earth. Therefore, serving as the spiritual leader of Argentina for so many years, with a primarily Catholic population but with large Jewish and Muslim communities, precisely required a broad perception of this issue of interreligious dialogue. We will develop this subject in depth when we discuss Pope Francis' deep ecumenism.

Another advantage that this name can provide Peter's current successor is related to its connection to religious orders within the Catholic Church, particularly to the power and influence that different orders have within the present structure of the Church. His own order, the Society of Jesus, manages a very powerful network around the world. Not only is this due to the number of its members, organized into ten "assistances" within ninety-one provinces, but it is also because, from its very origin, the Society has focused on education.

Impressive statistics published by the Jesuit Curia in Rome state that, in 2008, the order sponsored 231 universities, 462 secondary schools, 187 primary schools, and 70 professional and technical schools throughout 69 countries. In all of these institutions, there were 130,571 laypersons and 3,732 Jesuits working as educators and administrators. To this we need to add the Society's Educational Networks (particularly Fe y Alegría in Latin America), with 2,947 centers. The total number of students in attendance in Jesuit-run institutions today is estimated at three million around the globe. Among the most prominent alumni from these establishments we find people of diverse origin and accomplishment, including Descartes, Voltaire, Cervantes, Quevedo, José Ortega y Gasset, Antoine de Saint-Exupéry, Charles de Gaulle, Vicente Huidobro, Alfred Hitchcock, Fidel Castro, and James Joyce.

But by honoring the legacy of Saint Francis with his choice of name, the current pope sends a strong message to all mendicant orders that see in him an inspiring example. Not only Franciscans but Dominicans, Augustinians, Carmelites, Trinitarians, and Mercedarians, among others, will surely see that from the top of the ecclesiastical hierarchy, they are being recognized for the honor and importance of their work. A brief look at the Franciscans illustrates this point.

Franciscans are organized into three orders: Friars Minor, men; Order of Saint Clare, women (abbreviated in Latin as O.S.C.); Regular and Secular Franciscans, both men and women. The first order of friars, all men, is made up of approximately three branches: 17,000 of the Order of Friars Minor (O.F.M.), 12,000 of the Order of Friars Minor Capuchin (O.F.M. Cap.), and about 5,000 of the Order of Friars Conventual (O.F.M. Conv.). Third Order Regular and Secular Franciscans are made up of men and women, both vowed and unvowed, all of whom expect to live a life inspired by the principles and examples of Saint Francis and fellow pioneers.

The second order, also known as "Poor Clares," are contemplative nuns who follow the legacy of Saint Clare of Assisi. Another noble and rich contemporary of Saint Francis, she gave up everything to follow him and became the first woman to organize a feminine order that included a monastic rule. She lived longer than her mentor, reaching sixty years of age, with more than forty members secluded in a monastery dedicated to withdrawal and prayer. The symbolic link between the current pope and this woman could prove to be advantageous. As noted, in evocative and poignant gesture on his first Holy Thursday as pope, Francis washed the feet of twelve inmates in a youth detention center in Rome, including two women. Saint Clare's work as Saint Francis of Assisi's closest disciple could prove to be of use to him as he continues his outreach to women in the Church family.

The new pope's allegiance to Franciscans widely exceeds the choice of his name. He recently designated the Superior of the order, Spaniard José Rodríguez Carballo, only fifty-six years old, to second in command of the powerful Congregation for Institutes of Consecrated Life and Societies of Apostolic Life. This organization is in charge of the supervision and control of the more than 900,000 ordained men and women in the world who have vowed to live lives of chastity, poverty, and obedience. Replacing conservative archbishop Joseph Tobin, he will have to confront a major issue inherited from Benedict XVI's papacy: disciplinary sanctions applied to the Leadership Conference of Women Religious (LCWR), a group comprised of 59,000 North American nuns, for taking very liberal positions regarding feminism, priesthood, and homosexuality. By replacing the conservative archbishop with the Franciscan leader, the new pope sends a message of dialogue and rapprochement to his sisters in the Church.

Another interesting aspect is simply that the name Francis is very popular around the world. In Italy it was the most common male name for many years and is still quite popular today. It was used extensively in Spain and Latin America until recently, and it currently sits in ninth place in Poland and tenth in Portugal with respect to new baptisms. As we can see, there are many Catholics around the world who share their name with the pope and who may now better identify with the man who now leads the bishopric of Rome.

Similarly, we should not overlook the many locations and cities in the Christian world — San Francisco, San Francesco, Sao Francisco, Saint Francis, Saint Francois — that were also named in tribute to Saint Francis. There are at least seven in the United States, seven in Canada, seven in the Philippines, four in Portugal, six in Mexico, three in Colombia, three in Brazil, two in Cape Verde, and one in Argentina, Chile, Costa Rica, Dominican Republic, Ecuador, Guatemala, Nicaragua, and Panama, adding up to almost fifty. From the quiet city of San Francisco in the province of Córdoba, Argentina, with its 60,000 inhabitants and known for its farming and diary industries, to the San Francisco of the United States — one of the world's great metropolitan areas, a center of cultural influence and cutting-edge technology, with a population of more than seven million people from all over the planet — residents of these places might now reflect on the story and legacy of the saint who inspired the naming of their hometowns.

———————

A Jesuit who decides to call himself Francis, who comes from Earth's distant south, a Latin American of direct Italian descent who, from the utmost height of Vatican power, proclaims humility and the example of the saint who made history by renouncing all his wealth and offering himself completely to God. Perhaps these attributes, unusual to the papacy, simply make for an interesting conversation piece. More likely, this unique, virtuous combination of factors, properly utilized and sustained over time, will bring about a turning point in the recent tumultuous history of one of the most venerable religious institutions in the world.

His Holiness' examples of humility thus far seem to come from a most genuine place, as opposed to being a simple media ploy, feigning the principles of Saint Francis. A pope who presents himself stripped of luxurious clothing in his first public appearance; calls himself Bishop of Rome rather than Supreme Pontiff; bows before the crowd and, in an unprecedented gesture of humility, asking that they pray for him; travels by bus with the rest of the cardinals who chose him rather than alone in the papal limousine; refuses to live in the luxurious papal apartments; picks a gold-plated silver ring, as opposed to one of solid gold, to comply with protocol; washes the feet of society's dispossessed and forgotten; moves through the crowds without bulletproof safeguard — these are merely a handful of examples that seem to be illustrating Pope Francis' desired course for a revived Holy Roman Church.

A papacy, though, is obviously not reduced to these symbolic gestures alone. Governing the Church is far more complex, and the current agenda includes very serious matters with potentially very controversial resolutions. Some will generate massive arguments and will incite dissent and serious divisions within the institution. It will take a great helmsman to steer the ship amidst the choppy seas of current problems faced by the Church and the dangerous crags of hatred and resentment within the Roman Curia itself.

But Pope Francis' first steps are promising. And his very choice of name has proven to be the right one — no minor issue when we think of a spiritual leader whose life example is extremely important. No one expects the pope to renounce all his material possessions like Saint Francis did. Maybe something that extreme wouldn't even prove useful. However, he should continue to follow the teachings of the Saint Francis and come as close as reasonably possible in this modern world to the saint's way of life. He must remain coherent and, as he did throughout his entire religious career, bear daily witness to human sacrifice as a means of remaining connected with his highest mandate. If, to the humble Jorge Bergoglio, we add the determined Jesuit who, in Argentina, rose through the ranks of his order under some of the most politically challenging circumstances any man of God has ever faced, this combination could prove to revolutionize not only the Church, but the world itself.

Saint Francis of Assisi: Testament written in April 1226:

> Write that I bless all my brothers in Religion and all who shall be to the end of time. And since I am unable to speak because of my weakness, my pain and my sickness, I will briefly give in three words my

wishes and desires to all the brothers present and to come: namely, that in memory and remembrance of my benediction and last will, they shall always love each other mutually as I have loved them and as I still cherish them; let them always love and follow our Lady Poverty; and let them always faithfully obey the prelates and clerks of our Holy Mother, the Church.

Chapter 9

Poverty

JORGE BERGOGLIO'S FIRST intimate experience with true poverty occurred when he was barely 23, and its indelible impression is best illustrated in a letter he sent to his sister from Chile on May 5, 1960. The letter was
published in one of the country's major newspapers, *La Nación*. From Padre
Hurtado, a city around twelve miles outside of Santiago, Francis wrote:

> I am going to tell you something: I teach third and fourth-grade
> Religion in a school. The children are very poor; some even come
> to school barefoot. Often, they have nothing to eat, and in winter
> they experience the cold in all its severity. You don't know what that
> means, because you've always had food and when you are cold you
> get close to a heater. I'm telling you this so that you remember . . .
> When you are happy there are many children crying. When you sit
> at the table, many only have a piece of bread as a meal, and when it
> rains and it's cold, many are living in tin caves and they sometimes
> have nothing with which to cover themselves. Just the other day
> an old lady said: "Father, if I could only find a blanket, how great
> would that be! Because I'm very cold at night." And the worst part is
> that they don't know Jesus. They don't know him because there's no
> one to teach them. Do you understand now when I say that there's
> a need for many saints?

Although definitions vary, material poverty basically refers to the economic standing of the world's billions of impoverished. It can be defined

broadly as a denial of alternatives and opportunities, which equates to a strong violation of human dignity in that it generates an incapacity to effectively participate in society. Poverty is clearly illustrated in cases where there isn't enough to feed or dress a family, where there is poor to nonexistent infrastructure, or when there is no access to education or health care. It can also be related to a lack of land available to produce one's own food, no access to credit, or not making enough to earn a living. All of this causes the marginalization of both individuals and communities, and it perpetuates, in these fragile environments, a culture of despair.

According to criteria set by the World Bank, an individual with an income of less than $1.25 a day is living in extreme poverty. Although statistics show improvement in this area, as of 2015, an estimated one billion people will still fall below this line. The total number of people living on less than $2.50 a day may be as high as three billion.

If we concentrate on one of the most abhorrent elements of poverty, hunger, we see again that the situation has improved in the past twenty years. Food and Agriculture Organization of the United Nations (FAO) figures show that for the period 1990–1992, there were an estimated one billion undernourished people around the world, a number that dropped to 868 million for the period 2010–2012. By any measure, this is still an enormity and a tragedy.

Regarding access to health care as a barometer of poverty, consider life expectancy rates. According to the World Population Prospects 2010 report published by the United Nations Department of Economic and Social Affairs, Japan heads the list of 198 countries, with an average life expectancy of 82.73 years (79.31 for men and 86.96 for women). The forty countries at the bottom of the list are dominated by African nations (the exception being Afghanistan), with the Central African Republic at the very bottom with an average life expectancy of 45.91 (44.71 for men and 47.31 for women). The difference couldn't be more stark: inhabitants of the developed world live practically twice as long as those of the underdeveloped world.

Another indicator that underscores the harsh reality of poverty is infant mortality. The United Nations' Population Division publishes a list of the number of children that die during their first year of life out of every thousand that are born alive. In the list of 188 countries for the period 2005–2010, Singapore showed the lowest infant mortality rate with 1.92, followed by Iceland with 2.07. The bottom forty again are African countries, and closing the list is Afghanistan with an incredible 135.95.

Once again, the difference between developed and underdeveloped areas is enormous.

A fourth reality of poverty is lack of access to education. Even though there are more modern and sophisticated methods, a basic and traditional way of analyzing this issue has always been to measure literacy rate. The CIA World Factbook lists, among the worst places, Burkina Faso with a mere 21.8 percent of the population knowing how to read and write, South Sudan with 27 percent, and Afghanistan with 28.1 percent. The world average is 83.7 percent. There is still a long way to go to bridge this gap.

People lacking access to running water or sewers; people living under the scourges of disease and war — the sad statistics could go on. Although the past decade has witnessed the transfer of vast sectors of the world's lower-class population into a budding middle class, the situation is far from optimal. There are many millions who still suffer under the crushing weight of poverty.

From Jesus himself onward, the Church has played a key, hands-on role in helping to overcome poverty's causes and effects. Throughout its more than two-thousand-year history, the list of saints, martyrs, and consecrated people who have dedicated their entire lives to this task is practically endless. Along the way, many doctrines have grown out of this preferential option for the poor and vulnerable and have gone on to become central contributions to human thought. This includes the preservation of human life and its dignity; the right to work; the preservation of social institutions such as marriage; equal rights and social justice; charity; and respect for our environment.

Even though the Church has always been committed to the poor and dispossessed, it's fair to say that ever since Leo XIII's papacy, it decided to take a clear and precise stance on issues related to the economy and labor relationships. This Italian pope, who took office in 1878 and held Peter's throne for twenty-five years, was the first to take charge of an organization that, as a consequence of Italian unity, lost pontifical territories and practically all its power. Given this new condition, the pope was greatly concerned about establishing clear and very precise positions on different matters that were affecting society. The growth of the modern economy and the advance and consolidation of capitalism during the nineteenth century brought with it many abuses, prompting budding socialist ideas about the plight of workers, all of which influenced his thinking.

Thus, in 1891 Pope Leo XIII revealed his Rerum Novarum (Of New Things) encyclical, which confronted the labor issue, among other problems. This was a serious concern in Europe at the time, since decades of industrial revolution had generated a severe strain between capital and work. His encyclical, almost revolutionary at the time, outlined what would later become the Church's Social Doctrine. It recognized the right of workers to unionize in defense of their rights, and while it also reinforced the principle of private property, characterizing the latter as a means but not an end. And so began a long sermon given by different popes regarding these fundamental social issues.

Forty years later, in his Quadragesimo Anno (Fortieth Year), Pope Pius XI used the term "Social Doctrine" for the first time when referring to the content of the Rerum Novarum. Pius XI's encyclical recognized and summarized the contribution of Leo XIII's work, reaffirming the idea of building a middle ground between communism and capitalism by strongly condemning socialist collectivism while criticizing the abuse of rampant individualism. Fair wages, the right of workers to be able to sustain an adequate standard of living, and the importance of private property, once again as a means, not an end, were key issues.

In 1967, Pope Paul VI revealed the Populorum Progressio (Development of Peoples) encyclical calling attention to a crucial issue of the time: the imbalance between rich and poor countries. He addressed the problem of developing, so-called Third World nations, supporting the right of people's welfare and condemning neocolonialism to the extent of even justifying the possibility of rising up against a powerful oppressor. These contributions aside, the Populorum Progressio still held the position of prior encyclicals, outlining an equidistant stance between collectivist Marxism and unrestrained capitalism.

The Church's doctrinal concern on these matters continues with three encyclicals issued by Pope John Paul II. In 1981, celebrating ninety years of the Rerum Novarum, he revealed the Laboreum Exercens (On Human Work) encyclical, which continued to underscore the issue of workers' rights, but approaching it from a moral and spiritual standpoint. In 1987 he released Solicitudo Rei Socialis (Concern for the Social Order), honoring the twenty-year anniversary of the Poplorum Progressio, where he reaffirmed the validity of the Church's Social Doctrine and highlighted the constant balance between continuity and renovation, revisiting the issue of progress and integral development of the individual. Finally, he released Centesimus Annus (Hundredth Year) in 1991, which celebrated Rerum Novarum's first century, confirming its content and assigning a modern meaning to "New Things."

In 2009, during Benedict XVI's papacy, Caritas in Veritae (Charity of Truth) was released. It highlighted the work of all of Benedict's predecessors, but incorporated a concern for sustainable development through charity while analyzing the global financial crisis of the time. It even suggested the need for a world political authority in order to confront these new challenges.

One typically equates the concept of poverty with some of the issues we addressed earlier: hunger, a lack of housing, health care, or social justice. As mentioned in the previous chapter, another type of poverty in our modern world is spiritual poverty — the drying up of the soul. Lack of spirituality in our society causes the loss of a sense of transcendence. It is a serious disease that especially affects the people who have managed to satisfy their basic needs but still can't find their way. They are lost in an apparent material satiety.

Francis' relationship with this dilemma and his authentically Christian positions on the matter of both material and spiritual poverty have been apparent for years, as evidenced by the letter he sent to his sister from Chile. But after some time, and having risen through the Church's ranks to cardinal, he expounded on the matter in his remarkable conversations with Rabbi Abraham Skorka, published in book form in 2010 under the title *Sobre el Cielo y la Tierra* (*On Heaven and Earth*). Speaking of charity and poverty, he turned to the Gospel, to Matthew 25:35–36:

> For I was hungry, and ye gave me meat: I was thirsty, and ye gave me drink: I was a stranger, and ye took me in:
>
> Naked, and ye clothed me: I was sick, and ye visited me: I was in prison, and ye came unto me.

When the people in this parable of the final judgment asked the Lord when they had performed these acts of charity, Francis explained, "Every time they did it with one of the little ones in His kingdom, they did it with Him."

Clearly, here lies the essence of the mandate governing how one should act when confronted with poverty and the poor, with suffering and those who suffer. A commitment to help others is a commitment to serve God. It is the only path that a good Christian can take. And thus the cure for material poverty also becomes the cure for spiritual poverty.

Regarding when and how help to the needy should be implemented, Francis is very precise about where to start. "The first type of care for poverty," he says, "is aid: 'Are you hungry? Here, have something to eat.'"

Francis is sure to point out that it is every Christian's moral obligation to reach out to the needy with such tangible assistance whenever possible. And he is precise again when he emphasizes that to "reach out" means exactly that — not by writing a check or attending a charitable fundraiser, but "body to body . . . establishing direct contact with the needy . . . even when it causes aversion, repugnance."

But things shouldn't stop there. That personal attitude needs to be organized and given a collective meaning in order to alleviate poverty as a social problem. "The poor don't have to be perpetually marginalized . . . It is essential to incorporate [them] to our community as soon as possible, through education, art schools, and trades . . . so that they are able to succeed."

This is exactly the sort of pioneering work that Francis, as archbishop of Buenos Aires, implemented in the most impoverished areas of the city. He focused not only on charity, but enabling the poor to help themselves. Francis reminds us that "what is degrading to the poor is not having that oil that anoints them with dignity: work."

Francis is careful to point out the risks of aiding the needy as a means to subordinate them. This is something that is particularly prevalent in poorer countries where, often, behind the state's good intentions to help those in need lurks an interest to obtain votes. This practice ends up causing a dangerous distortion of charity — a patronage system that is often benefited by the perpetual existence of poverty in order to maintain the status quo. Francis believes that "the great danger — or great temptation — in aiding the poor dwells in falling in a kind of protective paternalism that, ultimately, will prevent them from growing."

A final point Francis has made about Christian charity sheds some light on his earthly inspirations for the doctrines he expounds above. As cardinal primate of Argentina, his predilection for supporting the slum priests in their work among the poor had raised some concern among the Church hierarchy. "This isn't a new phenomenon," Francis pointed out. "In northern Italy, in the kingdom of Sardinia, Don Bosco worked with the humble and also raised suspicions among bishops. Not to mention Don Cafasso and Don Orione. They were avant-gardes in regard to their work with the needy. They somehow forced some change in authorities."

———————

The Italian region of Piedmont was the birthplace of Francis' parents. Whether due to a twist of fate or through intercession of the Holy Spirit, the three Church figures mentioned by Francis as examples of the work he, too, was doing to assist the poor also hailed from the Piedmont region.

Giovanni Melchiorre Bosco was born in the hamlet of Becchi, in Castelnuovo D'Astia, in 1815, a year in which all of Europe was undergoing a profound change. The Congress of Vienna[1] had concluded, and monarchies were reinstated after the defeat of Napoleon at the Battle of Waterloo. The Boscos were a humble family struggling to survive in a time of poverty and famine, in an area recently ravaged by war between France and Austria. When he was only two years old, his father passed away, leaving his mother, Margherita, to raise her family alone. She would go on to play a vital role throughout his life and work.

From an early age, John Bosco began experiencing premonitory and revealing dreams that would serve as a spiritual guide throughout his life. The first one, at nine years old, invoked words of wisdom when, in the middle of an imaginary fight, someone told him, "Not with fists, but with politeness will you defeat those boys."

Amidst economic hardship and with great personal effort, Bosco managed to pursue an education with the help of his mother. With the constant need to support himself, he worked as a pastry chef, tailor, ironmonger, and shoemaker.

Once he finished high school, and due to lack of resources, he decided to join the Franciscan order. However, at twenty, the advice and help of a friend, coupled with his telling dreams, made him reconsider his decision and lean toward the diocesan seminary at Chieri. There he was ordained as a priest in 1841, at the age of twenty-six. Once ordained, he moved to the capital, Turin, where he formally began the work that would transform him into an influential force within the universal Church.

Piedmont's capital was a large industrial city at the time, and it had attracted numerous immigrant farmers, most of them young, some even children. These immigrants were crowded into and practically enslaved in the first industrial factories of the time. After several casual encounters with a few of them, Don Bosco started caring for and protecting them from their employers' abuse, seeking to liberate them from labor exploitation by finding them dignified jobs and negotiating favorable contracts on their behalf. By 1845, his network was comprised of more than four hundred young men, with whom he often appeared publicly, generating concern among civil and ecclesiastical authorities.

Don Bosco managed to build an oratory for his followers, and eventually his center incorporated a boarding school as well as shoemaking, tailoring, sewing, printing, and even light metallurgy workshops. He began teaching mid-level classes and even received authorization to function as a seminary, ordaining the first thirty-four priests in 1861. His work was inspired by the gentle teachings and spiritual theology of Saint Francis de Sales,[2] which he juxtaposed with the rigor and exaggerated discipline of the European Church at the time, influenced by the strict ideals of Jansenism.[3]

So much activity and so many followers kindled the mistrust of hierarchies, to the point of rousing fear in Count Cavour himself, a powerful ally of the ruling House of Savoy, who feared a revolution might be brewing. However, because Don Bosco's work was so powerful and his results so positive, he finally obtained authorization to constitute the Salesian Order. Given a series of government restrictions on ecclesiastical organizations stemming from tension between the crown and the papacy, he decided to form a civil society of ordained men, an atypical arrangement and an interesting precedent for the future. At the same time, and after meeting María Dominga Mazzarollo, he organized the women's branch of the Salesian Order, the Mary Help of Christians.

Don Bosco's work expanded to other Italian communities and eventually, through massive migration of Italian citizens, to South America. Thus, in 1875, the first Salesian mission arrived at the port of Buenos Aires. The order would soon concentrate in Patagonia, a vast region that had recently been incorporated to the Argentine domain. Barely reached by Spanish conquistadors, its inhabitants had little introduction to faith in Christ. Next the order moved into Uruguay in 1876, Brazil in 1882, Paraguay in 1886, and Ecuador in 1888. It was in this year that Don Bosco died in Turin at seventy-two, having lived a prolific life that completely changed the way in which the Catholic Church related to the poor and the young. His impact was such that his beatification process began two years later, ending in 1929, and Pope Pius XI canonized him as Saint John Bosco in 1934.

Don Bosco's work through the Salesian Order has endured through the present day. They form a network of almost 16,000 ordained men and women in 131 countries.

Another Piedmontese saint who has had a great influence on Francis was Giuseppe Cafasso. A contemporary of Don Bosco as well as his friend, confessor, and patron, Don Cafasso was most importantly his inspiration. He was born a few years earlier in 1811, in the same town, although to a wealthy family. They met in 1827 and, according to Salesian tradition, he was the one who obtained funding for a half scholarship in the seminary for a humble, young Bosco, who otherwise would have been unable to undertake his education and likely never carry out his subsequent work.

Don Cafasso was professor of moral theology at his friend's institute, where he went on to become rector, presiding there always in accordance with Saint Francis of Sales' philosophy of the potential for holiness within all people, in contraposition to Jansenism's rigor. Making the most of his family connections, he played an important role in soliciting donations to help with the expansion of the entire mission. But the place where he developed his apostolate the most, which would later lead to his sainthood, was the prisons of Turin. He was chaplain at the main penitentiary for several years where he worked in defense of the inmates, striving to improve their vile living conditions and ensuring that those on death row were not executed without receiving the sacraments of Confession and the Eucharist.

After suffering from a long illness, Don Cafasso died prematurely in 1860, at the age of forty-nine. He did not live to see the global expansion of the work he inspired. At his funeral, Don Bosco himself delivered the eulogy. Due to his life and example, Pope Pius XII canonized him in 1947.

The son of Piedmontese parents, Luigi Orione was born in 1872 in Pontecurone, around sixty miles west of Turin. He met Don Bosco when he entered the Valdocco oratory after a frustrated attempt, due to illness, at becoming a Franciscan monk. Don Orione entered the seminary at Tortona in 1889 and during that time alternated between his formation and his apostolic work, opening an oratory and a school. In 1895 he was ordained a priest, and four years later he formed the Little Work of Divine Providence, concentrating all his efforts on the marginalized and the differently abled. In 1903, the congregation was officially approved under the name of the Sons of Divine Providence.

In 1908, Don Orione moved to Sicily to help those affected by the Messina earthquake, where he was named vicar general. His work continued to grow and in 1913, he sent his first group of missionaries to Brazil. Two years later, he founded the congregation of the Little Missionary Sisters of Charity and opened the first *cottolengo* — a house of refuge for the poor and destitute — in Ameno, Italy. In 1924 he opened another in Geneva and ten years later he traveled to Argentina, where he opened the first Argentine *cottolengo* in Claypole, in the suburbs of Buenos Aires.

Don Orione passed away in San Remo, Italy, in 1940, concluding a life of dedication and devotion to the forgotten and disenfranchised. His work spanned more than thirty nations and survives in numerous *cottolengos*, professional schools, retirement homes, and youth and homeless shelters, which led to his beatification in 1982 and canonization in 2004 by Pope John Paul II.

Although these three saints began their work in Italy, they managed to cast their influence out across the Atlantic, all the way to Latin America, helping the poor, the exploited youth, the imprisoned, the disabled, and the homeless. The similarities of their origin, the work they carried out, and their apostolic sense of mission, without a doubt, exemplifies a tradition of charity that continues to live on in Pope Francis.

———————

Humanity is equipped to defeat poverty, to overcome it as an affliction of the past. Throughout history, we have repeatedly made decisions of similar magnitude and taken a morally qualitative leap forward. When, by the end of the nineteenth century, the recently constructed Federative Republic of Brazil became the last country to abolish slavery throughout its vast territory, our species formally abandoned that abhorrent institution, at least as a legal and accepted practice amongst nations. Obviously, this does not mean it disappeared completely. Even today there exist new forms of slavery, such as human trafficking and labor exploitation, which are still practiced in many places, albeit generally outside the law.

A similar transformation has taken place with regards to war as a means of conflict resolution among countries. Although humanity has not completely abandoned the urge to kill one another over territories, ideas, religions, resources, or political power, the last few decades have slowly generated a system of dialogue and coordination that has made it possible to avoid many armed conflicts. This becomes very clear if we consider the endless bloodletting of past centuries, or the massacres that were the two world wars of the twentieth century.

But still, there is poverty.

Argentine Marcelo Giugale, the World Bank's Director of Economic Policy and Poverty Reduction Programs for Africa, is an expert on the subject. Following his thinking, if the international community seriously sets itself to the mission, it could deliver the final blow to this monster that has stalked mankind since the dawn of time. Perhaps it's coincidence, but Giugale is yet another descendent of Piedmontese ancestors who has devoted his career to the issue of poverty, although this time from World Bank headquarters in Washington, DC, and using the most modern research tools at his disposal.

In his regular online columns and via various other media, Giugale manages to provoke his audience with his optimistic and audacious positions. In them he points out that it is indispensable to get to know the enemy that we intend to defeat, and that the enormous amount of data available in this age of information can enable us to direct available resources to the appropriate organizations and places for which they were intended, and where they are needed most. In order to do that, we need to access data that is comparable, consistent, and accessible. And to best utilize this seemingly unlimited well of information, we need to keep in mind a few factors.

Giugale asserts that our first priority is to establish precise goals for active policies in order to manage expenses more efficiently in regard to the desired effect. Ultimately, this may require creating a new system of supervision and evaluation of poverty programs worldwide.

Next, he indicates that a larger flow of information allows us to understand much more about the skills we should help develop so that marginalized sectors can overcome poverty and support themselves based on their own talents.

Finally, according to Giugale, we are now able to know how different personal circumstances affect human opportunities. He is referring to such factors as gender, skin color, place of birth, and family income. This has allowed for the development of a new indicator, the World Bank's Human

Opportunity Index, something that will forever change the way in which social policies are designed.

"We will be able to win the war against poverty when those who try to help the poor decide to literally start listening to them," concludes Giugale. This final, very Christian sentiment is what will allow us to connect these technical and social policy prescriptions with the indispensable approach toward the poverty-stricken to which Francis continues to refer. The Church will never renounce its welfare mission, or the work of slum priests, *cottolengos*, youth homes, and so many other modalities that, throughout time, have advanced Christ's mandate in spirit and practice. But this mandate will also have to inspire and influence the minds and policies of all humanity, through doctrinal definitions that are promulgated by the Catholic Church but universal in their appeal.

That is why the arrival of Francis, the Argentine pope of Piedmontese heritage, inspired by the saint of the poor and following the example of the other three saints born in the same Italian region, can make a difference. If technology and Christianity can be wedded in a common goal, we can begin to transform the idea of eradicating the world of poverty into a reality.

Chapter 10

Ecumenism and Interfaith Dialogue

W HAT WE NOW see as normal — respectful dialogue between dignitaries from different religions in order to discover commonalities and bridge differences —is actually a relatively new phenomenon. Throughout all of history, beliefs and faith have fueled the fires of division, rivalries, and war. In sharp contrast with their own teachings — love of God, respect and harmony between human beings — religions in conflict have been the cause of untold hatred, suffering, and deaths.

The Christian Church was born from such rivalry and bloodshed. Beginning with the vehement opposition to Jesus' teachings that resulted in his crucifixion, for the next few centuries there ensued an "age of martyrs," when Christians were brutally persecuted for their beliefs. In 312, before engaging co-emperor Maxentius at what came to be known as the Battle of Milvian Bridge, Roman emperor Constantine I was inspired by a revealing dream in which he was commanded to have his soldiers mark their shields with a symbol of Christ. His victory made him the sole emperor in the West, and in 313 Constantine the Great, together with Emperor Licinius I of the East, drafted the Edict of Milan, which granted religious tolerance throughout the empire and legalized Christianity. This would lay the groundwork for Christianity to begin flourishing throughout the Roman world. Later, with the First Council of Nicaea in 325, Constantine settled important matters of doctrine and canon law and helped unify competing visions of the meaning and practice of Christianity.

But Christendom was soon embroiled in further conflict, this time with adherents of a competing monotheistic faith that virtually exploded onto the world map in the seventh century: Islam. In the early eighth century, the Moors (North African Berbers), accompanied by Arabs, crossed the Strait of Gibraltar and invaded the Iberian Peninsula. Christian armies engaged the Muslim invaders in an ongoing struggle for control over the region, one that would last for over 700 years. War between Christians and Muslims continued with the Crusades, when legions of lords and knights sent by the Christian monarchies of Europe attempted to wrest control of the Holy Land from Islamic occupation. Extending from 1095 to 1291, the Crusades are considered an archetype of religious conflict.

The advent of the Protestant Reformation in the early sixteenth century initiated a series of internal conflicts in the Christian Church between those loyal to Rome and the Protestant reformers influenced by the ideas of Martin Luther and John Calvin. The battles that raged between Catholics and Protestants throughout Europe during this era are legion: German princes vying for power in the Schmalkaldic War of 1546–1547; the hunt for and massacre of Calvinists in France, including the Saint Bartholomew's Day Massacre of 1572; the Eighty Years' War between 1568 and 1648 in what we know today as the Netherlands, which concluded with the recognition of Dutch independence under the influence of the Calvinist family of Orange-Nassau, while Catholicism prevailed in the south; and the Thirty Years' War, 1614–1648, beginning in the fading embers of the Holy Roman Empire as a clash between Catholics and Protestants. Across the English Channel, power struggles in England, Scotland, and Ireland between 1639 and 1651 — collectively known as the Wars of the Three Kingdoms — included religious disputes among their causes.

The tendrils of this ancient armed conflict between Catholics and Protestants have extended into modern times. Beginning in the 1960s, "the Troubles" saw the Irish Republican Army (IRA) waging a decades-long resistance against Anglican England's control of Northern Ireland, while Irish "unionists" in the north pushed back against Catholic encroachment from the Republic of Ireland to the south. This fierce, tragic fighting claimed the lives of 3,500 people, and its echoes still reverberate in the British Isles to this day.

Contemporary to the sixteenth-century battles among Christians in Central Europe, Hapsburg Catholics vied with Islamic Ottoman Turks for control of vast areas of Eastern Europe and the Balkans. This friction between two major monotheistic religions persisted for years in different regions and in different manners. Its echoes, too, have been felt in the present day, from the fighting between Muslims and Christians that followed the break-up of Yugoslavia in the 1990s to the unconventional war between Islamic fundamentalists and the Western world that dominates today's headlines.

The constant and repeated persecution of the Jews deserves a singular mention. Although not embroiled in the vast geopolitical struggles of Catholic and Protestant monarchs or Christian and Muslim armies through the ages, the Jews were convenient, collateral targets in these campaigns. Persecution of Jews, both spontaneous and systematic, has been recorded over centuries throughout the Middle East and several European regions, culminating in brutal anti-Jewish pogroms in Russia in the eighteenth and nineteenth centuries and Nazi Germany's "Final Solution" for Jews during World War II — the Holocaust.

This brief historical review is but a glimpse of the sprawling conflicts that have haunted Christendom for more than two millennia. But it is necessary background in order to appreciate the focus of this chapter: an end to religious-based division and fighting; a new era of understanding, respect, and peace; and the new pope's role in helping to bring it about.

When discussing Christian ecumenism — the principle of promoting unity between different Christian denominations — our goal is not only to define the varying beliefs and practices among the different sects into which Christianity has divided, but to find points of agreement between them. It is like an attempt to reunite feuding siblings, reminding them that they have one common branch and recognize only one father. Although it might seem like a simple task given their shared origin, the proposed challenge is daunting. Taken alone, it is a complex issue given the theological, moral, doctrinal, liturgical, and disciplinary differences. But when we factor in history, and the extreme enmity and mistrust caused by years of opposition, the venture becomes yet more problematic.

On a grander scheme, the objective of interfaith initiatives is to bring large religions closer, especially monotheistic religions. Jews, Christians, and Muslims believe in the same one, true God, although their concepts differ in interpretation. We have seen, in our historical review, how this paradox has played out in unproductive ways; the idea of a unique supreme being, creator of all things, has more often been a source of division than union. At its most fanatical extreme, these divisions have brought about a true clash of civilizations. That is why the positions and attitude projected by the papacy become especially important today.

The notion of seeing the world's citizens unite under a single religious banner is, frankly, impossible. What is possible, however, is people of different faiths working together to avoid the conflicts of the past and present, guaranteeing a more peaceful and harmonious future. It is imperative that agnostics and atheists be included in this dialogue as well. In our times, millions have moved away from organized religion or spirituality altogether, and they, too, should be invited to participate in order to reach this higher goal.

Before we begin our analysis of ecumenism, it is necessary to dig a little deeper into the history behind the many disagreements within the Christian family today. With that purpose in mind, we need to focus on the concept of schism, derived from the Greek *schisma*, which means "cleft" or "division." The different versions under which faith in Christ is presented — Roman Catholic, Eastern Orthodox, Protestant, Anglican, and other denominations — are a result of breakaway movements from the original Church of Rome. They often began as a rebellion against local clergy or the respective bishop, particularly with respect to their position as intermediaries between believers and God, but the most committed movements ultimately reached all the way to Rome, rejecting the pope's authority as Christ's representative on Earth.

Most often, these competing interpretations of the Christian faith ended up being defined by the Church as heresy. Those breaking from the Catholic doctrine suffered excommunication and loss of all ecclesiastical benefits and dignities, including the right to receive sacraments or attend ceremonies and masses. Any relationship or sacred communication between loyal followers and the schismatic was forbidden. Some theologians and specialists make a distinction between "active schism," when the schismatic group or individual makes the decision to part, and "passive schism," when the Church provokes it through excommunication. In either case, the result has been the same: splinter groups coalesced into new branches of Christian church, and centuries of contention followed.

After reading José María Laboa Gallego's *Historia de los Papas, Entre el Reino de Dios y las Pasiones Terrenales* (*History of the Popes: Between the Kingdom of God and Earthly Passions*), we can establish that even among the very first followers of Christ there were arguments and divisions. What has been considered the first recorded schism involved several bishops with Judaizing tendencies in the year 63, and minor, localized schisms, such as ones in Carthage and Egypt, took place during the third and fourth centuries.

In the year 251, a priest named Novation unsuccessfully challenged Pope Cornelius for the papacy. His followers (*katharoi*, meaning "purists," "puritans," or "the pure") rejected the primacy of the Roman pope and endured excommunication and persecution for another four hundred years. In the centuries that followed, there occurred the Luciferian Schism,[1] the Donatist Schism,[2] and the Aquileia Schism (Schism of the Three Chapters)[3], until in the ninth century we arrive at the Photian Schism[4] between Rome and Constantinople, which paved the way for the first great division in Christianity.

The East-West Schism, also known as the Great Schism, was instigated in 1053 by the Patriarch of Constantinople's refusal to acknowledge the authority of Rome. The roots of the split sprang from the Eastern belief in the idea that the pope should be a *primus inter pares* (from the Latin, "the first among *peers*") who recognized the authority of councils made up of all the patriarchs rather than serving as an absolute monarch. There was also criticism of the privileged attention the Church in Rome was giving to Western matters. In the West, the ties between the Byzantine emperor and the head of the Church in Constantinople became problematic to the Roman pope. The differences ultimately proved irreconcilable, and Christianity split into the Eastern Orthodox Church and the Roman Catholic Church. Despite attempts at reunification at the Second Council of Lyons in 1274 and the Council of Florence in 1439, no reconciliation was possible, and these two branches of Christianity remain divided to this day.

That was not the end of schisms for the Catholic Church. In the twelfth century, Anacletus II ruled for a time as an antipope rival to Pope Innocent II, as did Felix V to Pope Eugene IV in the fifteenth century. The Western Schism (1378–1417) was a period of great turbulence for the Church that saw opposing popes seated in Rome and Avignon, France (and, for a time, in Pisa, Italy).

The second major division of the Roman Church occurred in the sixteenth century with the Protestant Reformation, led by Martin Luther in Germany and John Calvin, first in France and later in Switzerland. Their movement sprung from animosity toward the excessive avarice of the papacy, as well as the widespread abuse of the sale of indulgences, which they felt separated the Church from the teachings and examples of Jesus. Branding the Church of Rome with such colorful epithets as "Babylon of the Apocalypse," "Satan's Synagogue," and the "Antichrist Society," Luther and Calvin's movement quickly spread, especially throughout northern Europe, and gave birth to the different branches of Protestantism we know today.

Almost simultaneously in England, King Henry VIII, finding it difficult to obtain an ecclesiastically authorized divorce from his second wife, Queen Anne Boleyn, decided to break from the Catholic Church. In 1531 he was proclaimed Supreme Head of the Church of England — better known as the Anglican Church — by Parliament and the Clergy General Assembly.

Several smaller, lesser-known schisms followed. In Holland in the early eighteenth century, the Utrecht Schism allowed for the expansion of Jansenism, and, years later, another schism arose from the French Revolution with a failed attempt to construct the Constitutional Church.[5] In 1831, Abbé Chatel founded the French Catholic Church that would last only until 1842. In 1844, a schism of German Catholics endured until 1848, and in 1871, "Old Catholics" gathered in Munich in opposition to decisions made by the First Vatican Council, which gave rise to a separate church. Even the Swiss Church underwent a reformation in the late eighteenth century, dividing into several small groups.

Schisms are not only relegated to the annals of history. As recently as 1988, Marcel Lefebre, a French traditionalist bishop who opposed conclusions drawn by the Second Vatican Council, brought about a new schism. It ended years after his death when, in 2009, Pope Benedict XVI repealed the excommunication of the four bishops who followed him.

As we can see, dissension and divisions are entwined in the very fabric of the history of Christianity. Some events generated movements that quickly dissolved, while others took root and nurtured mainstream Christian denominations that today provide alternatives to the way in which Jesus' teachings are carried out. Yet the Church of Rome is still the core in terms of tradition, history, and influence.

The largest of all Christian churches, the Roman Catholic Church considers itself the direct heir to the faith founded by Jesus, with Saint Peter as its first leader. Its spiritual influence extends around the globe: Of the world's 1.2 billion practicing Catholics, Latin America and the Caribbean is home to 40 percent, Europe to 25 percent, Africa 16 percent, Asia, 10 percent, North America, 8 percent, and finally Oceania with 1 percent, according to figures supplied by the American Catholic Organization.

There are approximately 225 to 300 million members of the Eastern Orthodox Church, making it the second largest Christian church in the world. The church is organized into various branches, although the exact number isn't clear since it varies depending on recognition. Four branches are ancient and still senior to this day, while others came later. Following a tradition of autonomy typical of ancient Christianity, there isn't a single acknowledged leader of the entire church; rather, clerical importance is established by honor and seniority.

Of the four ancient branches, the first is the Orthodox Church of Constantinople, which currently represents about 3.5 million followers under the leadership of the Ecumenical Patriarch. The Orthodox Church of Antioch follows, with 1.2 million followers. The third is the Orthodox Church of Alexandria with 500,000 adherents, and last is the Orthodox Church of Jerusalem with some 200,000 followers. These original patriarchates used to coexist with the Patriarchate of Rome, which after the East-West Schism became the Roman Catholic Church.

The Eastern Orthodox Church also includes five junior patriarchates: the Russian Orthodox Church, presided over by the Patriarch of Moscow, over 140 million strong; the Serbian Orthodox Church, led by the Patriarch of Belgrade, with 11 million followers; the Romanian Orthodox Church, led by the Patriarch of Bucharest, with 20 million; the Bulgarian Orthodox Church, headed by the Patriarch of Sophia and containing close to 8 million people; and finally, the Georgian Orthodox Church with 4.5 million followers, led by the Patriarch of Tiblisi.

Another five divisions fall under the leadership of an archbishop (or "metropolitan") and are known as Autocephalous Archbishoprics. They include the Church of Cyprus with close to half a million followers, the Church of Greece with 10 million, the Polish Orthodox Church with 600,000, the Albanian Orthodox Church with 400,000, and the Czech and Slovak Orthodox Church with 75,000.

There are also special cases, such as the American Orthodox Church, with close to a million followers, whose patriarchate is disputed by Moscow and Antioch, and Orthodox churches in countries that became independent after the collapse of the Soviet Union in 1991. These include the Ukrainian Orthodox Church, with more than 22 million led by the Patriarchate of Kiev and another 11 million who still follow the Patriarchate of Moscow (the not entirely recognized split took place in 1995). To these two we must add the Ukrainian Autocephalous Orthodox Church with over 3 million followers, which obtained its autonomy from the Polish Orthodox Church in 1924.

Albeit divided and lacking a single visible authority, the various Eastern Orthodox churches maintain a common doctrinal and sacramental communion. However, given their tendency toward self-rule and the influence of nationalism, a great number of groups have proliferated that do not accept any of the other patriarchates and do not recognize each other, such as in Ukraine.

As a group, Eastern Orthodox Christians are an ample majority in Belarus, Bulgaria, Cyprus, Georgia, Greece, Moldavia, Montenegro, Macedonia, Russia, Romania, Serbia, and Ukraine. They represent substantial percentages of the population in Kazakhstan, Latvia, Bosnia and Herzegovina, Albania, Kyrgyzstan, and Estonia. Smaller populations exist in such countries as Lebanon, Uzbekistan, Turkmenistan, Syria, Croatia, Lithuania, and Uganda, among others.

The other great branch of Christianity, of course, is Protestantism. Protestant churches independent of Rome emerged after the excommunication imposed by the Council of Trent over those who supported Reformation ideas of the sixteenth century, as well as after the separation of the Church of England from papal authority. As greatly divided as the Eastern Orthodox Church, and lacking a single structure or authority like the Catholics, Protestantism currently totals close to 700 million followers scattered across the world.

Perpetuators of Luther and Calvin's ideas expanded rapidly across northern Germany, Scandinavia, the Netherlands, Scotland, Switzerland, Hungary, Poland, and France, although the reaction of Catholic monarchies soon reestablished papal authority in the latter three countries. Early Protestants took advantage of the contemporary invention of the printing press, which allowed them to publish versions of the Bible in every language without the supervision of Rome. Harnessing the energy of the growing division between Church and State, they found an open space to grow in places where monarchies did not impose absolute subordination to papal power. The rise of the United States, with its Protestant majority and tremendous cultural influence, helped its global dissemination.

According to statistics published in the *CIA World Factbook*, we see that Protestants are divided between the Lutheran Church, concentrated in Germany and the Scandinavian countries, totaling close to 75 million followers, and the three so-called dissident denominations: Methodist with 70 million, Presbyterian with 50 million, and Baptist with more than 100 million followers. To these we must add Congregationalists with more than 30 million, Adventists with 17 million, Mormons with more than 14 million, and Reformed Christians with 5 million. Rounding out this list are the Anabaptists, including Mennonites, Amish, and others, which represent close to 2 million followers around the world.

Finally, the most numerous Protestant group is formed by Pentecostals, originating in the United States in the nineteenth century and today encompassing more than 250 million followers. Although fragmented into a number of subgroups, the passionately evangelical Pentecostal movement has expanded greatly in recent years, especially in Latin America and Africa.

Even less than a century ago, the Christian world was still actively battling over competing interpretations of the teachings of Jesus. Today, Catholics, Orthodox, and Protestants, in all their denominations, have made tremendous strides in their attempt to come closer to each other in the spirit of Christ. But in order to consider the possibilities of reconciliation among Christianity's many branches, we must first summarize the issues over which they disagree.

The oldest of the major separations, the one that occurred in 1054 and resulted in the Roman and Orthodox churches, was the product of dogmatic, liturgical, and administrative issues. Regarding dogma, there were, and still are, four main areas of concern. First at hand is the issue of the origin of the Holy Spirit. In the beginning, all churches, in the West and East, recognized that the origin of the Holy Spirit was solely the Father. This derives straight from Scripture, where the Lord said, "But when the Comforter is come, whom I will send unto you from the Father, even the Spirit of truth, which proceedeth from the Father, he shall testify of me" (John 15:26). Over time this idea evolved, and in the sixth century, first in Spain and later in France, the notion of an origin for the Holy Spirit that also encompassed the Son expanded. This concept, initially rejected but later accepted by the supreme pontiffs, triggered protests by Eastern patriarchs, who recognized only the Fatherly origin of both the Son and the Holy Spirit.

Another dogmatic discrepancy has to do with purgatory. The Roman Catholic Church teaches that after death, souls go to purgatory where, after undergoing commensurate torments, they purge their venial sins in order to enter Heaven. The Orthodox do not believe in the concept of purgatory as a place where souls await final judgment, instead maintaining several nuanced schools of thought on the matter.

Far beyond the subtleties of this issue, the disagreement over the notion of purgatory was more centered around a practical and earthly consequence: indulgences. The Catholic pope and his bishops had the authority to grant indulgences under certain circumstances, which granted the remission of penance and torment in purgatory owed for any remaining sins after absolution, both for oneself and for other souls already in purgatory. This practice was rejected by Eastern Orthodoxy.

The third great difference in belief is related to the notion of the Immaculate Conception. The Church of Rome believes that Saint Anne, the Virgin Mary's mother, conceived her daughter exempt from original sin as well as its transmission. The Orthodox Church dismisses this precept, contending that it removes Mary from the rest of humanity and suggests that she was above redemption, thus in no need of a savior. The Immaculate Conception is commonly mistaken for the doctrine of the Perpetual Virginity of Mary. Although the Orthodox don't subscribe to the belief of Anne's immaculate conception of Mary, they do hold faithful to the virginity of the Mother of God.

The final dogmatic disagreement pertains to the pope's infallibility with respect to matters of doctrine, faith, and morality. Papal authority was elevated to this level by the First Vatican Council in 1870, and Eastern Orthodox churches reject it.

As far as liturgical differences are concerned, the bread used in the Orthodox Church for the Eucharist contains yeast, while in the West it is unleavened. The West argues that this was the type of bread that would have been present during the time of the Last Supper, but the Orthodox Church differs due to its varying interpretation of the New Testament. Furthermore, in the West a person can participate in Communion only when they are old enough to distinguish right from wrong, while in the East they can participate from the very moment they are baptized so that no one has to die without the possibility of experiencing the Eucharist.

Another aspect related to liturgy has to do with baptism and confirmation. In the East, both sacraments are imparted simultaneously and the ceremonies can be performed by both bishops and priests. In the Roman Church, bishops and priests can baptize newborns, but only bishops can confirm adolescents. The Orthodox maintain the practice of baptism by immersion (dunking in water) and the Catholics by infusion (pouring of water).

When delivering the liturgy or sacraments, in the East there is the belief that the principal medium is Divine Grace and not the presiding priest, who is a mere instrument. For that reason, they say, "It baptizes . . ." "It anoints . . ." "It forgives . . ." In the Roman Church, the belief is that the action dwells in the priest's person, which is why they use the formula, "I baptize . . ." "I anoint . . ." "I forgive . . ."

Other disagreements over liturgy involve the clergy's celibacy, a requirement in the West but not in the East, and the presence of statues in houses of worship, which the Orthodox prohibit but Catholics allow.

Turning now to matters of administration, we come to one of the bedrock differences between the Eastern Orthodox and Roman Catholic traditions: authority. While the Orthodox consider the Ecumenical Council of all their patriarchs the supreme authority, Roman Catholics believe that this power belongs to the pope alone. The supremacy of the bishop of Rome stems from the fact that he is the successor of Peter, who was the superior among the apostles. In Jesus' own words in Matthew 16:18, "And I say also unto thee, that thou art Peter, and upon this rock I will build my church; and the gates of hell shall not prevail against it." However, because of differing versions of the Petrine texts of the New Testament, the Orthodox Church contends that Peter was not above the other apostles in the eyes of Jesus, directly opposing the doctrine of papal supremacy.

An administrative matter of great concern to the Orthodox involves the right to primacy of the different patriarchs. According to Orthodox tradition, the transfer of authority of the Western bishops to the presiding bishop of Rome and that of the Eastern bishops to the one in Constantinople is a temporary and political matter that originally relating to the location of the imperial capital in the Roman Empire. While the capital was in Rome, the head bishop had the privilege of sitting at the emperor's right; however, when the capital was transferred to Constantinople or Byzantium, the Orthodox feel such right to primacy moved as well and did not remain with the bishop of Rome. Therefore, the Orthodox believe that when the pope renounces his alleged authority over the churches around the world, he will be considered the first of all patriarchs, even above the one in Constantinople, and will be respected as a *primus inter pares*.

Another conflicting aspect of administration is marked by the position of Vatican chief of state that the supreme pontiff holds. The Eastern Orthodox Church contends that this contradicts what the Lord said in John 18:36 ("My kingdom is not of this world") and Matthew 22.21 ("Render therefore unto Caesar the things which are Caesar's; and unto God the things that are God's").

After considering the main dogmatic, liturgical, and administrative differences that separate the Eastern Orthodox Church from the Church of Rome, it is worth analyzing the particular case of one Orthodox sect that parted ways during the Great Schism of 1054 and, four centuries later, rejoined the Catholic family. The Ukrainian Greek Catholic Church, with four million followers scattered throughout several countries, conforms the largest autonomous eastern Catholic Church in full communion[6] with the Hole See.

The story begins when Byzantine missionaries under the leadership of the Patriarch of Constantinople evangelized territories of what we know today as Ukraine. These messengers successfully converted peoples and princes that governed from Kiev, who embraced Christ's faith *en masse* a few years before the Great Schism. Once the division was in place, they followed the same path as other Eastern churches and stopped recognizing the pope's authority. After a period of decline as a consequence of the Mongol invasions, Moscow assumed authority over the Eastern Orthodox Church, and it was then that Ukrainians tried to gain a degree of religious autonomy, negotiating their return to the great Catholic family directly with Rome. With that objective in mind, they participated in the Council of Florence in 1439, where they agreed to a union in the face of rigid opposition from the Patriarchate of Moscow. This reunification continued to strengthen and, in 1596 at the Union of Brest, the Ukrainian Greek Catholic Church declared the "Official Communion" between Rome and Kiev.

As a case study that could prove useful to ecumenical conversations between present-day Orthodox and Catholics, it is important to note that Ukrainians were allowed to keep mostly all of their liturgical practices, and a high degree of autonomy was respected. There was, however, a demand for total acceptance in terms of dogma, as well as absolute subordination to the authority of the pope. Time will tell if these same conditions will someday be accepted by patriarchs of the East, bringing about reconciliation and reuniting that which became separate almost a thousand years ago.

———————

Regarding ecumenism and Protestant churches born as a consequence of the Reformation and of Henry VIII's separation in England, the analysis of orthodox differences with Rome is no less complicated.

To start, Luther's concept of *sola scriptura* (by scripture alone) refers to the Protestant tenet that Christ is the head of the church since no human being is infallible, and therefore the only authority lies in the Word of God recorded in the Holy Scriptures. While Catholics acknowledge the authority that lies in the Scriptures, they hold that supreme authority on Earth lies with the pope. He is considered to be infallible and has absolute and compulsory authority *ex cathedra* (from the chair) in terms of faith and practice, given that he is Peter's successor and Christ's Vicar.

Regarding interpretation of the Bible, Catholics argue that it can only be done correctly and appropriately by the Church of Rome. Protestants, when arguing that God sent the Holy Spirit to dwell inside each and every human being, believe He gave that capacity to all believers. As well, Protestants don't believe in a single, true, and universal church like Catholics do. They believe there can be several, and all are valid.

Another key difference between Protestants and Catholics lies in salvation. Following the principle of *sola fide* (by faith alone), Protestants believe that salvation is attainable simply by having faith in Christ. Catholics believe that, albeit very important, simple faith is not enough. For salvation to be reached, Catholics require strict adherence to receiving the seven sacraments (though the sacraments of Marriage and Ordination are not compulsory, and the latter does not apply to women).[7]

With regards to the Sacrament of Ordination, commonly known as Holy Orders in Catholicism, Protestants reject the notion of priests as God's mediators, having special dispensation that enables them to bestow God's grace. As such, they also reject the title "priest" in favor of "pastor" or "minister." Celibacy is compulsory for Catholic priests, while it is voluntary for Protestant clergy members. And as for the sacrament of the Eucharist, Protestants believe that the transubstantiation of bread and wine into the body and blood of Christ can be administered by any of their faithful. The Catholic Church only grants priests the right to administer the Eucharist.

Catholics accept the virginity of Mary, Jesus' mother, whom they adore and sometimes place almost at the level of her son, a dogma that is rejected by Protestants. Such is also the case of the more than four thousand saints, exemplary men and women sanctified by the Catholic Church, to whom intercession before God is asked. There is no such tradition in Protestant faith.

───────────

This succinct description of the different branches into which Christianity has divided and the main differences in dogma, liturgy, and administration that separate them sets the stage for the challenges faced by those who seek reconciliation and reunion among the Christian faithful. To advance the concept and practice of ecumenism, all Christians will need to minimize the differences among them and maximize opportunities for contact, dialogue, and mutual respect.

The Christian family's movement toward ecumenism originated at a local level in the late eighteenth and early nineteenth century in some regions, such as Scotland, mainly through the efforts of the Pentecostal and Evangelical churches. However, this push toward reunion wasn't generalized among Protestant churches until the early twentieth century. At first, it merely consisted of initiatives such as the Week of Prayer for Christian Unity (conceived in 1908), and it was generally met with tough opposition from the papacy, which considered a return to Catholicism as the only way to guarantee a reunion. Among these early campaigns, the work of Nathan Söderblom, bishop and head of the Swedish Lutheran Church, stands out. His ecumenical efforts earned him the Nobel Peace Prize in 1930.

This tendency toward reunification led to the creation of the World Council of Churches, formally established at a meeting in Amsterdam in 1948. From then, more general assemblies were held in Evanston in 1954, New Delhi 1961, Uppsala 1968, Nairobi 1975, Vancouver 1983, and Canberra 1991. The organization strives to coordinate efforts among Christ's followers, although it doesn't expect conformity within one world church. Currently, it joins 345 churches from 110 countries, with close to 560 million followers, including most Orthodox churches and a great many Anglican, Baptist, Lutheran, Methodist, and Reformed churches. The Catholic Church is not a member, although it holds a joint meeting with the council every year, among other links with the group.

In recent years, there has been a significant shift within the Catholic Church regarding reconciliation with other Christian traditions. It began in 1960, when Pope John XXII created the Pontifical Council for Promoting Christian Unity, a preparatory commission for the Second Vatican Council that participated as an observer at the World Council of Churches' New Delhi assembly in 1961. The Pontifical Council, whose very existence is remarkable given the stances of the Roman Church, emphasized in several of its decisions the necessity for Christian reunification. The *Unitatis Redintegratio* Decree on Ecumenism that came out of the Second Vatican Council stands out in particular. It establishes six paths to advance ecumenism: renovation of the Catholic Church in biblical as well as liturgical matters; a true "change of heart" among all Christians to live holy lives; constant and unanimous prayer for unity; mutual knowledge of the doctrine, history, spiritual life, and religious psychology of fellow Christians; ecumenical formation and cooperation among Christians; and an improvement in the depth and preciseness of the language that expresses faith.

Later popes continued to deepen this encouraging discussion. In 1995, John Paul II issued the *Ut Unum Sint* (That They May Be One) encyclical, urging the unity of Christ's followers through fraternity and solidarity at the service of humanity. On the very first day he occupied Peter's throne, Benedict XVI pointed out that this objective would be one of the central motivations of his papacy.

As far as concrete possibilities of reunification and attending to discrepancies that separate them, it is fair to say that the least complicated situation is the one between the Catholic and Orthodox churches. Both branches have many aspects in common, yet the one, likely insurmountable matter lies in acknowledgment of the pope's absolute infallibility and authority.

There has been much improvement in relations between the Catholic and Anglican families, although recent decisions by the Church of England regarding bioethical issues, women and priesthood, and homosexuality threaten to slow this progress. In 2009, Benedict XVI approved an Apostolic Constitution, the highest level of decree within his power that urges those prelates who have decided to abandon the Anglican Church due to its movement toward liberalism to enter into full communion with the Catholic Church. They are offered the possibility to create a personal prelature, similar to the status given to Opus Dei and military ordinariates,[8] which links their clerical authority not to a diocese but to the people whom they serve, wherever they happen to serve them.

One complicated aspect in the progression toward ecumenism is the widespread atomization and numerous denominations under the Protestant umbrella, each with its own deeply held convictions on matters of practice and faith. Still, there has been some progress among the entire Christian family in such areas as recognition of baptisms, interdenominational marriage, and related moral, social, and cultural issues.

As we can see, there is an earnest effort underway to advance the cause of Christian reconciliation and reunification. Equally promising, great strides have also been made in establishing commonality among the great faiths of the world that believe in one God — Christianity, Islam, and Judaism.

From the Church of Rome, Pope Paul VI instituted the Secretariat for Non-Christians in 1964, and John Paul II followed his steps in 1988 with the Pontifical Council for Interreligious Dialogue. Both initiatives were reaffirmed by several similar outreach measures sponsored by Benedict XVI. These decisions, made at the highest level, have given rise to countless encounters, seminars, commissions, and other forums in an attempt to encourage unity among God's faithful.

Naturally, our focus shifts to a cardinal, who in the midst of witnessing this effort toward alliance and understanding among God's children, now heads the Catholic Church as its greatest champion.

Jorge Bergoglio has always had a tendency for dialogue — in all matters, in every sense, and with all interlocutors. He is a man who is perpetually willing to lend an ear to the meek and powerful alike, showing a natural predisposition to honest discourse that very clearly defines his personality. Therefore, he is expected to continue the ecumenical and interfaith work he began from the Buenos Aires Cathedral in Argentina now that he sits in Saint Peter's Basilica, expanding upon the progress made by his predecessors.

An interesting illustration of his thoughts on these matters can be found in his celebrated conversations with Rabbi Abraham Skorka. In it, then

Cardinal Bergoglio pointed out that everything begins with an attitude — symbolic gestures that will later facilitate administrative, liturgical, and, most challengingly, dogmatic progress. He describes how, as the presiding archbishop at the traditional Te Deum ceremony, he would accompany the president of Argentina to the door of the cathedral while representatives of other denominations would stand to the side "like showcase dolls." Francis put an end to such show of favoritism toward a Catholic prelate. "Now," he says, "the president comes up and greets the representatives of every creed."

Francis also discusses his participation in religious ceremonies of other creeds, especially evangelical Protestants who constitute the main challenge to the Catholic Church in Latin America, given their newfound propensity toward broadcasting their beliefs and criticisms via mass media. In the book, he talks of the day he attended an Evangelical service at the Luna Park arena in Buenos Aires, and the presiding pastor requested permission to pray for Francis and his ministry. Francis continues: "When everyone was praying, the first thing that came over me was to kneel down, a very Catholic gesture, to receive the prayer and blessing of the seven thousand people that were there."

This seemingly simple gesture — which once again shows Francis' spontaneous and fearless style — gained him not only attention worldwide, but the awe of his followers. It was a dramatic public demonstration of his commitment to respect and dialogue among brothers in Christ.

That attitude, so genuine and deep felt, extends beyond the Christian circle. "Even with an agnostic," Francis adds, "from his doubt, we can look up together and search for transcendence. Each person prays according to their tradition. What is the problem with that?"

We move now from Buenos Aires to Rome, where one of the first steps taken by Pope Francis continued this theme of public displays of interfaith goodwill. On the very day of his nomination and in a gesture customary to Argentines, he sent a letter to the chief rabbi of Rome, Ricardo Segni, in which he expressed his desire to contribute to the progress of relations between both religions.

Soon after, at the enthronization ceremony in Saint Peter's Square, an extraordinary and historically transcendent event took place. For the first time since the Great East-West Schism of 1054, Ecumenical Patriarch Bartholomew, *primus inter pares* of all the Eastern Orthodox churches, traveled from his headquarters in Istanbul to participate in the appointment of one of Peter's successors. Surely as a gesture of welcoming acceptance, on that occasion they sang the gospel in Greek instead of Latin.

The next day both leaders met in the Clementine Hall of the Apostolic Palace, and Bartholomew himself expressed a gracious sentiment when he said, "We wholeheartedly rejoice for your election inspired by God, and by your appointment as bishop of Rome."

Simple words, perhaps, but coming from an Eastern Orthodox archbishop of Constantinople and addressed to a Catholic bishop of Rome, they are words burdened with the weight of history. Yet, just as Ecumenical Patriarch Bartholomew commended Francis' simplicity and humility as something that "fills the hearts of all the people of the world with hope," so, too, did his congratulatory statement provide a sense of hope — hope for all who pursue the ecumenical dream within the Christian family, and hope for all who seek a world of peace and harmony between people of every faith.

The New Challenges

THE PURPOSE OF a spiritual institution is to serve as a moral compass for humanity, guiding it in faith so that it may transcend the many adversities that seek to destroy it. In order to achieve this, it needs to be firm and permanent in its principles and values, and not at the whim of current trends and tendencies. It must manage to mold the public's opinion rather than follow it.

At the same time, a spiritual entity must be sufficiently in touch with the modern world so it does not lose relevance for its followers. It must acknowledge and confront opposing visions that come in the form of competing religions and pseudo-religions, as well as societal influences and pressures that threaten to rob humanity of its faith.

Pope Francis has clear positions on the issues that are at the forefront of this ongoing struggle. Through a lifetime of sermon and evangelization, he stood on the front lines of the Christian mission, working hand in hand with those in most desperate need, as well as asserting his convictions via the pulpit and the written word, even when it meant speaking out against the Church and the presidency of his native Argentina. In doing so, Francis has piqued the interest of the entire world, as it watches with anticipation for signs of his capacity to enact real change.

The following is an overview of some of his concerns and thoughts on the relevant issues of the day, which stand as an indication of what may lie ahead for the papacy, and thus for humanity.

Atheism and Religion

One of the main problems in the world in which we live is the growing distance between humanity and God and religiousness. Clearly, the creation of a theocratic society, such as the one endured in Iran, is not the answer; that would be regressive, not to mention impossible. Rather, the idea is to thoughtfully consider humanist answers to the complexities of life through a prism of spirituality and transcendence. Such a perspective can give meaning to the increasingly powerful tools available to us, such as advances in science and technology, and to understand that much of what today is worshipped as a means to an end only acts to keep us from reaching a higher spiritual ground.

In the face of this dilemma, Francis advises that in order to find God in our modern society, the key is to look within, to embark on a spiritual journey with an open mind and open heart, "looking for Him and letting Him look for you."

To reconcile that which comes from within and that which comes from without is to tap into one's own individual inner spirit. This space that exists deep within each of our souls is unique, private, and intimate. It has more to do with what each person offers as a contribution to the greater good than what is imposed by any state or collective organization. In this regard, Francis tells us that we don't need to look far at all to find the living God; He is closer than we could ever imagine Him to be.

Once we discover God in our own hearts, we will understand that everything has a meaning; we will be empowered to take charge of and perpetuate the gift given by the creator. On the contrary, when we decide not to follow God's plan and to place all of our faith in self, we are answering the call of the one who seeks our demise — one of the fallen angels who rebelled against his creator's mandate and masterpiece. Francis himself has admitted, "I believe the Devil exists. Maybe his biggest success nowadays has been to make us believe he does not exist, that everything can be fixed on a purely human level."

An atheist society, one without God, is like an empty shell, with no content. However, that does not mean that people who do not experience faith are insignificant. On the contrary, they can be very virtuous and, from a Christian perspective, just in need of help, waiting to be encouraged to dive into their own hearts. When Francis encounters atheists, his preference is to initiate a respectful dialogue on shared human concerns, discussing matters of belief only if encouraged.

By doing so, Francis places faith in the concept that the experience of finding God must be personal. Religion can help this intimate process take place, but it cannot force anyone down that path, and it certainly cannot use coercion or violence to do so. God, Francis believes, respects all people and cultures. The belief in God and the mystery of faith may translate in different ways in different cultures, but Francis recognizes the significant common ground shared by all His children. "God," he has said, "is open to all people. He calls upon everyone to look for and discover Him through creation."

This brings us to the concept of holy war and the belief that it is permissible to kill in the name of God as a means to convert the unfaithful. Although history has been plagued with those who have misinterpreted God's message in this way, many in the name of Christ, humanity is only now beginning to comprehend how these ideologies are the antithesis to the creator's mandate of love and forgiveness. Francis is direct on the matter: "Killing in the name of God is blasphemy." He cites the dangers of "the vanity of power" and invokes not only the example of Christians murdering nonbelievers during the Middle Ages but Nazis killing Jews, Communists killing Slavs, and Turks killing Armenians as manifestations of fallible human beings straying as far from godliness as one can go. "Those who do this," he says, "self-establish themselves as God."

Science and Education

A related aspect to this überfaith in man over God is the realm of science. We are living in a time when, together with technology, science is aggrandized and treated as an end in itself. In a Godless society without transcendence, the means become the end.

The current pope is no enemy of scientific progress, saying it must be "respected and encouraged," and that the Church should never infringe on the autonomy of scientists to pursue their work. But he warns of areas where science begins to encroach on matters of transcendence. Nuclear energy, Francis has acknowledged, can been harnessed for the betterment of mankind, but it has also been an agent of existential terror and profound destruction. When the pursuit of scientific progress outpaces questions of morality, it can, unwittingly or not, open doors better left closed. As Francis has put it, "When man becomes arrogant, he creates a monster that walks with him hand in hand."

Clearly, we must reconcile science and technology with the mystery of faith. That may well be the primary task religion has at hand, as seen from a twenty-first century perspective. The need for faith and the material universe to occupy the same space is more apparent than ever; the time to reject archaic thinking, to emerge from the shadow of an institution that proclaimed Galileo a heretic, is upon us. The idea is not to favor the elimination of all progress and return to those times, but rather to find the meaning that should be designated to scientific advancement. Underscoring this shift in paradigm and supporting the idea that science and faith can coexist is the fact that, before Francis turned his life over to God, he was a chemist.

Another key issue, very much interconnected with the previous one, is education. Taking into account that the Roman Catholic Church is the greatest supplier of this service in the world after the state, the thoughts of its current leader are very relevant. However, Francis is well aware that both he and the Church must wield this powerful tool extremely gingerly. Anything that could be interpreted as overbearing could lap into arguments over the separation of church and state, with proponents of purely state-sponsored education working to dilute or eliminate altogether the Church's long and respected role in this arena.

This leads to an area of concern that continues to worry Francis: religion within the curriculum of public schools. He does not advocate a sole focus on Catholicism, but he does believe that schooling in religion and religious thought is important "as one more element in the broad range provided in classrooms."

Family plays a big part in any discussion about education. Although in many countries the state assumes this role, one that is often constitutionally consecrated, parents continue to be the lead actors in their children's development. In this regard, Francis has recognized that "each man and woman has the right to educate their children within their religious values." The alternative, he warns — when the state assumes so much control over public education that it actively seeks to counteract the religious viewpoints of families — has led societies down the road to totalitarianism.

Vocation and Celibacy

Another important matter to be reconciled in the modern age is the rigors of commitment to the priestly vocation. If the Church wants to extend its influence both globally and within each country it serves, it must increase its legions of followers. This is not accomplished as within a private enterprise, with newspaper ads or the help of employment agencies. Religious vocation is something much more profound, felt within the most intimate part of the soul, and once conscious, those who seek it must respond with total, lifetime dedication to God. No easy feat.

In John 15:16, Jesus says to his disciples, "Ye have not chosen me, but I have chosen you, and ordained you" — a powerful calling from the Lord. However, the calling must fall upon fertile land to avoid frustration. Francis speaks of the Christian concept of "the integrity of the intention" upon first feeling the calling of a life dedicated to God. At first, he says, "it is all very mixed up because we are all sinners." But as the individual continues down the path toward a consecrated life, he must aspire to the concept of "saintliness," an elevated level of virtue, holiness, and complete dedication to God. This is especially so when they start becoming leaders of the faithful.

The celibacy of priests has been greatly discussed behind closed doors within the Church, and now, more than ever, has become a very public issue. It is one of the key points that divide and differentiate the Roman Catholic Church from other branches of Catholicism, the wider family of Christianity, and other monotheistic philosophies, and the topic is integral to advancing ecumenical and interreligious dialogue. But the current pope's stance is unequivocal: "At the moment, I'm in favor of maintaining celibacy with all its pros and cons, because there are ten centuries of good experiences overweighing the faults."

Very clear and specific.

Women and the Church

Another current issue is the role of women both within the Catholic Church and society. To many experts, one of the most significant trends of our time is precisely the growing influence of women in practically all roles, many of which were previously reserved only for men. Such modern leaders as Angela Merkel, Dilma Rousseff, Cristina Kirchner, Ellen Johnson Sirleaf, Michele Bachelet, Condoleezza Rice, and Hillary Clinton are evidence that women clearly hold a firm position in the arena of politics and power. It's a welcome phenomenon that extends to many other areas of life and human activity.

The Catholic Church seems to have avoided this obvious societal shift by continuing to deny women a role in the priesthood. The former Archbishop of Buenos Aires clarified this position when he explained the theological tradition behind it — that priesthood is a function of men in the Church because the first priest, Jesus, was a man. The function of women in Catholicism, he maintains, is reflected in Mary, the mother of Christ, "who embraces society, comforts it, and is mother to the community."

Though Francis supports the Church's tradition of a woman's role within the evangelical structure, he does not view them as in any sense lesser than men, and he is quick to point out the unjust nature of their marginalization. It is no secret that this gender has been perpetually degraded throughout history, especially when it comes to objectification. His attitude on the matter was beautifully portrayed during his first Holy Thursday celebration, when he became the first pope in history to wash the feet of women — two young inmates in a juvenile detention center — during the ritual. The bold departure from centuries of tradition was rich with symbolism, showing the new direction of his papacy in its stances toward women.

Regarding feminism, or the defense of the rights of those who represent more than half of humanity, in keeping with his tendency toward pragmatism, the pope accepts this movement in more moderate terms, though not in its exaggerated and fundamentalist forms. He honors the historical accomplishments of the feminist movement but departs from it when it assumes an aggressively anti-male posture. As such, he says, "it runs the risk of becoming chauvinism with skirts."

Abortion

Abortion is a front and center debate the world over, and it promises to remain a hotly contentious issue for years to come. Like divorce a few decades ago and same-sex marriage today, it is an issue that deeply divides societies, especially those with Catholic traditions. Legislation that authorizes some sort of pregnancy termination at the woman's request has already been approved in sixty countries. Like a hoisted flag, especially within certain feminist groups, arguments for the legality of abortion are generally based on practical reasons connected to the proliferation of illegal interventions that would occur otherwise, and the risks such procedures pose for the pregnant woman's health.

The Church has staked out one of its most steadfast positions on legalized abortion, and it actively campaigns everywhere to impede its progress. Francis continues to rally against abortion, regarding which he is very clear and emphatic: "The person's genetic code is created in the moment of conception. A human being already exists at that point. . . . To abort is to kill a defenseless person."

Old Age, Euthanasia, and Death

Like the great abortion debate at the beginning of life, there is also the one regarding death and euthanasia at the end of one's physical existence.

Life after death is an issue that clearly distinguishes the faithful from those who believe that everything ends when the heart stops or the brain shuts down. As a lifelong Christian and the leader of the Roman Catholic Church, the matter is not one of doubt for Francis. He rejects the notion that religion is an elaborate defense mechanism concocted in the minds of the human species as a way to assimilate and calm the natural distress the idea of death produces.

Comfortable in his faith, Francis accepts his own aging with grace. He knows he will die, but, he says, "I don't let that distress me, because the Lord and life prepared me." But he remains concerned for the treatment of the elderly in their final days. In an increasingly hedonist, narcissist society, our aged citizens become "disposable people." Everything operates so quickly in many of our lives that there is no time left to attend to the dignity of those who gave us life. He is similarly critical of institutions and systems that provide health care only to a point, a "hidden euthanasia" that deprives adequate medicine or care until death arrives.

Once the end is inevitable and extending life only prolongs unnecessary suffering, the issue of euthanasia, or dignified death, comes to light — another extensive debate that divides societies. On this subject, Francis holds a humane and quite flexible position. The object is not to prolong life for the sake of doing so but to do whatever is necessary to maintain the dignity and minimize the suffering of the patient. Morally, a line is crossed when such care devolves into active euthanasia. On that matter, he is again unequivocal: he considers it murder.

Finally, a very sensitive and complex subject emerges: suicide and its interpretation. The Catholic Church rejects suicide on both spiritual and pragmatic grounds. The *Catechism of the Catholic Church* states, "We are obliged to accept life gratefully and preserve it for his honor and the salvation of our souls. We are stewards, not owners, of the life God has entrusted to us. It is not ours to dispose of." Providing a more earthly perspective, it notes, "If suicide is committed with the intention of setting an example, especially to the young, it also takes on the gravity of scandal." As pope, Francis adheres to the merciful message of the *Catechism* — "by ways known to him alone, God can provide the opportunity for salutary repentance." While he can never condone suicide as a means to salve life's many difficulties, of the suicide victim he says, "I do not reject this person; I leave him or her at God's mercy."

Divorce

This debate seems to have faded into the distance, since there are only two countries — the heavily Catholic Philippines and the Vatican — that have not approved legislation that authorizes it. However, studying the Church's present attitude toward divorcees and those who have remarried may give us insight into its future direction on other current, controversial issues, such as same-sex marriage.

The Church has always been against legally undoing what God had united; however, dysfunctional unions not entered upon in love had become so commonplace that the pressure to reconsider this stance became increasingly intense. In the end, acceptance of divorce expanded even in the most conservative places, such as Ireland and several Latin American nations (although some of which only recently acquiesced). It's interesting to note what the current pope said regarding this issue in Argentina. Although those who've divorced may not represent the mainstream of Catholic doctrine, "divorced and remarried believers are reminded that they are not excommunicated . . . and are asked to join the parochial life."

An important change in attitude that could set the course for the future.

Same-Sex Marriage

If there is one issue on the social agenda generating strong worldwide controversy, it is same-sex marriage, or, as its defenders call it, egalitarian marriage. It's an institution that emerged in liberal European countries and has slowly been approved by parliamentary actions, judicial decisions, and popular referendums around the world.

Its legal recognition began in 2001 in liberal Holland, then continued in Belgium in 2003, followed by its surprising acceptance in Catholic Spain in 2005. Canada came on board that same year, followed by South Africa in 2006, Sweden and Norway in 2009, Argentina and Iceland in 2010, Denmark in 2012, and recently Uruguay in 2013. There are also provinces and states in such places as Brazil, Mexico, and the United States that have locally approved legislation supporting same-sex marriage. Today, this union still occupies a space outside the traditional, legal definition of marriage in Finland, France, Germany, Luxemburg, the United Kingdom, Andorra, New Zealand, Nepal, and Taiwan. It's likely that these countries will soon take the next step to full legalization, just as in previous cases where the process was incremental while a compromise between morality and legality was sought.

The acceptance and legalization of same-sex marriage was the result of a long process of demands carried out by organizations that represent gays, lesbians, and transsexuals, which see in it a type of validation of their lifestyle. It is also seen as a vindication of their rights, overcoming the discrimination these minorities have suffered throughout history.

Francis has very strong, personal opinions on this matter given that it has sparked much debate with respect to the traditional Catholic mores of his homeland, Argentina. The City of Buenos Aires approved civil unions in 2002, becoming the first place to do so in all of Latin America. The capital was later followed by the province of Rio Negro and some places within the province of Córdoba. Subsequently, the supporters of these reforms began a long fight to achieve judicial approval on a national level, which was met with the Church's distinct opposition. Finally, as previously mentioned, in 2010, the Argentine Congress approved the law at a national level.

The Archbishop of Buenos Aires and Primate of Argentina himself energetically took sides in this debate and frequently expressed harsh opinions, describing these legislative initiatives as "the Devil's move." He urged his followers to join "God's war," encouraging them to participate in defense of traditional marriage between a man and a woman. He warned them not to be naïve since "this is not a simple political fight, it's the destructive ambition against God's plan" and he asked "Saint Joseph, Maria, and Baby Jesus to defend the Argentine family," according to newspapers at the time.

Francis defended his right to debate the issue. As the leader of the country's Catholic Church, he unabashedly advocated the institution's traditional positions, acknowledging that in his role, "one must speak clearly of values, limits, commandments."

Regarding homosexuality and the idea that his opposition to egalitarian marriage could be interpreted as a condemnation of it, Francis contends that he is not at all contemptuous of homosexuals. His recent headline-grabbing comments in an informal press conference on the return from his 2013 trip to Brazil only confirms this: "Who am I to judge a gay person of goodwill who seeks the Lord? You can't marginalize these people." He acknowledges that homosexuality has existed throughout history, and that has been tolerated, even admired, to different degrees in various places at various times. But he invokes the anthropological position that same-sex marriage and traditional marriage cannot be likened, because members of the opposite sex are biologically programmed to procreate, in accordance with God's creative design.

Francis' platform on the issue of adoption by same-sex couples goes beyond civil union, which only stands to impact the lives of two consenting adults. He believes that "everyone needs a male father and female mother to help shape their identity."

A common argument of those in favor of adoption within this type of union is that the chance for orphaned or abandoned children to be adopted by a couple, regardless of their sex, who raises them with love and dedication, is always better than being left to wander through the system, being institutionally raised. Francis vehemently refutes this by pointing out that neither situation is ideal and that the state, NGOs, churches, and other organizations need to address red tape and streamline processes so it is not so difficult for willing couples to adopt. "The state's failure" in this matter, he says, "does not justify another failure of the state."

As we can see, Francis is a man of strong conviction, and his opinions do not only remain in rhetoric. When the time comes, Francis stands in defense of his beliefs, confronting whomever necessary. It's a much more courageous attitude if you take into account that Argentina's public opinion very much favored the approval of the same-sex marriage law. A December 2012 survey on egalitarian marriage done by Raul Aragon, director of the public opinion program at the Universidad Nacional de La Matanza, reported that 68 percent of Argentines were in favor and 28.5 percent were against it — a forty-point difference.

Pedophilia

The issue of pedophilia within the Catholic Church's structure is one that has shaken it to its very foundations. Reports of priests abusing minors are multiplying exponentially around the world. It's a pathology that affects a very small portion of the general population, but it seems to happen more often than normal with people leading consecrated lives.

At the heart of the situation are the wrenching stories of hundreds of abused children who, as adults, are not able to overcome their trauma. Similarly damning was the discovery of serial abusers within the clergy, made worse by the cult of secrecy perpetuated by ecclesiastic authorities.

Although the problem was suspected and rumored, it wasn't until the first few cases came to light and reached justice in the early 1990s, mainly in the United States and Australia, that the true breadth and depth of the disgraceful cover-up would be realized.

Thousands of people from different countries began to come forward and report similar incidents that took place in their childhood and adolescence, most of which occurred in the latter half of the twentieth century. In an attempt to mitigate the negative impact of public opinion on the vocation of priesthood, many Catholic organizations publicly played down the number of pedophilia cases at hand when compared to the general population. Behind the scenes, clerical authorities had been dealing with the matter by reassigning and hiding the accused within their own system, placing them out of sight and above the law. Yet the flood of reports would not cease, until it became the bane of the modern Catholic Church's existence, distancing its followers as well as potential leaders.

The attitude of the last two popes confronting this enormous moral scandal changed with time, from John Paul II's initial bewilderment to Benedict XVI's clear disapproval. Nevertheless, some organizations that defend the rights of the victims have suggested that both popes bore some responsibility for failure to report fully on the matter as they received more information.

In any case, Benedict XVI took on a very clear position of condemnation when he asked for the forgiveness of Catholics in Ireland for the abuses, and he did the same in repeated opportunities with the victims themselves. He also called for the guilty to respond to the accusations before the courts.

Beyond the psychological explanations behind these abhorrent behaviors, these scandals heavily damage the Church's credibility. Thousands of news articles, columns, reports, and interviews have generated a very unfavorable public opinion not only against the directly implicated priests, but also against the institution itself.

Yet another side to this scandal is its economic impact on the Church. Justice departments have ordered the Church to pay millions of dollars in compensation to the victims. According to the August 2012 issue of the *Economist*, it is estimated that more than three thousand reported cases occurred in the United States within the last four decades, costing the Church more than $3.3 billion, $1.3 billion in California alone, at approximately $1 million per victim. This situation has already caused the bankruptcy of the dioceses in San Diego, Tucson, and Milwaukee, a path that could be followed by many more of the 196 dioceses in the United States.

The decision to allow individual dioceses to go bankrupt is an attempt by the Church to contain the financial damage by charging each bishopric with its own responsibilities, thus avoiding action against the Church as a whole or against the very profitable educational and health institutions it manages throughout North America. For this reason, some dioceses, such as the one in Boston, have been forced to liquidate assets, among them some very valuable properties, including several churches and chapels.

Although the severity of the many devastating facets of this situation is not at all lost on Francis, he vehemently rejects the idea that pedophilia could be considered a product of celibacy. "If a priest is a pedophile," he says, "he was so before becoming a priest." But that does not equate to an excuse for this sickness within the priestly ranks. He continues: "It is not possible to have a position of power and destroy another person's life." During his time in Buenos Aires, when he was informed of a pedophilia case in the diocese, he demanded that the abuser's licenses be revoked, that he be barred from continuing to serve in the priesthood, and that he be tried in the canonical court of the diocese. He would brook no suggestion that the accused be shuffled and hidden within the Church's structure in order to protect the larger institution's image.

As the newly elected pope, only a few hours prior to officially assuming his role, Francis sent a strong message when he went to the Papal Basilica of Santa Maria Maggiore to thank the Virgin for his appointment. At the basilica, he learned that eighty-two-year-old Cardinal Bernard Law — a man who covered up more than 250 pedophile cases between 1984 and 2000 — resided there. Cardinal Law had shockingly found refuge in Rome to avoid facing North American courts for his crimes. Francis immediately ordered Boston's former bishop to evacuate the premises within twenty-four hours.

A few days later, he received in an audience Monsignor Gerhard Ludwig Müller, prefect of the Congregation for the Doctrine of the Faith, the entity in charge of dealing with this issue. Reiterating his position condemning these abuses, Francis directed that, following Benedict XVI's line of thought, Müller's group should act decisively in all that was connected to sexual abuse cases. He wanted them to promote protective measures for minors, help those who suffered such violations in the past, take necessary action against the guilty parties, and commit the Episcopal Conferences to formulate and act upon guidelines to prevent the future occurrence of such atrocities. He also made sure to keep the abuse victims present in his attention and prayers.

These are very clear gestures and words that must quickly be translated into actions if Francis has any hope of turning the page on one of the most regrettable and damaging chapters in the Catholic Church's recent history.

Chapter 12

Spotlight on Latin America

To **UNDERSTAND THE** Latin American mindset, it is essential to delve into the region's history. Although they may seem culturally balanced and homogeneous to the outsider, these lands and their people are actually a kaleidoscope of different realities and huge contrasts.

Like all territories on this side of the Atlantic, the nations of Latin America were established through European exploration and colonization. Spurred by competition among kingdoms, expeditions to the New World began in earnest after the historic journey of a Genovese sailor commissioned by the Crown of Castile in 1492.

Inspired by Christopher Columbus and the Spanish, Portugal immediately followed with its own commissioned expeditions, as did France, England, and Holland. Gaining control over vast new territories teeming with valuable resources, the Old World kingdoms accumulated formidable wealth and power. In every case, but especially so in Madrid and Lisbon, acquisition of earthly power was always accompanied by a parallel agenda: the expansion of faith in Christ. This entailed converting the original inhabitants, considered "infidels" by the imperialists.

The conquerors held the sword as well as the cross, but they were confronted with disparate realities in these new lands. On several occasions they found themselves face-to-face with civilizations that were quite advanced and willing to fight tooth and nail to resist European attempts to impose a new order. This clearly happened to the Spaniards in present-day Mexico and Peru, where they highly underestimated the power and will of the Aztec and Inca Empires. Yet conquistadors Hérnan Cortés and Francisco Pizarro ultimately managed to subdue and subjugate these societies, causing the implosion and collapse of both pre-Columbian cultures. The colonizing campaigns of the Portuguese, French, English, and Dutch had the same result on the indigenous inhabitants in their spheres of influence.

Aside from a handful of French and Dutch enclaves, most of the vast territories of the southern cone of South America were divided between the two competing crowns of the Iberian Peninsula. As early as 1493, Pope Alexander VI issued a series of papal bulls[1] that were later accepted by the the Kingdom of Portugal and that of Castille and Aragon. Both signed the Treaty of Tordesillas a year later in which they agreed to divide control of newly discovered lands along a meridian located a thousand miles west of Cape Verde, Africa.

The coexistence of European and indigenous cultures in any part of the world was never easy; however, history records few cases where one culture imposed itself so quickly and completely over another as occurred in the New World territories. In little more than fifty years, practically the entire region was under the newcomers' control, and millions of people were serving a new king and worshipping a new God. The consequences of this process forever conditioned the children of this land.

In those places where there was evident wealth and a substantial native population, such as Mexico and Peru, the Spaniards exercised ironclad colonization practices and intense exploitation of resources. Mexican and Bolivian silver and Peruvian gold fed the exhausted chests of a crown that, thanks to this sudden and seemingly bottomless source of financing, swiftly became the leading European power. According to modern calculations, Madrid's court received the equivalent to what today would be worth more than $50 billion from the silver mines in Potosí (in present-day Bolivia) during Philip II's reign alone.

Areas with less-valuable natural bounty still offered economic advantages given their land and climate, producing sugar, coffee, tobacco, and other profitable tropical and subtropical products. But to support such rapid growth in the Caribbean Islands, the warm countries in Central and South America, and the Portuguese section of Brazil, the European colonists had to increasingly import a workforce to compensate for a small indigenous population, thus opening the door to one of the most abhorrent practices in the history of humankind: slavery. Similar to what later became entrenched in the southern regions of the United States, millions of Africans were shipped across the Atlantic as slaves, enduring bondage

and inhumane conditions to perpetuate the economies of key colonial out-
posts of the crowns of Europe.

The sparsely populated southern flatlands of South America, like its
equivalent in the northern tip of the continent, did not initially require intense labor. But years later, when a global food market was established, the
region proved to be highly valuable and productive, and soon immigrants
and pioneers, especially from Europe, arrived to work the lands.

This is the historical backdrop that today provides Latin America with
its many faces and multifaceted cultures. The area's demographic profile
shows a combination of local native population mixed with the blood of
the colonizing Europeans and their descendants. Add an African imprint
from the legacy of slavery and a final splash of immigrants and settlers
from around the world (though mainly European), and the result is a cultural melting pot that makes it impossible to speak of one uniform Latin
America. There *is*, however, one common denominator that unites them
all: since these nations were mainly colonized by Spain and Portugal, all
are primarily Catholic.

———————

Another characteristic that unites the nations of Latin America is the way
they emerged into independence, with an important distinction between
former Spanish and Portuguese colonies. In the early nineteenth century,
when the Iberian Peninsula was devastated by Napoleon Bonaparte's armies
during the Peninsular War, each kingdom's distinct reaction provided very
different fates for their Latin American territories. While King Ferdinand
VII of the Bourbons became prisoner of the French, John VI of Portugal, of
the Braganza family, set out on a tactical withdrawal together with his entire court, treasures, and archives and established himself in Rio de Janeiro,
from where he managed his global empire. He remained there several years,
even longer than the Napoleonic occupation of his homeland, and when
he returned to Lisbon, he left his son, Peter, in charge, who later claimed
the title emperor of Brazil and was then succeeded by his own son. This
consistent imperial presence unified under one banner a vast population
and explains the enormous size of this Portuguese-speaking country today.

Throughout the rest of the continent, the gigantic territory previously
dominated by Spain, spanning from Northern California to Patagonia,

suddenly found itself without a monarch. Revolutionary movements filled the power vacuum, many inspired by the revolutions in France and North America decades earlier. After battles for independence and internal civil wars, more than twenty Spanish-speaking countries had been established by the time the monarchy was restored in Madrid in 1874.

Although most Latin American countries abolished slavery once they gained independence, their autocratic governments were turbulent and unstable, resulting in a weak development of institutions and individual rights. Brazil, on the other hand, managed to maintain political unity within the same governing family for more than eighty years, although on the shoulders of a very unjust society, being the last country in the world to abolish slavery when it finally passed the Lei Áurea (Golden Law) on May 13, 1888.

This history of conquest and autocracy instilled in the psyche of many Latin Americans a profound sense of resentment with respect to central authority. At first it was against the European colonists who radically abused the indigenous population and ransacked their resources and wealth to maintain the luxurious lives and finance the endless wars of far-off courts. Decades later, these sentiments were transferred, often in an exaggerated fashion, to the United States, which in many countries, especially in Central America and the Caribbean, took on a role of control and paternity previously exercised by the Europeans. Through most of the twentieth century, revolutionary movements were spawned in reaction to the alliance between the United States and Latin American governing elites, an alliance that was often seen as subservient to US interests over the national interests of the people.

The profound, almost chronic social injustices and the deterioration of exchange terms greatly weakened the economies of Latin America. This caused a bewildering succession of governments, with weak democracies giving way to military dictatorships that constantly vied with leftist revolutionary groups for power and influence during the Cold War era and beyond. Some of these groups looked to the Soviet Union as an ideological blueprint and gladly accepted funds and even arms to support their cause. This was a familiar tactic from Moscow, used with equal deliberation in such places as Angola, the Congo, Malaysia, and Vietnam in its struggle against the United States for global hegemony.

Shortly before the fall of the Berlin Wall in 1989, Latin America seemingly exhausted its era of military governments and revolutionary fervor, and democracy spread like wildfire. Although political liberties made a comeback, from a financial and social standpoint the situation did not improve until twenty years later, in the twenty-first century, when shifts in the global financial landscape brought with it a reversal of exchange terms and the rise of emerging economies as big consumers. This increased commodity prices to unimaginable levels and transformed long-suffering Latin American nations into viable economies themselves.

———————

Throughout this turbulent history, the Catholic Church played a key role. From the first days of European colonization, the Church aligned closely with imperialist powers and, in the process, garnered much power of its own. When the conquerors arrived and began to occupy the land in the name of the kings of Castile and Portugal, they were accompanied by priests whose job it was to spiritually comfort the European envoy while converting the indigenous population. From the start, this generated a feeling of a governing church closely tied to earthly powers.

Practically every city in the widespread terrain of Latin America was founded with a central plaza, containing within it, among its official buildings, the temples of the various Catholic orders and congregations. This is readily evident when analyzing the early blueprints of the region's capital cities. The cathedrals, basilicas, chapels, convents, monasteries, and retreats of Franciscans, Jesuits, Benedictines, Augustinians, Dominicans, Mercedarians, Carmelites, and Clares were all part of a network of property of incalculable value, and all were assigned by the monarch to the Church, guaranteeing the containment of the spirit and morals of the people — as well as their ongoing loyalty to the crown.

The job carried out by religious orders during Latin America's conquest, although rightly reviled for its often savage imposition of a culture and faith upon millions of people, was indisputably indispensable in amalgamating such a vast and varied region. With the passing of generations, a worldview emerged acknowledging that, in addition to spreading a common language and similar history, the rooting of Christianity fostered a cultural unity seldom seen in other parts of the world — a key component of the very essence of being Latin American. As good Christians, the representatives of the different orders carried out other social roles, although clearly adapted to those times. They cared for the poor and dispossessed, spread knowledge and culture, attempted to calm the souls of the people, and gave transcendence to the fate of different villages. Cardinal Bergoglio himself has pointed to the example of such "peaceful men" as Fray Bartolomé de las Casas, the Dominican friar who bravely resisted institutional abuse of native populations, earning him the nickname "Defender of the Indians."

The holy work of men like Bartolomé notwithstanding, the institutional Latin American Church historically remained close to the governing power of the state. Without ceasing to help the needy, it never distanced itself much from those central plazas where important decisions were made. But certain local clergy, being close to the ground and keen observers of the social condition, knew where their allegiance should lie. In the wars of independence, some of them stood by the rebels, consecrating their tasks to different saints and virgins. Once the new independent governments were established, practically all of them made an oath to God and the Holy Gospels, and this divine coexistence between the Church and the new generation of rulers would endure for decades. (In fact, the modern tendency of the separation of Church and state would not take hold in most Latin American countries until well into the twentieth century.)

There is still a perception in Latin America that this sometimes incestuous relationship between spiritual and earthly power has not changed much from when the region was governed by autocratic *caudillos* and military dictatorships. For this reason, there has always existed the critical view that the Church didn't do much for the original indigenous inhabitants, the slaves who followed, or the victims of state persecution of recent years. However, it's always difficult to generalize the wide range of the Church's role in Latin American society, often contradictory in itself, and it is precisely this fact that allows for the other side of the story to be told. As noted, there were those from religious orders who blessed the armies led by Simón Bolívar and José de San Martín[2] in the struggle for Latin American independence. Clergy members such as Bartolomé de las Casas actively participated in the battle for native and slave rights. Indeed, many of the revolutionary movements that emerged against authoritarianism and dictatorship were inspired by fathers and priests who served as true apostles of these new ideas.

The Church's presence and influence does not end there. Its role in educating the people of the region is undeniable and remains indispensable today.

Elementary schools, high schools, universities, and technical schools found-ed by the different orders began to spread not only throughout the region but around the world. Today, the Catholic Church is the largest provider of education outside of government-run systems. Pope Francis' own religious career can serve as an example: a concerned Jesuit who consecrates his life to service to the poor, who exercises spiritual power and challenges earthly powers, while dedicating a significant part of his work and time to education.

The presence of the Society of Jesus in this part of the world is particu-larly noteworthy. In the seventeenth and eighteenth centuries, it acquired so much strength and power that it threatened the absolute authority of reigning kings, who not only expelled Jesuits from their territories but convinced Pope Clement XIV to sign the dissolution of the order in 1773. Yet the work they carried out in the missions, especially in Paraguay, northern Argentina, eastern Bolivia, and southern Brazil, was astonish-ing. In contrast to the government (which often perceived their efforts antagonistically), the society managed to serve enormous territories, al-most all populated by the Tupí-Guaraní ethnic group, developing within them a social model that was much more respectful of the native popula-tion. Called "Jesuit Reductions," these indigenous settlements allowed the Church to Christianize the people while simultaneously governing them and protecting them from maltreatment. Although the main goal of these settlements was to impart Christianity, the Jesuits also insulated the people from European cultural imposition, enabling them to maintain their own identity and traditions. Pope Francis himself has singled out these Jesuit Reductions as "an example of human promotion."

The current state of affairs in Latin America show that in recent years, al-though there have been important advances in social inclusion and GDP growth, there are still many serious matters with which to contend.

Perhaps the most complicated issue is precisely the one front and center on Pope Francis' agenda: poverty. Although poverty figures have declined through a combination of increased economic activity and more active and efficient distributive policies, they are still very high. Bearing in mind that statistical methods can often cause a varied reality, under any measure the percentage of those who fall below the poverty line is unacceptably high in most Central American countries, especially Honduras and Nicaragua, and in some South American countries, such as Bolivia.

However, a more pressing issue — both the root of the region's extreme poverty and the cause that perpetuates it — is inequality. Although much progress has been made recently, Latin America is still the most economically and socially unbalanced region in the world. The Gini index measures income distribution, going from 0 for a hypothetical situation of absolute equality to 100 for absolute inequality. Based on this scale, Latin America leads the world with the highest overall score. This is confirmed by 2009 figures compiled by the United Nations Economic Commission for Latin America and the Caribbean (CEPAL in Spanish). Many attribute this imbalance to a sum of causes related to lack of opportunities, mainly regarding access to quality education; high inflation as a result of region-wide, decades-long, misguided fiscal policies; overdependence on production and exportation of raw materials; lack of credit, especially for small producers and small and medium industries; and an inefficient distribution of social aid. All of this is complicated to the extreme by a third societal albatross in Latin America: endemic corruption.

Corruption is a true calamity south of the Rio Grande. Putting aside media coverage and popular perception of the issue, a few indicators are available to actually quantify it in a systematic way. If we look to annual figures in the Corruption Perceptions Index sponsored by Transparency International, where 100 represents absolute transparency and 0 total corruption, we can see that in 2012, out of 176 countries, Brazil occupies position 69 with 43 points, Argentina at 102 with 35 points, Mexico at 105 with 34 points, until we reach the extreme cases of Paraguay at 150 with only 25 points and finally Venezuela at 165 with 19 points. It's a very poor performance and speaks of one of the darkest characteristics of Latin American political practices.

Finally, if the previous data hasn't succeeded in putting a human face to the region's challenges, there is another disturbing reality to consider: many of its residents live in a state of constant fear. As if the combination of poverty, inequality, lack of opportunities, absence of state assistance, and general corruption (both among civil authorities and security forces) weren't enough, the overall sense of insecurity has been multiplied in recent years by the eruption of organized crime, especially drug-trafficking gangs and cartels. When analyzing the indicators used to measure the impact of the drug trade, there's a clear correlation between the production, transportation, and sale of illegal drugs and the violent murder rate per every 100,000 residents. Figures from the United Nations Office on Crime and Drugs show that Central America, with a "score" of 28.5, is only surpassed worldwide by the southern African region, with 30.5, while all of South America averages 20. However, if we look at figures for each country individually, we find that Latin America holds the first 10 positions on the list of 207. This is the tragic reality of life in much of the region.

As we have recounted in other chapters, the pope knows of this issue all too well, having preached at the epicenter of the poorest and most violent areas of Argentina's capital. Internal and cross-border migration patterns fueled by the almost chronic economic crisis doubled the number of residents in the *villas miserias* of Buenos Aires. These impoverished corners of the most modern and European-influenced city in Latin America are slowly falling into the hands of powerful drug traffickers.

To overcome these difficulties, a plethora of solutions have been tested, many of which have been worse than the problems themselves. As well, a lingering resentment of the region's colonial past and the local perception of an unjust international order continue to act as a roadblock to real progress.

It is an interesting fluke of history, with repercussions that play out on the world stage to this day, that the most successful revolutionary movement in the entire region occurred on a strategically located Caribbean island: Cuba. Like a geopolitical anachronism, Cuba and Puerto Rico remained Spanish colonies until the end of the nineteenth century, while the rest of Hispanic America launched on the road to independence from European colonialists as early as the Napoleonic invasion of Spain in 1808, and had achieved it by the early 1820s. (Belize was the one outlier, gaining independence from the United Kingdom in 1981.)

Cuba's proximity to the United States had an inevitable effect on the island nation. Transitioning from servitude to Madrid to a newly independent regime, it could not resist being pulled into the orbit of US influence. In fact, American intervention in the Cuban War for Independence was crucial in the Spanish defeat and withdrawal of 1898. With the defeat of a traditional, although decadent, European power, the Spanish-American

War marked the entrance of the United States into the ranks of world powers, and as a result Cuba claimed its independence from Spain, while the territories of Puerto Rico and the Philippines were passed on to Uncle Sam.

A fitful democracy was established and a series of moderate governments followed in Havana until 1952, when Fulgencio Batista gained total power through a coup d'état with the American ambassador's consent. Based on the "devil you know" philosophy, the US felt that it was preferable to have someone corrupt yet familiar as an ally rather than allow leftist movements to flourish ninety miles off the Florida coast in those early years of the Cold War.

Batista turned out to be a cruel and corrupt dictator who crushed a growing opposition movement and personally profited from the exploitation of Cuba's economy. He was eventually deposed by a group of young revolutionaries led by brothers Fidel and Raul Castro and Argentine guerrilla Ernesto "Che" Guevara, among others. Once in power, they began to take steps that suggested a democratic alternative to the authoritarianism of the Batista regime. However, whether due to hostility from the United States or their desire to stay in power by avoiding a risky election, their regime slowly mutated into a Soviet-style state. Thousands of Cubans were forced to emigrate and hundreds were executed, many with practically no trial. Elections were suspended and the economy took a sharp turn toward socialism. Ever since, Cubans have endured an excessively oppressive regime against their individual liberties while subsisting in a depressed economic state, although with some notable achievements in such areas as health care and education.

Relations with Washington became extremely tense during this transformation, and such failed attempts to overthrow the Cuban government as the Bay of Pigs invasion only turned up the heat. This was followed by an almost total US economic embargo of the island and the alignment of Havana and Moscow through the remaining years of the Cold War. Essentially a Soviet satellite, the Caribbean island became an export industry for revolutionary movements around the world, and especially throughout the region. Oftentimes taking on the Russians' dirty work, since they came into power the Castro brothers have instigated every armed revolution attempt in Latin America, some of which have been very bloody.

An extremely interesting aspect to this brief overview is the tense relationship between the Cuban revolutionaries and the Catholic Church.

The Church had been present on the island since the arrival of the first Spaniards with Columbus, and the Castro government considered it part of the previous regime's establishment. Inspired by a toxic mix of Marxist atheism, Soviet inspiration, and anti-imperialist airs historic of the region, Christian priests, nuns, professors, and thinkers were persecuted and expelled. From high-ranking offices down to the streets, a godless society was encouraged, an objective that, despite the government's constant efforts to smother religious expression under a blanket of socialist state propaganda, was never fully accomplished. Just as what transpired in all the countries behind the Iron Curtain, the people held true to their beliefs.

The relationship between Cuba and the Catholic Church gradually improved as the Soviet Union descended into crisis, and since its demise in 1991, the relationship has gained definite momentum. Faced with the prospect of following in the footsteps of the former socialist republics in Eastern Europe and on the Russian frontier, the Castros decided to mend their relationship with the Vatican. In November 1996, Pope John Paul II received Fidel Castro in an audience in Rome, and in January 1998, concluding the island's first papal visit ever, celebrating mass in front of one million people gathered in Havana's Plaza de la Revolución.

Despite this recent détente, the Cuban Revolution experience and its influence throughout Latin America made a lasting, negative impression on the Catholic Church. Since then, from all of its most official positions, it allowed its expansion efforts throughout the continent to wither. The hostile experience endured by Catholics and Orthodox in Eastern Europe and Russia under Marxist regimes further reinforced this position. This distancing caused the Church to be in direct conflict with its own precepts, since Christ's mandate clearly required its clerics and clergy to seek out and tend to the weak and persecuted. Doing so, however, would force it to coexist with atheist, authoritarian dictatorships, and the Church had lost its nerve for the fight. The world's most significant Catholic population, with its five-hundred-year history in the region, was seemingly raffled off overnight — quite a difficult dilemma for the many local priests dedicated to serving the poor, among which stood the Argentine Jesuit Jorge Bergoglio.

After a difficult period of adjustment following the Soviet Empire's demise, the shrewd Castro brothers found a helpful dose of oxygen from a least-expected source: a Venezuelan army official and coup leader who became a revolutionary and Cuban admirer — Hugo Chávez.

Chávez' 1999 election to the presidency, in a country with the largest oil profits in the entire region, was somewhat expected. Venezuela had been an imperfect and highly corrupt democracy, excluding millions of people from the benefits of a booming petroleum industry. Sloppy management of a serious economic crisis facilitated the rise to power of this lieutenant colonel, who in 1992 had initiated an unsuccessful coup against President Carlos Andrés Pérez. Once he settled into the Palacio de Miraflores, Chávez unfolded a platform for rule that, inspired by a combination of Argentine Peronism and Cuban Revolution, he pompously called "Twenty-First Century Socialism."

No one can argue against the fact that the profound injustices existing in Venezuela and its elite's abandonment of the masses legitimized the arrival and consolidation of Chávism. The legality of his terms in office cannot be questioned either, since they were always ratified by elections that, although not entirely clean, were considered representative of the popular will. Their legitimacy was even recognized by such prominent international observers as former US President Jimmy Carter, a long-standing champion of free and fair elections around the world.

Unfortunately, elements of a free society under the Chávez government soon began to suffer, including a lack of regard for democratic institutions, the subjugation of minorities and opponents, and a crackdown on individual rights, among them freedom of expression. The poor's situation improved, although many critics note that it was (and still is) due strictly to a rickety oil-profit distribution system rather than a countrywide economic revival. These critics point out that this sort of system is most prevalent in countries with an enormous income, such as Venezuela, and less so in more constricted economic realities without the largesse of a natural resource like oil from which to draw. Once the high-priced, international commodity bonanza subsides, nothing will be left to inherit; the fish will all be distributed, and no one will know how to fish. Yet the people of Venezuela have acquiesced to this scenario, all, obviously, in exchange for an almost complete loyalty and obedience toward *el jefe*.

To maintain and further his regime, Chávez drew on Venezuela's long since lost sense of national pride, resurrecting the anti-imperialist flag. In this way he began to influence the Bolivarian movement[3] in different countries, which has taken root in Ecuador and Bolivia and has greatly influenced the governments of Nicaragua and Argentina. This anti-imperialism has also led to provocative maneuvers aimed at Washington, as

Chávez began forging relationships with well-known antagonists of the United States — Iran, Libya, Syria, and Belarus — as well as supporting the emaciated Cuban system with gifts and donations. The moral authority of this strategy, however, is hard to understand coming from a regime that sells a good amount of its cheap oil to its supposed enemy to the north — Venezuela exports 40 percent of its oil to the United States, whereas only 14 percent is exported to Cuba.

Regarding its relationship with the Church, the Twenty-First Century Socialism situation is more subtle than the Cuban Revolution. Chávez never encouraged atheism as an ideology, although he maintained tense relationships with the ecclesiastic hierarchy in Venezuela, something that has become the modus operandi in all the countries under his influence. Evo Morales in Bolivia, Rafael Correa in Ecuador, Daniel Ortega in Nicaragua, and Nestor and Cristina Kirchner in Argentina have followed this path by often considering bishops and cardinals as part of the established order that they intend to change. No religious persecutions have been reported, nor has land and property been expropriated or state-sponsored atheism encouraged, as occurred in Castro's Cuba. What has been reported, varying country to country, is an internal argument regarding certain issues that collide with the Church's traditional positions. Abortion, the decriminalization of drug consumption, and same-sex marriage are all issues that have caused tension between these governments and the religious hierarchy. This confrontational stance is not exclusive to Bolivarian governments; the more moderate, European-style, traditional socialism predominant in Chile, Uruguay, and Brazil in the past few years has produced similar friction with the Church.

However, the Vatican's main concern regarding Latin America has more to do with its very future under these neo-populist regimes disguised as revolutionary socialism. In general, in these environments, loyalty to the state takes precedence over freedom of the individual, allegiance to any authority other than the state is suppressed, and a form of idol worship toward a nation's leader is encouraged. In a region that constitutes 40 percent of the Church's followers, this ideology threatens the future growth of the institution.

Although it is still too soon to predict with certainty what influence Pope Francis will have on the region, we can risk a few attempts. To do so, we shall analyze Argentina's case, since it was where he served throughout his clerical career and where his elevation to the papacy had the most immediate repercussions.

In Argentina, Cardinal Bergoglio's election took everyone by surprise, both friends and enemies. The initial reaction from Kirchnerism's toughest sectors was very negative, comparing Francis' ascension to the papacy and its impact in Latin America with that of John Paul II and the earthquake he produced in Eastern Europe under Soviet dominance. Some even maintained it was an imperialist ploy to cut short the budding liberation movements in the region. They even tried to resurrect stories of his ties to the last military dictatorship, saying that he hadn't stood up to officials when faced with the disappearance of two Jesuit priests — an accusation that has not been legally proven. This scandalous attack, nourished by Argentine governmental rumor mills, finally forced the Vatican's own spokesperson to intervene, putting the matter to rest.

Quick to act, and aware that backing Francis was directly related to her own popularity, President Cristina Kirchner modified her initial stance in favor of a position that was more supportive of the newly elected pope. In a notable gesture from Francis, she was invited to the enthronement ceremony as an esteemed guest and was the first head of state to be received by His Holiness prior to any other on the planet. Both appeared before the press, joyful and reconciled at the following gift exchange and luncheon.

This does not mean Francis has forgotten their prior disagreements, nor her work that, through marriage to his greatest opposition, Nestor Kirchner, has governed the nation since 2003. On the contrary, this attitude shows that the pope forgives and will be occupied with more transcendental issues than the backbiting, inside politics of Argentina or Latin America. He knows that he does not have to come down to earth for his impact to modify reality. To this end, sermons and homilies are no longer necessary; signs and examples will suffice.

The pope's popularity in his homeland is astounding. A survey published in the Buenos Aires newspaper *La Nación* one month after Francis' designation as pope, 90 percent of Argentines had a positive image of him, 5 percent had an average impression, and only 2 percent had a bad one. Regarding the impact on Argentina, 74 percent consider it will be positive and 11 percent negative. Surveys also show his countrymen believe the pope will be able to make changes within the Church, with 51 percent thinking they will be big and 34 percent moderate. These figures would be the envy of any active politician.

If Francis manages to put some of his potent ideas and reforms into effect, combining his Jesuit skillful efficiency with his Franciscan humble simplicity, it is expected that in a few more years, the people of Latin America will begin to seek presidents and leaders who authentically emulate his example.

Chapter 13

A Pope from the End of the Earth

THE WORLD IS changing. The previous century witnessed the fading of old orders and the rise of new. The titanic struggles against the forces of fascism and communism triggered the end of an exhausted Europe's long reign as the world's hegemon, and the United States emerged as the world's sole superpower, a position it still holds at the dawn of the twenty-first century.

But orders may be shifting again. As the United States and its European allies groan under the burden of international responsibility and financial crisis, a new set of players have taken a place at the table, eager to enter the game. China, of course, heads the list, and India, Brazil, and a reviving Russian Federation all have pieces on the board.

But what of Latin America? As a region, it was more of a pawn than player over the last five hundred years, first in the hands of competing European colonizers, then in the long game between the United States and Soviet Union. But today, represented by one of its sons on the grand stage of world affairs, the region may yet play a surprising role in our future.

To put into context Latin America's position among the major world powers and the global impact that the region will likely have now that one of its own has been elected to the papacy, it is important to first discuss the strengths and weaknesses of the most influential and dominant nations. Examining these factors will enable us to shed light on the issues that Pope Francis will need to confront in order to ensure a vibrant role for the Catholic Church in the twenty-first century.

Despite the profound changes underway in the geopolitical order, the United States will remain a leading world power, at least for the immediate future. Its superiority is notable on several levels.

According to the International Monetary Fund (IMF), in 2012, the United States had a GDP of $16.6 trillion, doubling China's $8.2 trillion, which occupied second place on the list, whereas the GDP of emerging market Brazil was slightly less than $2.4 trillion. However, the US figures are far more impressive if you take into account its per capita wealth, since, with only 5 percent of the world's population, it holds 25 percent of global production.

America has a relatively young and dynamic population, which several specialists say is a key to defining the future viability of societies. In 2012, based on the *CIA World Factbook*, the birth rate in the United States was 13.68 per 1,000 total population. Niger was in first place with 50.6; other notable countries include India with 20.6, Brazil with 15.2, China with 13.31, and Russia with 12.3. This is an important trend to monitor, because societies with elderly populations face the prospect of having too few younger, active inhabitants in the workforce to fund services for older, passive inhabitants, a serious crisis currently playing out in several European countries.

Another strength of the United States is its strong network of educational opportunities. American universities dominate lists that rank the world's top institutions of higher education, and its capacity for research and development is without equal. This is always a good barometer of a nation's overall capacity for growth.

This strength in numbers and opportunities translates into primacy on the military level. A look at the US defense budget revealed by the Stockholm International Peace Research Institute (SIPRI), that it totaled $7 billion in 2012. This figure constitutes almost 40 percent of aggregate military spending worldwide. According to historian Jonathan Freedland, we'd have to go back to the Roman Empire to find a similar disproportionate situation of such magnitude.

Based on these statistics, it is clear that America's decline is still far off, although serious domestic economic difficulties indicate a dangerous leveling out. However, the more complex issue is philosophical and related to the US citizenry's perception of their country's role in the world. There is a growing fatigue within the United States of its role as the "planet's police," sacrificing resources and lives in regions that oftentimes do not value or even need them. The US government must respond to the voice of public opinion; its Caesar, elected by the people, must respect an independent press and bear the opposition's criticism. Such are the vicissitudes of a democratic republic and twenty-first century empire.

When the United States assumed its role as a world power after the demise of the British Empire, it began a relentless mission to expand its political, economic, and social model — in short, the American system. As the world's leading torchbearer of Judeo-Christian ideals, the task, just as it had been for other great powers over the centuries, was to convince outsiders to ascribe to their beliefs. The United States proceeded on the assumption that once a culture experienced the superiority of its model, it would willingly abandon centuries of tradition in favor of a new set of practices. This worked well in postwar Germany and Japan; it has not in Afghanistan and Iraq today.

In its heightened sense of Christian morality lies one of the United States' greatest strengths. In the original inclusive spirit of its forefathers, arising from the foundations of those thirteen colonies that dared to break free from the English king, the freedom for all creeds and religions to flourish allowed for the development of a type of homogenous spirituality. This is why the most powerful country on Earth constitutes a reservoir of moral values that will likely be high on the list of considerations for the new pope as he maps the direction of his Church. US Catholics, mainly descendents of Italians, Irish, and a burgeoning Hispanic population, total almost eighty million and represent an influential bloc of the faithful in the pope's body politic.

The main weakness of the United States as a supreme power is not its ballooning budget deficit, drug issues, immigration law disputes, or the noticeable division between its political parties. Those are all undeniably important issues, but to many thinkers, its deficiency lies in an existential paradox. Americans seek to export their socioeconomic system; centered on democracy and the free market, it usually produces prosperity and growth in places that adopt it. But some of the more successful cases have grown to the point where they have gathered the strength to defy their inspirer. China — which imported aspects of free market economics to revolutionize its broken model of central planning — may now be poised to assume the mantle of the world's primary economic engine, along with all the privileges that status bestows. China's formidable growth illustrates that the strength of America's imperial model is simultaneously its greatest weakness.

Across the Atlantic we find Old Europe — the cradle of Western civilization that governed the planet's fate since the Age of Discovery. Dominance changed hands from Spain's supremacy, a direct consequence of the immense wealth it plundered from American lands on the backs of an enslaved workforce, to the French court, and then to England, Queen of the Seas, which constructed a truly global commercial empire. The end of World War I brought with it the decline of England as superpower of the world, and Washington took the role for good after World War II, with all its rewards, responsibilities, and consequences.

Following the cataclysm of two world wars, Europe understood it had to overcome centuries of hate and rivalry to join forces and become one if it wanted to regain its status as a key global power. In order to do this, it began a slow but steady process of integration that culminated in the creation of the European Union (governing political and economic matters) and Eurozone (a monetary union, epitomized by the zone's single currency, the euro). The process has been a true success, in that it has brought forth the longest period of peace and growth on the continent in its entire stormy history. If the European Union manages to avoid being dragged down by the anchor of weak economies and lackluster leadership of its southern member states, it will emerge as a stronger, more efficient entity.

But Europe must overcome other challenges. We've already noted the potential calamity of its aging population and its effect on the continued viability of its expansive social security programs. Another noteworthy hurdle is the absorption of millions of immigrants into European society. Despite the egalitarian rhetoric of governments, these newcomers oftentimes find a hostile climate marked by a lack of openness in places where they've chosen to restart their lives.

Aside from these challenges, the EU still represents a sizable economy, and its collective military capabilities compete with the US in terms of troops, equipment, and technology (and, to a smaller degree, nuclear weapons). Europe's cultural capital, accumulated over centuries of patronage and expansion of the arts, sciences, and letters, is one of the greatest achievements of mankind. The region may no longer set the rules of world affairs, but it will never be discounted from the game.

One can not discuss the global big leagues without mentioning the Russian Federation, primarily due to the many lessons its history has provided. From the original dukedoms and princedoms that, in the eighteenth century, united the Slavic tribes of the enormous plains east of the Ural Mountains, to the mighty Soviet Union and its colossal empire, this nation has clearly demonstrated the profundity of its expansive spirit. This has partly been due to its massive, continental span of harsh, frozen terrain, inspiring a constant search for warmer, more viable waters. A more deeply rooted element of this expansion has been security. The global intelligence company Stratfor and other scholars have noted that the Russian homeland has been on the receiving end of some of the greatest invasions in all of history, from the Mongol hordes of the thirteenth century, to Napoleon's doomed march on Moscow in 1812, to the brutal blitzkrieg of Hitler's Operation Barbarossa, opening up the bloody Eastern Front of World War II. The result has been an almost desperate campaign to establish buffer zones around the motherland.

Always armed with a cause, be it cultural, racial, religious, ideological, or geopolitical, the Russians advanced where they could, conquering, subjugating, converting, or convincing entire nations to come under its sway. First it was spreading the faith of Christ from their Orthodox perspective, akin to the agenda of the Roman and Byzantine Empires. Later, with Peter and Catherine the Great, the leitmotif was the determined, somewhat forced Europeanization to "civilize" its own people. And so we arrive to the Soviet oligarchs and their attempt to impose a centralized command economy and atheist ideology on the nations of the world. In this last effort, for almost half a century, they competed against the United States for world power and almost won.

Although the economy of today's Russian Federation shows a structural weakness — a by-product of almost seventy years of trying to put Marxist principles into practice — it is still a country with an enormous supply of natural resources, especially food and energy, as well as a large and sophisticated military and a nuclear arsenal that's among the largest on Earth. To many observers the Russian bear is only hibernating, and it's only a matter of time before it awakes from its assumed slumber and once again tries to become a dominant world power.

This is something Pope Francis must take into consideration as he looks to the east and considers the Vatican's long-sundered relationship with its Eastern Orthodox brothers. He has already shown his sensitivity to the matter at the start of his reign, when he presented himself solely and simply as the Bishop of Rome rather than Supreme Pontiff. It was a compelling sign for the Eastern Orthodox churches, among which is the huge Russian

Orthodox Church. It has no desire to bow to an absolute and infallible monarch; it would, however, welcome a *primus inter pares* relationship with the Vatican.

––––––––––––

Chinese civilization represents a completely different paradigm of thought than the West: the emphasis is on social stability and harmony rather than progress and individual rights. It is very much inspired by the legacy of Confucius, a great thinker and proponent of order and discipline. The first three hundred years of Chinese civilization saw tremendous innovation and advances in some of the most fundamental aspects of modern life — writing, language, institutions, government bureaucracy — but rather than build on this progress, they simply maintained the status quo. Many specialists claim that this was the best way to contain an excessively large population. Order and discipline were branded in the minds of millions of human beings, who transmitted these values from one generation to the next. The typically Western ideas of change and progress, with the evolution that this implies, was hardly understood or conceived in this hemisphere, and neither was faith in one God that could lend significance to life's journey.

A crucial difference between the Eastern and Western models is precisely the lack of missionary and expansive spirit of "the Civilization," as the celestial Peking throne liked to call it. China never sent an invading army to any country or region it did not consider within its orbit — its vital space. The Chinese defended themselves against outside threats partly through the construction of huge walls that protected their frontier from the horseback Mongol hordes who swept in from the central steppes of Asia, or when they decided to close their door for centuries to avoid any type of foreign contamination. Yet in almost all history, it was the most populated region of the planet — an immense market that, to European crowns and mercantile powers, could not be set aside. The pressure, at first timid and later quite violent, aimed at prying open the door of commercial trade with the imperial court resulted in a legacy of conflict between China and the West, and the history books list a string of confrontations: the First and Second Opium Wars with Great Britain, the Boxer Rebellion (a violent uprising against Western imperialism and Christian missionary encroachment), US president Teddy Roosevelt's "gunboat diplomacy" to intimidate China into doing business, and others.

The story of modern China's transformation from Maoist basket case to economic behemoth is well known. But China's embrace of the new global capitalism has been done in its own way, without altering key components of its social organization, political structure, or philosophical thinking. Since 1978, it has experienced unprecedented growth — the most significant recorded in history. As critics points out, the most populated country on Earth is transitioning from an economy based on investment and exports to one centered on consumption and internal demand. The inclusion of millions of people in a new urban middle class is key to understanding China's shift from being the world's factory for cheap goods to a leading consumer market. The World Bank calculates that in the next ten years, China's GDP, closely tied to consumer spending, will grow more than $10 trillion — almost 60 percent of North America's economy. According to the Chinese National Bureau of Statistics, its GDP increased seventy times in thirty years since it put into practice Deng Xiaoping's reforms. China, consciously self-contained for centuries, has clearly been a sleeping giant.

These extraordinary figures are reinforced by an enormous accumulation of reserves, a result of a surplus of foreign trade, especially with the United States. Chinese multinational corporations travel the world in search of business opportunities and raw materials, and education indicators show considerable improvement in the last years. As well, the People's Liberation Army — the world's largest, with its nuclear arsenal and burgeoning naval capabilities — is increasingly flexing its muscles in the Asian theater.

There is one potential hurdle that prevents China from assuming the mantle of the world's primary superpower, and that is its lack of interest in exercising the role, an attitude that, as we have seen, has strong historic antecedents. But if Beijing were to eclipse Washington on the world stage sometime in the near future, the reason may lie not in its size and strength but rather the risk its increasingly prosperous citizenry will take to finally demand political rights and individual freedoms. If that were to occur, it would be a true revolution, one of the most momentous of modern times, although the Confucian strand in the DNA of Chinese society may ensure a far more orderly hive than Western values can achieve.

An interesting aspect to this analysis is a lack of a widespread religious heritage in the Chinese people, a reality since the days of the empire and reinforced through the Communist Party's regime. The persecution of different religions and an attempt to nationalize the relatively small lo-cal Catholic Church hints at what could happen in a world where Beijing reigns supreme — another key perspective the new pope needs to consider as he sets forth to reinstill spiritual values in a world where they are seem-ingly on the decline.

Some experts claim that the next dominant power to emerge from Asia may not be China but India, the other giant that is slowly awakening. With almost the same population, 1.2 billion to China's 1.3 billion, its somewhat chaotic economy still leaves much to be desired. Although it celebrates a similarly long history as China, New Delhi's lack of systematic, govern-mental order cannot be ignored.

According to the International Monetary Fund (IMF), in 2012, India ranked tenth in the world in terms of GDP, with slightly more than $1.9 trillion. If measured per capita, however, that ranking takes a sharp de-cline to number 130, at $3.6 billion. In comparison, the US GDP in 2012 exceeded $16 trillion, and China's was more than $8 trillion. As we can see, this country would have to triple the size of its economy to reach the Chinese level. And it would need to start by resolving its endemic poverty and profound social inequalities maintained through centuries of an ab-horrent, functioning caste system.

India is not without its advantages, many of which come from its British colonial past: it is a well-functioning democracy, and its people, many of whom speak English, tend to purse higher education. It has been main-tained that while China prepares factory workers, India prepares engi-neers and technicians (albeit something that is now changing in Beijing). Its population has a rich spiritual life, with more than 93 percent actively involved in religious practice, roughly 80 percent of whom are Hindus and almost 10 percent Muslims. All these factors bode well for long-term sta-bility, barring a political crisis such as another war with Pakistan.

However, what the Indian government shares with China's is a tendency to not get involved in situations beyond it borders that do not concern them. India's powerful armed forces and nuclear arsenal are maintained because of its almost existential conflict with its Muslim brother, Paki-stan. Historically, it has never shown expansionist tendencies beyond wars among the different regions and peoples that make up the quilt of this ancient civilization.

Being the planet's dominant power has never been easy. It must be earned through effort and commitment, which means it must be desired.

That is the main reason why the presence of a missionary spirit regarding one's culture, way of life, ideology, or religion is fundamental to nourish the enormous sacrifice this all implies. Though not all have the same ability or desire to do so, every monotheistic religion that encourages evangelization and conversion holds within it this seed.[2] Throughout history, this force within major religions has served to spread and consolidate the political power of the moment; hence, the constant conflict between Christians and Muslims.

It is also true that being the world's leading power brings with it important benefits, such as the management of global economic variables, the possibility of issuing a currency of international value, the policing of conflicts to one's advantage — in short, establishing the global order and the rules of the game. But with that comes high costs, represented by the enormous military forces that must be maintained, participation in conflicts and wars in which innocent lives are lost, and resentment and hostility from the rest of the world. Since World War II, the United States has assumed the negative and in exchange has enjoyed the positive, something that is expected from a great power.

But, as we said at the beginning of this chapter, the world is changing. We will go through a period of transition in the years to come, where the unipolarity of US dominance will become multipolar. We will always need Washington, but Washington will increasingly have to look to places like Berlin, Moscow, New Delhi, and Beijing for consensus. And we will undoubtedly need to add Brasilia to that list, as the capital of the largest country in the region that spawned the most influential spiritual leader on the planet.

By any measure, the institution governed by Pope Francis is impressive. As mentioned, the Roman Catholic Church represents close to 1.2 billion followers, 17 percent of the world's total population. Catholics — from the Greek *katholikos*, or universal — are found all over the world: around 495 million Central and South Americans practice the faith, 296 million Europeans, 190 million Africans, 100 million North Americans, and 10 million inhabitants of Oceania.

Having such an extensive global reach, the Catholic Church must adhere to an efficient and hierarchic organization. Based on the BBC and information published in the newspaper *L'Osservatore Romano*, by 2006 the Church employed 945,210 consecrated people dedicated to different tasks. From this group — its "army" if you will — 753,400 were women and the remaining 191,810 men, of which 136,171 were priests.

This gigantic structure is ruled at the top by three levels of authority. At the pinnacle is the pope, the Bishop of Rome and the Holy See's head of state. He is aided by the Roman Curia, the executive and administrative offices of the Vatican. The Holy Father is elected by the College of Cardinals, from which he may also receive advice and counsel.

Any baptized Catholic male can be chosen as pope, although since 1389, Peter's throne has always been occupied by a cardinal. Cardinals are bishops who receive this honorary title, but they can also be theologians or distinguished members of the Roman Curia.

The entire structure of the Catholic Church is divided into twenty-three autonomous churches, of which the most extensive is the Latin Church with more than 1 billion followers; the other twenty-two are the so-called Eastern Catholic churches. Although they are self-governing, they recognize Rome's supremacy in regards to doctrine. The twenty-three churches are organized into 2,795 dioceses, headed in all cases by a bishop, who governs the local church district. In turn, this district is divided into parishes, led by priests, who dedicate themselves to managing the various sacraments and liturgical celebrations. Parallel to this structure, although respecting local ecclesiastical authorities, are the special congregations and religious orders.

The pope and his curia; the bishopric; parish priests — the entire organization has been controlled for two thousand years within these three strata.

The Church's earthly influence can be gleaned through the finances and the resources it moves around the world. Its exact value, however, is not easily accessible — a product of the long-standing tradition of secrecy and discretion that has allowed the institution to survive for more than two millennia. Taking into account the lack and/or reliability of source material, the *Economist*, also in its August 2012 issue, published a series of estimates. In the United States alone, the Catholic Church spent $170 billion in 2012, much of it managing more than 6,800 schools, 630 hospitals, 244 colleges and universities, and close to one million employees. The income required to fund such massive expenditure would amount to almost 60 percent of the Church's worldwide total, the *Economist* article speculates. Despite the lack of transparency in Vatican finances and without hard figures to analyze, it is nonetheless indisputable that the Roman Catholic Church represents an enormous earthly power.

However, to base the pope and his organization's influence solely on a balance sheet would paint an extremely misleading picture of his true power. The business of managing a significant portion of the health and education infrastructure in many countries is important, but given the enormous flock over which he presides, it's the political power derived from his spiritual authority that is truly distinguished. One gesture, one attitude, one speech, or one of the pope's ideas conveniently distributed through the vast network he heads creates ripples that have far-reaching effects on projects and initiatives around the world.

The political and geostrategic role the Catholic Church has played in the past has always been crucial to the organization's advancement. Since the end of the fourth century, when Christianity became the state religion of the Roman Empire, church officials and clergy have known how to skillfully use the institution's spiritual lineage to their advantage, including wielding its financial and ideological power to influence earthly issues. For centuries, practically every European monarch was either crowned by the pope or solicited his intervention to resolve an assortment of issues.

One of the papacy's more recent geostrategic initiatives was spawned from the ideological alliance among US president Ronald Reagan, British prime minister Margaret Thatcher, and Pope John Paul II. The three leaders coordinated a series of actions that precipitated the fall of the Soviet Empire. Given its authoritarian Marxism and active atheism, with wide reach into profoundly Catholic lands in Eastern Europe, the Soviet Union constituted a serious challenge for Western democracies and a huge threat to the Vatican.

In his native Poland and its neighboring countries, one cannot deny the enormous influence exercised by John Paul II. He incited the people to rally against the injustices of Soviet occupation, igniting their desire to once again become a part of democratic Europe. The close relationship between John Paul II and Lech Walesa, the leader of the Polish trade union known as Solidarity (and the country's first president elected by popular vote), was a crucial factor that set in motion the momentous events that would lead to the fall of the Berlin Wall and the collapse of the Soviet Union — arguably the historical culmination of the twentieth century.

The transition phase of Benedict XVI's papacy — focused on reaffirming orthodoxy and reestablishing internal discipline, a logical product of Cardinal Joseph Ratzinger's intellectual nature — has ended and a new phase is upon us. There exist lingering issues within the Church, many so serious, such as the sex abuse scandals and ongoing issues with the Vatican Bank, that they continue to strongly affect its credibility. But while not ignoring these problems, Francis' primary focus is outward, toward a new horizon.

It is no coincidence that the pope comes from Argentina, a long-suffering country that fulfills an essential role in maintaining Latin American unity. This is relevant if we take into account his influence as spiritual father to the heavily Catholic Spanish-speaking world, combined with his preferential relationship with Brazil. Argentina, which for many years was the leading regional power, in the past few decades has relinquished this position to its giant neighbor and accepted a new order of coexistence and harmony. Both countries, for example, agreed to abandon the possibility of competing for nuclear power. Although they have access to the necessary technology, they have deliberately decided to follow a common path in peace. Together, these two nations cooperate in all areas and project themselves onto the international scene as peaceful powers, participating in several humanitarian missions sponsored by the United Nations and other international organizations.

Its admirable partnership with Brazil aside, Argentina epitomizes the face of the region, having successfully assimilated its original indigenous culture, the heavy imprint of the Spanish colonizers, and the enormous influence of its mainly European immigrants. It is a place where adversaries from foreign lands have managed to become allies in a new world. And like Argentina, Francis is a living melting pot, an ideal blend of European heritage and Latin American culture that makes him an ideal leader in the uncertain climate ahead for the twenty-first century Church.

Obviously, Francis' election has already instilled renewed energy in Catholics around the world. The European and North American faithful connect with the new blood and bold style he represents, and those in Latin America, Africa, and Asia view him as their own — someone who understands their problems and shares in their suffering. It is likely that the Church will gain strength in those three regions, given the number of followers already there and the possibilities for growth. His presence alone, his history of working with and for the disadvantaged, and his frank and friendly style almost guarantee the success of this objective.

The task that lies ahead for Francis is one of great magnitude, but he is not alone; other sectors must take on their share of the responsibility as well. The G20 (the Group of Twenty Finance Ministers and Central Bank Governors) may not be able to fully resolve the financial crisis that is threatening to overwhelm the developed world; indeed, many observers believe the 2008–2009 financial crisis marked the beginning of the end of US and G7 dominance and with it the end of United States supremacy. If the emerging countries of Brazil, China, India, and, to a lesser degree, Russia, continue to grow and interrelate, it will force the United States and Europe to add them permanently to the negotiation table. The result will be a new world order — a true global society.

As this scenario plays out, another region is poised to take an important lead. Perhaps surprisingly, it is Latin America that has the potential to assume the role of the United States in the transformative years to come.

In the vacuum of Europe's postwar decline, America crucially served as the counterweight to an expansionist Soviet Union and the communist, authoritarian, atheist world it sought. Today the world is faced with a similar dilemma, with the possibility of global hegemony being transferred to another mechanical, godless regime, this time governing from Beijing. Although China does not evidence the aggressively imperialistic tendencies of the Soviet Union, it almost uniquely combines the two antagonistic systems that divided humanity during practically the entire twentieth century: communism and capitalism. And an overabundance of either does not bode well for a global order centered on moral and spiritual values.

It goes without saying that this transitional phase, ending with China as the dominant and supreme power, is a worrisome scenario. With this in mind, Latin America, a Christian counterweight to Communist China, is likely the last hope for our civilization. It would not necessarily replace or even directly augment the United States' leadership; rather, it would be a bastion of traditional Western principles and way of life — respect for democracy and individual rights, and for financial development as well, but always putting man's dignity and spirit first. It is a great paradox that the fate of the world could possibly rest in one of its corners that for so long was marginalized and virtually forgotten.

Decades after Old Europe ceded its reign to the power across the Atlantic, today we can look to the South as a steadfast home of Western values and the civilizing compassion of its Christian traditions. This vision requires enormous moral authority to carry out, in the same spirit of truth upon which Peter built his church. Therefore, to bless and strengthen this monumental task, who better than the pope of the poor and for the poor, who comes from the end of the Earth. An Argentine Jesuit, son of Italians, who calls himself Francis.

Endnotes

Chapter 2

1. When Francis was chosen as Pope, the media searched for anecdotes that reflected the pontiff's previous life. In one of these pieces, Amalia maintained that, ever since that fatherly scolding, she never spoke to Francis again. At present, the woman still resides in Flores and has said, referring to the new pope, "When I saw him on TV, I stood up and said, 'Jorge, I embrace you with the affection of a lifetime.'"

2. In Argentina, children attend high school between the ages of thirteen and eighteen.

Chapter 3

1. Active during the '60s and '70's, the Montoneros were an Argentine, urban, leftist guerilla group. They staged many bloody attacks against the pólice and dictatorship, but were effectively run off by 1980.

2. On October 26, 2011, after twenty-two months of debate and testimonies of more than 250 witnesses, judges Daniel Obligado, Ricardo Farías, and Germán Castelli, convicted eighteen defendants accused of the kidnap, torture, and homicide of eighty-six victims, including writer and journalist Rodolfo Walsh, French nuns Alice Domon and Leonie Duquet, and Azucena Villaflor, Mary Bianco, and Esther de Careaga, founders of the Mothers of Plaza de Mayo. Among the convicted was Alfredo Astiz, known as the "Blond Angel of Death," who received twenty-five years in prison for his crimes. In France, he was sentenced in absentia to life imprisonment.

3. Berisso, Avellaneda, Lanús, and Lomas de Zamora are cities located no more than thirty miles from Buenos Aires.

Chapter 4

1. On August 5, 1973, *La Nación*, the oldest newspaper in Argentina and the one closest to the Catholic Church, published a brief sidebar with a photo of a thirty-six-year-old

priest, hair slicked back and displaying a sullen expression, titled, "The Jesuits Have a New Provincial." And below were his name and the initials S. J., for "Sacerdote Jesuita" or Jesuit Priest.

2. Guardini was an important Catholic theologian of the twentieth century. His work influenced the final recommendations of the Second Vatican Council of the 1960s, whose goal was adapting the Church to the modern world.

3. Words offered by the Reverend Monsignor Jorge M. Bergoglio S. J., for the twentieth anniversary of the document "Historia y Cambio" (History and Change), uploaded to the Universidad del Salvador's official website, http://www.usal.edu.ar/en/history.

4. A titular bishop, designated in name (title) only, is typically appointed to a diocese that is no longer functional.

5. The term "cardinal" comes from the Latin *cardo* or "hinge" and suggests a role to which they are commended: they are the "hinges" around which the whole Church building turns.

6. "Conclave" comes from the Latin *cum clave* (with key) and refers to this moment of isolation and solitude. It has been celebrated this way, without change, since Pope Gregory X established the Ubi Periculum (rules of papal conclaves) in 1274. The first official conclave was held in January 1276.

Chapter 5

1. The Beagle conflict of 1978 was a dispute between Chile and Argentina over the Picton, Lennox, and Nueva islands and control of the waters surrounding them. The islands are located at the southern tip of South America, in the Beagle Channel.

2. The Movement of Priests for the Third World, known in Argentina as Movimento de Sacredotes para el Terser Mondo (MSTM), was organized mainly by priests and active between 1967 and 1976. Like Pope Paul VI, they wanted to incorporate the modern reforms of the Second Vatican Council into the Argentine Church. However, the MSTM sought a strong social and political presence within the Church and community, especially with regards to their work within the many depressed neighborhoods, or the *villas miserias*. At the behest of the papacy, Nucio Laghi was to minimize the social and political power of the MSTM.

3. When King Ferdinand V of Aragon married Queen Isabella I of Castille in 1469, the two kingdoms merged to create the foundation of present-day Spain.

4. A book containing prayers, psalms, hymns, and readings, a breviary is meant to be read at the canonical hours (daily, ritualistic prayer time, during which set liturgical rites are read). These prayers and readings are specifically chosen by the Roman Catholic Church or other Christian sects (with respect to varying versions).

5. In a homily he gave in Constitución, one of the poorest neighborhoods in the City of Buenos Aires, then bishop Bergoglio slammed what he called "modern slavery," saying, "A dog is better taken care of than these slaves of ours. As long as slaves still exist in Buenos Aires, I will continue to say the same thing: slavery in this city is widespread. There have been street kids for years, I don't know if there are more or less now, but there are a lot. This city has failed and continues to fail in freeing us from this structural slavery."

6. Francis always considered Susana Trimarco's case as paradigmatic. This woman managed to free 129 girls from involuntary servitude, yet her daughter has yet to turn up. "In this city, some girls stop playing with dolls and enter prostitution dives because they were stolen, sold, or betrayed," pointed out Francis in another of his homilies.

7. In Christian belief, the Thursday before Easter commemorates the Last Supper of Jesus and his apostles before his crucifixion. After supper, Jesus washed the feet of each of his apostles as a gesture of humility.

8. The Once Tragedy occurred on February 22, 2012, when a train that was arriving at the Once de Septiembre station, one of the four main stops in Buenos Aires, was unable to brake and crashed against the station's bumper system. Twelve hundred people were on the train. Fifty-one died and more than seven hundred were injured. Among the deceased was Graciela Bottega's daughter, Tatiana.

9. A gold, ornamental token, Popes annually present this blessed offering to countries, military officials, churches, and sanctuaries. Traditionally blessed by His Holiness on the fourth Sunday of Lent, the Golden Rose is offered as a sign of admiration and respect.

Chapter 6

1. Getulio Vargas was a four-term Brazilian president, advocate of the main labor laws that favor workers, and an ardent nationalist.

2. The Corpus Christi (Body of Christ) feast is celebrated on Holy Thursday (Thursday before Easter Sunday). In Catholic and Christian religions, the feast celebrates the tradition of the Eucharist — the consecrated bread and wine offered up as the body and blood of Christ, commemorating that which Jesus offered as his own body and blood to his disciples at the Last Supper. After Mass, a solemn procession is held.

3. Putsch is a term used to refer to civil-military uprisings. It's use stemmed from Munich's Putsch or the Beer Hall Putsch, the November 8 and 9, 1923, failed coup d'état in Munich, carried out by members of the Nationalist Socialist German Workers' Party (NSDAP), which became the reason why Adolf Hitler and Rudolf Hess, among other Nazi officials, were sentenced to prison.

4. The Justicialist Party, known as the *Partido Justicialista* (P.J.), is a Peronist political party which constitutes the main body of the Peronist movement.

5. "Option for the poor" or "preferential option for the poor" (*opción/preferencial opción por los pobres*) was a phrase popularized in '70s Latin America, most often used to represent the class struggle taking place there. The phrase, however, is known to have deep, biblical roots which can be traced back to Jesus' teachings regarding service and ministry to the poor.

6. The Southern Andes Mountain Range forms Argentina's long, western border with Chile.

Chapter 7

1. In the Old Testament, the Twelve Minor Prophets each have their own book. The prophets/books are ordered as follows: Hosea, Joel, Amos, Obadiah, Jonah, Micah,

Nahum, Habakkuk, Zephaniah, Haggai, Zechariah, and Malachi. These prophets/ books are ordered differently in Orthodox Christian bibles. The Major Prophets of the Old Testament, considered so because their books are much longer, are Isaiah, Jeremiah, Ezekiel, and Daniel.

2. Located in the Nothern Kindom of Israel and mentioned in Genesis, Bethel was an important religious center.

3. The centrist ideology, or centrism, is a term that defines those whose political beliefs are pragmatic and solution oriented, without bias, and not based on right or left political orientation. The centrist approaches politics via moderation and concession.

4. The Society of the Catholic Apolstolate, also known the Pallottines, are an apostolic sect (like the Jesuits) within the Roman Catholic Church.

5. Also referred to as media populism, neo-populism is an early 21st century cultural and political ideology amalgamates and redefines left and right ideals in order to bring about economic and social change, spreading its message via electronic media. Aside from its use of media, Neo-populism differs from 20th century populism in that its goal is to empower the individual, whereas the for goal of the former was to empower the community in their class struggle against the wealthy and privileged upper-class. Neo-populism is especially particular to Latin American countries.

6. The Latin American Episcopal Coucil (known as CELAM for its Spanish name) conferences in Puebla Mexico in 1979 and Santo Domingo, Dominican Republic in 1992, both innaugurated under Pope John Paul II, yeilded significant results in defining the Church's evangelical misión. The documents that bear their names contain the conclusions of these conferences. CELAM, made up of Latin American Roman Catholic bishops, was created in 1955.

7. A leftist movement led by late Venezuelan president Hugo Chávez, the Bolivarian Revolution was named for 19th century Venezuelan leader Simón Bolivar,

8. The usual duty of the Camerlengo, a cardinal of the Holy Roman Church, is to verify the death of the pope and oversee all aspects of the conclave to replace him. He also supervises the property and revenues of the Holy See.

9. Situated adjacent to Saint Peter's Basilica, Saint Martha's House is a guesthouse for clergy visiting the Holy See. Its construction was completed in 1996 under Pope John Paul II.

Chapter 8
1. Granted to patrons of the Church, plenary (complete) indulgences provide remission from the punishment of sin, recognized on Earth and in the eyes of God in the Kingdom of Heaven.

2. During the late middle ages, Saracen (those of the Sinai Peninsula as defined by Ptolemaic geography) was a term used for Muslims by Europeans.

Chapter 9
1. Somewhat of a predecessor to the League of Nations and United Nations, the Congress of Vienna attempted to address issues of international boundaries, peaceful balances of power, and logical spheres of influence in Europe.

2. Saint Francis of Sales' famous book, *Introduction to the Devout Life*, is a layman's guide to achieving holiness in one's life. It was a revolutionary tract of spiritual guidance for ordinary people.

3. Growing out of the writings of Cornelius Otto Jansen, this Roman Catholic movement sought to reconcile man's free will and divine grace.

Chapter 10

1. During the late fourth century, Bishop Lucifer of Cagliari, in Sardinia, broke from the Church due to his vehement opposition to Arianism (teaching of Arius of Alexandria that put forth that God the Son was inferior to God the Father).

2. Many early Christians avoided persecution by renouncing their faith (known as apostasy). In 311, when an apostatic was ordained Bishop of Carthage, many Christians were outraged. Named for Donatus of Carthage, this sect broke away from the church in the early fourth century by setting up their own bishopric (ordaining Donatus their bishop in 315).

3. As an attempt to win over Midddle Eastern Christians, the Churh decided to condemn certain texts, known as the Three Chapters. Under the leadership of Macedonius of Aquileia (northern Italy), a group of bishops that rejected the condemnation of these texts broke from the Chruch in 553.

4. Between 863 and 867, the Western Church's opposition to the appointment of Michael III as Byzantine emperor led to a schism between Rome and Constantinople.

5. On July 12, 1790, the French National Assembly approved the Civil Constitution of Clergy, by which the state would govern the church. This Constitutional Church divided the people of France.

6. Ecclesiatical organizations that recognize each other's practices while retaining their distinct identities are said to be in full communion with one another.

7. The seven sacraments recognized by the Roman Catholic Church are: Baptism, Reconciliation (Penance), Eucharist (Communion), Confirmation, Marriage, Ordination (Holy Orders), and Annointing of the Sick (Last Rites).

8. Ecclesiastical body of the Roman Catholic Church responsable for the miliary's pastoral care.

Chapter 12

1. A papal bull is a specialized character or stamp used as a seal by the pope.

2. In the early nineteenth century, Venezuelan leader Simón Bolivar, fighting for Latin American independence, liberated his own country as well as Colombia, Ecuador, and Bolivia. He also assisted José de San Martin, Argentine general, in the liberation of Peru.

3. Named for Simón Bolívar, the Bolivarian movement was established by Hugo Chávez and his fellow military officers in the 1980s. This leftist social movement sought to implement democracy, fair distribution of revenues, economic independence, and an end to political corruption.

Chapter 13

1. The other great monotheistic religion, Judaism, is distinguished by its inward-looking nature, as conversion is not one of its central tenets. By establishing more rigid conditions for belonging, such as tracing Jewish "membership" through maternal bloodlines, it becomes a more closed group. This explains the comparative demographics of these three groups: with more than 2 billion Christians, 1.2 billion of which are Catholic, and 1.5 billion Muslims, there are only 13 million people on the planet that belong to the Jewish faith.

Bibliography

"'*Addio ai Monti*' dal Captiolo VIII de '*I Promessi Sposi*' di Alessandro Manzoni," CRDC: Coro Drammatico Renato Condoleo, accessed March 30, 2013, http://www.cdrc.it/TestiCDRC%5CManzaddio.html.

Andreassi, Cecilia. "History of Peronism, Part I." *The Argentina Independent*. October 11, 2011. http://www.argentinaindependent.com/currentaffairs/analysis/the-history-of-peronism-part-i/.

ANS: Agencia Info Salesiana. "Papa Francisco y los Salesianos." *ANS: Agencia Info Salesiana*. March 19, 2013. http://www.infoans.org/1.asp?Lingua=3&sez=1&doc=8992.

Argen, David. "In Buenos Aires Slum, Church Counters Drugs, Evangelicals." *Catholic News Service*. March 18, 2013. http://www.catholicnews.com/data/stories/cns/1301244.htm.

Bergoglio, Jorge, and Abraham Skorka. *Sobre el Cielo y la Tierra*. Buenos Aires: Sudamericana, 2010.

Blustein, Paul. "Argentina Didn't Fall on Its Own: Wall Street Pushed Debt Till the Last." *The Washington Post*. August 3, 2003. http://www.washingtonpost.com/wp-srv/business/articles/argentinatimeline.html.

Brienza, Hernán. *Maldito Eres Tú: El Caso Von Wernich, Iglesia y Represión Ilegal*. Buenos Aires: Marea Editorial, 2003.

Camarasa, Jorge A. *El Verdugo: Astiz, un Soldado del terrorismo de Estado*. Buenos Aires: Planeta, 2009.

Carpena, Ricardo. "Entrevista con Luiz Inácio Lula da Silva: 'No Puedo Imaginar a Brasil y la Argentina Sperarados." *La Nacion*. April 19, 2009. http://www.lanacion.com.ar/1119713-no-puedo-imaginar-a-brasil-y-la-argentina-separados.

Castro, Jorge. *Dios en la Plaza Pública*. Buenos Aires: Agape Libros, 2012.

"Catechism of the Catholic Church," The Holy See official website, last accessed July 19, 2013, http://www.vatican.va/archive/ENG0015/_INDEX.HTM.

Catholic News Service. "Timeline of the Life of Pope Francis." *Catholic Review*. March 17, 2013. http://catholicreview.org/article/home/timeline-of-the-life-of-pope-francis.

Chossudovsky, Michael. "'Washington's Pope?' Who is Pope Francis I? Cardinal Jorge Mario Bergoglio and Argentina's 'Dirty War.'" *Global Research: Centre for Research on Globalization*. March 16, 2013. http://www.globalresearch.ca/washingtons-pope -who-is-francis-i-cardinal-jorge-mario-bergoglio-and-argentinas-dirty-war/5326675.

"CIA World Factbook," Central Intelligence Agency online global statistics, last accessed June 22, 2013, https://www.cia.gov/library/publications/the-world-factbook/.

Crassweller, Robert D. *Perón and the Enigmas of Argentina*. New York: W.W. Norton & Company, 1988.

D'Alencon, F. Ubald. *The Writings of St. Francis of Assisi*, trans. Countess Constance De La Warr. London: Burns & Oates, 1907. PDF, e-book. http://archive.org/details/ writingsofstfran00fran.

Dapelo, Santiago. "La Pobreza, a Preocupación Que lo Desvela Desde Joven: En una Carta de 1960, el Papa Habla de los Que No Tienen qué Comer." *La Nacion*. March 18, 2013. http://www.lanacion.com.ar/1564349-la-pobreza-una-preocupacion-que -lo-desvela-desde-joven.

Díez, Carlos Collantes. "Liberación y Opción Preferencial por los Pobres." *Misionero Javeriano*. http://www.javerianos.org/MaterialAnimacion/Formacion/LaMision/ LaMision12.htm.

"Do You Speak Ignatian? A Glossary of Terms Used in Ignatian and Jesuit Circles," webpage by George W. Traub, S.J., hosted by Xavier University, 2002, http://www. mountmanresa.org/documents/2008/Do_You_Speak_Ignatian.pdf.

Englebert, Omer. *St. Francis of Assisi: A Biography*. Ann Arbor, MI: Servant Books, 1979.

El Litoral. "Es un Papa que Tiene Sintonía con lo que la Pasa a la Gente." *El Litoral*, March 14, 2013. http://www.ellitoral.com/index.php/diarios/2013/03/14/ internacionales/INTE-06.html.

El Nuevo Herald. "Papa Francisco Nació a la Fe en la Iglesia de Gardel," *El Nuevo Herald*. March 20, 2013. http://www.elnuevoherald.com/2013/03/20/1435385/ fotogaleria-20-03-112313.html#.

Evita Perón Historical Research Foundation, Dolane Larson, trans. "To Be Evita, Part II, The Day Which Split History: October 17, 1945." April, 1997. http://www. evitaperon.org/part2.htm.

Frederick, John, and Laura Giubergia. *Crónicas de la Calle: Apuntes sobre los excluidos* (blog). April 4, 2009. http://cronicasdelacalle.wordpress.com/2009/04/04/la-droga -en-las-villas-despenalizada-de-hecho/.

Gallego, Juan María Laboa. *Historia de los Papas: Entre el Reino de Dios y alas Pasiones Terrenales*. Madrid: Esfera de los Libros, 2011.

"Ignatian Spirituality," Society of Jesus' official website, last accessed June 7, 2013, http://www.jesuit.org/spirituality.

Irigaray, Juan Ignacio. "Jorge Mario Bergoglio, el Primer Papa Jesuita: Duro con los Kirchner, Blando con la Dictadura." *El Mundo*. March 14, 2013. http://www.elmundo. es/elmundo/tags/9f/francisco-i.html.

Jenkins, Philip, "The Pope from Beyond the Seas. Philip Jenkins." *The Chronicle of Higher Education: The Conversation* (blog), March 13, 2013, http://chronicle.com/blogs/conversation/2013/03/13/the-pope-from-beyond-the-seas/.

"Jesuit Education," Jesuit Curia in Rome official website, last accessed June 22, 2013, http://www.sjweb.info/education/.

"Jesuits and Heraldry," webpage hosted by Sancta Maria Abbey,Nunraw, last accessed May 29, 2013, http://www.nunraw.com/SACMUS/jesuitheraldry/cardinals.htm.

Koepsel, Rachel. "Mothers of the Plaza de Mayo: First Responders for Human Rights." Case-specific briefing paper for Humanitarian Assistance in Complex Emergencies, University of Denver, 2011. http://www.du.edu/korbel/criic/humanitarianbriefs/rachelkoepsel.pdf.

La Gaceta. "El papa Francisco goza de una 'salud de hierro.'" *La Gaceta*. Sunday, March 17, 2013. http://www.lagaceta.com.ar/nota/537004/mundo/papa-francisco-goza -salud-hierro.html.

Lagos, Ovidio. *Principessa Mafalda, Historia de dos Tragedias*. Buenos Aires: El Ateneo Editorial, 2009.

La Nacion. "Bergoglio, El Cardenal Que No le Teme al Poder." *La Nacion*. July 26, 2009. http://www.lanacion.com.ar/1153060-bergoglio-el-cardenal-que-no-le-teme-al -poder.

———. "Fervor por el Papa: El 90% Tiene una Imagen Positiva de Francisco." *La Nacion*. April 14, 2013. http://www.lanacion.com.ar/1572528-fervor-por-el-papa-el -90-tiene-una-imagen-positiva-de-francisco.

"La Vita di Don Orione," Sito Ufficiale della Piccola Opera della Divina Provvidenza, last accessed February 22, 2013, http://www.donorione.org/#.

Lynch, John. *Argentine Caudillo: Juan Manuel de Rosas*. Lanham, MD: SR Books, 2006.

Martin, José Pablo. *El Movimiento de Sacerdotes para el Tercer Mundo*. Buenos Aires: Universidad Nacional de General Sarimento, 2010.

Mignone, Emilio Fermín. *Iglesia y Dictadura*. Buenos Aires: Colihue, 1986.

Mon, Hugo Alconada. "'Soy Bergoglio, Cura': Vida Intima y Obra del Papa que Llegó del Fin del Mundo." *La Nacion*. March 17, 2013. http://www.lanacion.com. ar/1564072-soy-bergoglio-cura-vida-intima-y-obra-del-papa-que-llego-del-fin-del -mundo.

Nassar, Ricardo Acosta. "The Contribution of the CELAM Conclusion Conferences in Puebla and Santo Domingo Concerning Inculturation." Taken from: Martínez Ferrer, and Luis and Ricardo Acosta Narssar. *Inculturación: Magisterio de la Iglesia y Documentos eclesiásticos*. San José, Costa Rica: Promesa, 2006. http://www.inculturacion.net/phocadownload/Ensayos/Acosta,_Contribution_of_Puebla_%20and_Sto_Domingo.pdf.

"On the 25th Anniversary of the Pueble Conference," by Card. Alfonso López Trujillo, The Holy See official website, February, 2004, http://www.vatican.va/roman_curia/pontifical_councils/family/documents/rc_pc_family_doc_20040212_trujillo-puebla_en.html.

Page, Joseph A. *Perón: Una Biografía*. Buenos Aires: Grijalbo, 1991.

Peregil, Francisco. "La Iglesia Argentina Dio la Espalda a la Mayoría de los Crímenes de la Dictadura." *El País*. March 23, 2013. http://internacional.elpais.com/internacional/2013/03/23/actualidad/1364057234_327032.html.

Pigna, Felipe. "La Gente Venía del Sur." Related testimonial of Sebastián Borro, a worker who participated in October 17, 1945 demonstration for the liberation of Perón. Originally appeared in *La Opinión Cultural*, October 15, 1972 issue. *El Historiador*. http://www.elhistoriador.com.ar/articulos/ascenso_y_auge_del_peronismo/17_de_octubre_de_1945.php.

"Plenary Indulgences," New Advent: The Catholic Encyclopedia online, last accessed May 14, 2013, http://www.newadvent.org/cathen/07783a.htm.

Potash, Roberto. *El Ejército y la Política en la Argentina*. Buenos Aires: Sudamericana, 1971.

Premat, Silvina. *Curas Villeros*. Buenos Aires: Sudamericana, 2009.

"Rereading of the Document 'History and Change' on its 20th Anniversary: Words Spoken by Your Emminence Jorge M. Bergoglio, S.J.," USAL: Universidad del Salvador, last accessed May 14, 2013, http://www.usal.edu.ar/en/history.

Riccardi, Andrea. *Juan Pablo II: La Biografia*. Buenos Aires, San Pablo, 2011.

Rubin, Sergio, and Francesca Ambrogetti. *El Jesuita: Conversaciones Con el Cardenal Jorge Bergoglio*. Buenos Aires: Javier Vergara Editor S.A., 2010.

———. *El Jesuita: La Historia de Francisco, el Papa Argentino*. 2nd ed. Buenos Aires: Javier Vergara Editor S.A., 2013.

Rush, Cynthia R. "Argentina: Center of Global Economic Battle." *EIR: Executive Intelligence Review*. December 10, 2004. http://www.larouchepub.com/eiw/public/2004/eirv31/eirv31n48.pdf.

"San Bonaventura: Leyenda Mayor de San Francisco," Directorio Franciscano, accessed March 30, 2013, http://www.franciscanos.org/fuentes/lma00.html.

"San Francisco de Asís," Directorio Franciscano, last accessed April 30, 2013, http://www.franciscanos.org/sfa/menud.html.

Sanguinetti, Julio María. "Argentina: ¿Fue o Es?" *El País*. June 21, 2001. http://elpais.com/diario/2001/06/21/opinion/993074410_850215.html.

Seaone, María, and Felipe Pigna. *La Noche de los Bastones Largos*. Buenos Aires: Caras y Caretas, 2006.

Shah, Anup. "Poverty Facts and Stats." *Global Issues*. Page last updated Monday, January 7, 2013. http://www.globalissues.org/article/26/poverty-facts-and-stats.

Terra. "Bergoglio Presenta su Renuncia Como Arzobispo de Buenos Aires, Aunque Seguirá en el Cargo. *Terra*. December 15, 2011. http://noticias.terra.com.ar/politica/bergoglio-presenta-su-renuncia-como-arzobispo-de-buenos-aires-aunque-seguira-en-el-cargo,148ef548c2444310VgnVCM20000099f154d0RCRD.html.

The Economist. "The Catholic Church in America: Earthly Concerns." *The Economist*. August 18, 2012. http://www.economist.com/node/21560536.

"The Remission of Temporal Punishment: Instructions Regarding Indulgences," Catholic Doors Ministry website, last accessed April 9, 2013, http://www.catholicdoors.com/teaching/book2/2-9.htm.

Tornielli, Andrea. "A Cardinal on the Subway: An Excerpt from *Francis: Pope of a New World*." The Catholic World Report. April 18, 2013. http://www.catholicworldreport.com/Item/2193/a_cardinal_on_the_subway.aspx.

———. "Jorge Mario Bergoglio, Francesco I, 'Vengo quasi dalla fine del mondo.'" *Vatican Insider, La Stampa*. March, 14, 2013. http://vaticaninsider.lastampa.it/vaticano/dettaglio-articolo/articolo/conclave-23131/.

Valente, Marcela. "RIGHTS-ARGENTINA: Priest's Life Sentence Draws Widespread Praise." *IPS: Inter Press Service*. October 10, 2007. http://www.ipsnews.net/2007/10/rights-argentina-priestrsquos-life-sentence-draws-widespread-praise/.

Vedia, Bartolomé de. "La Quema de Iglesias: Furia Contra los Templos." *La Nacion*. June 12, 2005. http://www.lanacion.com.ar/712038-la-quema-de-iglesias-furia-contra-los-templos.

Verbitsky, Horatio. "Cambio de Piel." *Pagina 12*. March 17, 2013. http://www.pagina12.com.ar/diario/elpais/1-215961-2013-03-17.html.

"Vida de Don Bosco," Official website of Don Bosco, Argentina, accessed May 12, 2013, http://donbosco.org.ar/vida_de_don_bosco.php.

Wagner, Luis Agüero. *Esther Ballestrino: Madre de la Plaza de Mayo; Homenaje del Movimiento Feberista F17 a 30 Años de su Desparación*. Buenos Aires: F17, 2007.

"World Bank 2008 World Development Indicators: Poverty Data," World Bank supplement, last accessed May 31, 2013, http://siteresources.worldbank.org/DATASTATISTICS/Resources/WDI08supplement1216.pdf.

"World Economic Outlook Database," April 2012 Edition, International Monetary Fund official website, last accessed March 22, 2013, http://www.imf.org/external/pubs/ft/weo/2012/01/weodata/index.aspx.

Index

A

Abbé Chatel, 140

Abortion, 92, 158, 179

Abrolhos, Brazil, 10

"Active schism," "passive schism" vs., 138

Administration, in Eastern Orthodox vs. Roman Catholic Church, 145–146

Adoption, by same-sex couples, 162

Adventists, 143

Afghanistan, 124, 125, 185

African-American civil rights movement, 75

Agnostics, 138, 151

Albania, 142

Albanian Orthodox Church, 141

Alexander VI, Pope, 168

Alhena (ship), 9, 10

Almagro district, Buenos Aires, Argentina, 19, 20

Álvarez, Alejandro "Gallego," 79–80

Amalia (childhood girlfriend), 24–25

Amaziah, priest of Bethel, 86

Ambrogetti, Francesca, 82

Ameno, Italy, 132

American Orthodox Church, 141

Amish, 143

Amos (prophet), 76, 85–86, 88

Anabaptists, 143

Anacletus II, 139

Anglican Church, 140, 149–150

Angola, Africa, 37

Animals, Saint Francis of Assisi as patron saint of, 115

Anne, Saint, 144

Anne Boleyn, Queen, 140

Antico, Gustavo, 42–43

Aparecida, Brazil, 96–97

Aparecida Document, 97–98, 97–99

Apartheid, 75

Apostolic Constitution, 100, 149–150

Apostolic Palace of Castel Gandolfo, 100

Aquileia Schism, 139

Aragon, Magister Raul, 162

Archbishop Primate of Argentina, 47

Argentina

    corruption in, 174

    Dirty War, 30, 71, 81–82

    economic recession, 1998-2002, 86, 87–88

    Falkland Islands War, 103

    Feast of Our Lady of Luján in, 63–64

    Francis' May Revolution homily on (1998), 86–87

    higher education system in, 44–45

    emigration from Europe to, 4–7

    Iron Guard in, 79–80

Mothers of the Plaza de Mayo
    kidnapping in, 29–31
Peronism in, 31–34, 67–68, 69–70
Principessa Mafalda sinking on trip
    to, 9–15
reaction to Pope Francis' election in,
    180–181
relationship with Brazil, 194
same-sex marriage in, 160, 161
slums in, 58–61
Society of Jesus in, 173
Sons of Divine Providence in, 17
split among Peronists in, 70–71
youth group and camp in, 20–21
youth movement on university
    campuses (1960s), 77–78
Argentinean Revolution period, 77
Argentine Communist Party, 39
Argentine Federal Police, 77
Argentine Team of Forensic
    Anthropology, 30
Arrupe, Pedro, 79
Asia, expanding Catholic Church in, 107
Astiz, Alfredo, 30, 31
Atheism, 138, 154–155, 177, 179, 193
*A Theology of Liberation: History, Politics,
    and Salvation (Gutiérrez)*, 74
Auca, Bishop of, 46–47
Autocephalous Archbishoprics, 141
Auxiliary Bishop of Buenos Aires, 46
Aztec Empire, 167–168

B

Bajo Flores, 81
Banderas, Antonio, 33
Baptism, 145
Baptists, 143, 149
Barletta, Leónidas, 69
Bartholomew, Ecumenical Patriarch,
    151–152
Bartolomé de las Casas, Fray, 172
Base Communities, 74
Batista, Fulgencio, 176
Battle of Milvian Bridge, 135
Bay of Pigs invasion, 176
Beagle conflict, 52

Becchi, Italy, 16
Belarus, 142, 179
Belgium, 160
Belize, 175
Benedict XVI, Pope, 80, 101, 114, 118
    Aparecida Document, 97
    Caritas in Veritae encyclical, 127
    ecumenism and, 149, 150
    election of, 94–95
    excommunication of bishops repealed
        under, 140
    on pedophilia, 163
    resignation of, 99–100
    transition phase of papacy of, 193
Berbers, North African, 136
Bergoglio, Jorge Mario. *see also* Francis, Pope
    appointed as Auxiliary Bishop of
        Buenos Aires, 46, 52–54
    as Archbishop of Argentina, 47, 57
    on Argentina's higher education
        system, 44–45
    birth, 16, 22
    as Bishop of Auca, 46–47
    calling to priesthood, 34–38
    as Cardinal, 47–48, 58, 92–93
    in Córdoba, 45–46
    early female influences on, 28–31
    employment during teen years, 26–27
    female influences on, 16, 17, 23–25
    on financial social crisis, 1998-2002,
        89–90
    in Germany, 43–44
    home in Buenos Aires Cathedral,
        54–56
    Iron Guard and, 78–79
    Kirchners, relationship with, 90–92
    letter from grandmother to, 41–42
    at Luján feasts, 63–64
    ordained a priest, 78
    ordained as deacon, 42
    parents, 19
    on pedophilia cases, 164–165
    Peronism and, 31–34
    political interests and affiliations,
        38–39, 67, 68–69, 70, 77, 78–79, 80,
        90–92
    poverty, first experience with, 123

"practical" religion of, 62
priesthood, 42–43
as professor, 40–41
relationship with father, 25–26
residences, 55–56, 89–90
in seminary, 39–40
slum priests/slum work and, 58–62
succession to John Paul II and, 93–95
Te Deum messages of, 86–87, 88, 90
Bergoglio, Juan, 4, 15
Bergoglio, María Elena (sister), 38, 76
Bergoglio, Mario José Francisco (father),
6, 15, 16, 19, 22, 25–26
Bergoglio, Regina Maria Sivori (mother),
22, 23, 38
Bergoglio, Rosa Margarita Vasallo de
(grandmother), 3, 4–8, 15–16, 38,
41–42, 57
Bergoglio Palace, 4
Bernardone, Giovanni di. See Francis of
Assisi, Saint
Bertone, Tarcisio, 101
"Bertonians," 101
The Betrothed (Manzoni), 24
Bianco, Mary, 30, 31
Bible, the, 142, 147
Bishops
administrative authority of, 145–146
Aparecida Document, 97–98
auxiliary, 46
baptism/confirmation and, 145
coup d'état of 1976 and, 52
right to primacy, 145–146
Second Vatican Council, 73
in structure of Catholic Church, 192
"Black Front," 79
Boff, Leonardo, 75
Bolivar, Simón, 172
Bolivarian Revolution, 98
Bolivia, 173, 174, 178
Bolivian immigrants, 59
Bonafini, Hebe de, 104
Bonaparte, Napoleon, 37, 169
Bonaventure, Saint, 113–114
Book of Amos, 86
Borges, Jorge Luis, 19, 40–41
Borro, Sebastián, 33

Bosco, Giovanni (Don Bosco), 16, 20, 37,
129–131
Bosco, Saint John, 131
Bosnia and Herzegovina, 142
Bottega, Graciela, 62
Boxer Rebellion, 188–189
Brazil
Aparecida, 96–97
Argentina's relationship with, 194
Base Communities in, 74
birth rate, 184
Getulio Vargas phenomenon, 68
liberation theology, 74–75
in new world order, 195
Principessa Mafalda and, 9, 10
Salesian Order in, 130
same-sex marriage in, 160
slavery in, 132, 170
Sons of Divine Providence in, 17
Brienne, Gaulterio de, 109
Buenos Aires, Argentina
civil unions in, 161
emigration from Europe to, 5–6
Plaza de Mayo, 32, 33, 34, 69
Santa Cruz Church, 29, 30, 31
slums, 47, 58–61
student youth movement, 77–78
Buenos Aires Cathedral, 46, 47, 53–55, 92
Bulgaria, 142
Bulgarian Orthodox Church, 141
Burkina Faso, 125
Bush, George H.W., 52

C
Cabildo, 32
Cafasso, Giuseppe (Don Cafasso), 129, 131
Calabresi, Ubaldo, 46, 51–52, 57–58
Calvin, John, 93, 136, 139, 142
Calvinists, 136
Canada, 119, 160
Carballo, José Rodríguez, 118
Cardinals, 192
Careaga, Esther Ballestrino de, 27, 28–31,
39, 68–69
Caritas in Veritae (Charity of Truth)
encyclical, 127

Carlotto, Estela de, 103–104
Carrara, Father Gustavo, 61–62
Carter, Jimmy, 178
Casa chorizo, 22
Casa Loyola (Jesuit seminary), 39–40
Casa Rosada, 32, 33, 88
Castellano, Ramón José, 41
Castille
    Kingdom of, 54, 168
    Crown of, 167
Castro, Fidel, 176, 177
Castro, Raul, 176
Castro brothers, in Cuba, 97
Catechism of the Catholic Church, 159
Cathars, the, 111
Catholic Action movement, 74
Catholic Church
    breakaway movements from, 138
    Cuban revolutionaries and, 176–177
    Eastern Orthodox Church and, 139,
        143–146
    England's breakaway from, 140
    finances, 192–193
    First Vatican Council, 71, 73, 140, 144
    Great Schism and, 139
    hierarchical structure of, 191–192
    international influence of, 140–141,
        192–193
    new phase of, 193–194
    political and geostratic role, 193
    Protestantism, 136, 139–140, 147–148
    role during Argentina's dictatorship,
        52
    role in Latin American government
        and culture, 171–173
    role in overcoming poverty, 125–127,
        134
    Second Vatican Council, 52, 71,
        72–74, 149
    on suicide, 159
    Twenty-First Century Socialism and,
        179
    Western Schism and, 139
    women's role in, 157–158
Catholic Corpus Christi procession, June
    11, 1955, 69
Catholic Worker's Circle, 63

Cayetano, Saint, 64
Celibacy, of clergy, 145, 147, 157
Center for Legal and Social Studies
    (CELS), 81
Centesimus Annus (Hundredth Year)
    encyclical, 127
Central African Republic, 124
Central America. see also Latin America
    drug trade in, 175
    poverty in, 173–174
Central Federal Commission, 33
Chapel of San Antonio de Padua, 19, 20, 21
Charity, Pope Francis on, 128–129
Chávez, Hugo, 97, 98, 177–179
Chieri, seminary at, 129
Chile, 17, 52, 76–77, 179
China
    birth rate in, 184
    Catholicism in, 107
    GDP, 184
    history, 188–189
    in new world order, 183, 185,
        189–190, 195
Chinese National Bureau of Statistics, 189
Christian ecumenism. See Ecumenism
Christianity. see also individual
    denominations
        conflict with Muslims, 136–137
        divisions and dissension within,
            138–140
        early persecution of Christians, 135
        schism concept and, 138
        Christianity and Revolution, 81
Chrysostom, Saint John, 62
Church of Cyprus, 141
Church of England, 149
Church of Greece, 141
Church of Rome. See Catholic Church
Church's Social Doctrine, 126–127
CIA World Factbook, 125, 143, 184
Cicconi, Cesare, 102
Civil rights movement (United States), 75
Clare of Assisi, Saint, 118
Claypole, Argentina, 132
Clementine Hall, Apostolic Palace, 152
Clement XIV, Pope, 108, 173
"Clement XV" name, 108

Clergy. *See* Priests/priesthood
Codrenau, Cornelieu, 78
Cold War, 73, 176
Colegio de la Inmaculada Concepción de
    Santa Fe, 4040
Colegio del Salvador, 44
Colegio Maximo de San Jose, 40, 42
College of Cardinals, 48–49, 93, 102, 192
Colonization, in Latin America, 167–169
Columbus, Christopher, 167
Communion, 144–145
Communist Party, 39, 69
Company of Jesus, 79, 108
Company of Jesus Church, 45
Concentración Nacional Universitaria, 78
Conclave, 71, 72, 93, 100–102
Confirmation, 145
Congregationalists, 143
Congregation for the Oriental Churches, 81
Congress of Vienna, 129
Constantine I, emperor, 135
Constantine the Great, 135
Constantinople, 139, 145–146
Constitutions, the, 42
Convertibility, 88
Córdoba, 38, 45–46, 51, 53, 92
Corralito, 88
Correa, Rafael, 179
Corruption, 174
Corruption Perceptions Index, 174
Cortés, Hérnan, 168
Costa, Nino, 57
Cottolengo, 132
Council of Florence, 139, 146
Council of Trent, 73, 142
Croatia, 142
Crossing the Threshold of Hope (Messori), 95
Crusades, the, 136
Cuba, 97, 175–177
Cuban War for Independence, 175
Curas villaros (slum priests), 58, 89
Cypress, 87
Cyprus, 142
Czech and Slovak Orthodox Church, 141

D
Da Cunha family, 9
Da Vinci Code saga, 99
Death, 159–160
Dei Filius (Son of God) doctrine, 71
De la Rúa, Fernando, 86, 88
Deng Xiaoping, 189
Denmark, 160
Diocesan Seminary of Villa Devoto, 39
Dioceses, 192
Di Paola, Father José María "Pepe." See
    Pepe, Father
"Diplomats," 101
Dirty War, 30, 69, 71, 81–82
Divorce, 160
Doctrine of the Perpetual Virginity of
    Mary, 144
Dogmatic discrepancies, between
    Catholic and Eastern Orthodox
    Churches, 143–144
Dolan, Timothy, 101
Dominican Republic, 77
Dominus ac Redemptor, 108
Domon, Alice, 29
Donatist Schism, 139
Don Bosco (Bosco, Giovanni), 16, 20, 37,
    129–131
Don Bosco Explorers, 20
Don Cafasso (Cafasso, Giuseppe), 129, 131
Don Orione (Orione, Luigi), 16–17, 129,
    131–132
Don Segundo Sombra (Güiraldes), 40
Dostoevsky, Fyodor, 40
Drug trade/crime, 60–61, 174–175
Duquet, Sister Leonie, 29

E
Eastern Orthodox Church, 139, 141, 142
    administrative differences between
        Roman Catholic Church and,
        145–146
    baptism in, 145
    bread used for Eucharist in, 144
    dogmatic differences between Roman
        Catholic Church and, 143–144
    ecumenism and, 149, 151–152

on Immaculate Conception, 144
liturgical differences between Roman
    Catholic Church and, 144–145
East-West Schism (Great Schism), 139
Economic crisis, 1998-2002, 87–88
Economic Policy and Poverty Reduction
    Programs for Africa, 133
Economist, 162, 192
Ecuador, 130, 178
    Salesian Order in, 130
Ecumenical Council, 145
Ecumenical Patriarch, 141
Ecumenical Patriarch Batholomew, 151–152
Ecumenism
    administrative differences, 145–146
    branches of Christian churches,
        140–143
    divisions/schisms with Christianity,
        138–140
    dogmatic differences, 143–144
    dogmatic discrepancies, 143–144
    explained, 137–138
    Islam-Christian conflict, 136–137
    in late eighteenth and early
        nineteenth centuries, 148
    liturgical differences and, 144–145
    Pontifical Council, 149
    Pope Francis' efforts for, 150–152
    Protestant-Catholic differences, 136,
        139–140, 147–148
    reunification and reconciliation
        efforts, 149–150
    Ukrainian Greek Catholic Church,
        146–147
    World Council of Churches, 148–149
Edict of Milan, 135
Education
    in Argentina, 44–45
    Catholic Church's role in Latin
        American, 172–173
    poverty and access to, 125
    religion in, 156
    in United States, 184
Egan, Cardinal Edward, 95–96
Eighty Years' War (1568-1547), 136
"El Cuervo" (Juan José Jaime), 55
El Cura Lorenzo (film), 22

Eliade, Mircea, 79
El Jesuita (Rubin/Ambrogetti), 82
El Mundo, 67
Encyclicals, 126–127, 149
England, 136, 140, 186
Englebert, Omer, 108, 109
Entre Ríos, Argentina, 4
Environmental concerns, 115–116
Episcopal Pastoral Vicar for Slums in
    Crisis, 58
ESMA (Escuela Mecánica de la Armada),
    29, 30, 81, 82
Estonia, 142
Ethiopia, 4
Eucharist, 144–145, 147–148
Eugene IV, Pope, 139
Europe, 186
European Union, 186
Eurozone, 186
Euthanasia, 159–160
Evangelical churches, 148
Evangelization, 191
Evita (musical and film), 33
Evita (person), 31, 34
Ezeiza Airport, Buenos Aires, 70

F
Faith, ways of arriving at, 59
Farrell, Ederlmiro J., 32
Fasci Italiani di Combattimento, 3
Feast of Saint Cayetano, 64
Federative Republic of Brazil, 132
Felix V, Pope, 139
Feminism, 118, 158
Ferdinand VII of the Bourbons, King, 169
Fe y Alegría, 117
Fifth Crusade, 112
Fifth General Conference of Bishops
    of Latin America and the Caribbean,
    Aparecida, Brazil, 96, 97
First and Second Opium Wars, 188
First Council of Nicaea, 135
First Vatican Council, 71, 73, 140, 144
Flores, Buenos Aires, church of, 35
Food and Agriculture Organization of the
    United Nations (FAO), 124

Forzosos de Almagro (The Force of
   Almagro), 21
Fourth Lateran Council, 111
France, 111, 142
Francis, Pope. *see also* Bergoglio, Jorge
   Mario
   on abortion, 158
   on aging and euthanasia, 159–160
   Aparecida Document, 97–98, 97–99
   on atheism, 154–155
   breaking tradition, 102–103
   conclave appointing, 100–102
   on divorce, 160
   Eastern Orthodox Church and,
      151–152, 187–188
   ecumenism and, 150–152
   on homosexuality/same-sex marriage,
      161–162
   on hypocrisy in the church, 63
   on inequality and oppression, 77, 86
   influence on Latin American region,
      179–181
   inspirations for working with poverty,
      129–132
   international recognition of, 95–96
   on justice, 64–65
   linked to kidnapping of priests, 1976,
      80–83
   name choice by, 107–108, 114–119,
      120
   position on material and spiritual
      poverty, 127–129
   qualities and characteristics of,
      103–104, 119–120
   on science, 155–156
Franciscan Order, 111–112, 117–118, 129
Francis of Assisi, Saint, 6
   biography, 108–113
   canonization of, 113
   name of Pope Francis and, 107, 108,
      117
   physical description of, 113–114
   Pope Francis on, 72–73
   Saint Clare of Assisi and, 118
   teachings of Jesus and, 75–76
   Testament written in April 1226,
      120–121

Francis of Sales, Saint, 131
Francis Solano, Saint, 108
Francis Xavier, Saint, 107
Franco-Prussian War, 71
Freedland, Jonathan, 184
Freire, Paulo, 74
French Catholic Church, 140
French Revolution, 140
Friars Minor order, 118
Fulbo, 20
Funes, María Elena, 81

G
G20 (Group of Twenty Finance Ministers
   and Central Bank Governors), 194–195
Gabrielle, Paolo, 100
Gallego, José María Laboa, 138
Garay, Juan de, 54
Garda de Fier, 78
Gay marriage, 92, 160–162, 179
GDP. *See* Gross domestic product (GDP)
General Labor Alliance, 33
General Management of "Urban Order,"
   77
Georgia, 142
Georgian Orthodox Church, 141
Germany, 43–44, 140, 142, 143, 185
Giménez, Darío, 62
Gini Index, 174
Giugale, Marcelo, 133–134
Giulio Cesare (ship), 8, 15
Great Schism, 139, 146
Greece, 87, 141, 142
Gregory III, Syrian, 101
Gross domestic product (GDP)
   Argentina, 87
   China, 189, 190
   India, 190
   United States, 184, 190
Grote, Father Federico, 63
Guardia de Hierro (Iron Guard), 78–79
Guardini, Romano, 43–44
Guerrilla movements, 70, 75, 83
Guevara, Ernesto "Che," 176
Güiraldes, Ricardo, 40
Gutiérrez, Gustavo, 74

H

Hapsburg Catholics, 136
Henry VIII, King, 140
Heresy, 138
Historia de los Papas: Entre el Reino de Dios y las Pasiones Terrenales (History of the Popes: Between the Kingdom of God and Earthly Passions) (Gallego), 138–139
Hitler, Adolph, 4, 187
Hölderlin, Friedrich, 17
Hole See, 146
Holland, 140, 160
Holocaust, the, 137
Holy Land, 112, 116, 136
Holy Orders of Catholicism, 147
Holy Roman Empire, 109, 136. *see also* Roman Empire
Holy Spirit, origin of, 143–144
Holy Thursday ritual, 59–60
Homosexuality, 118, 161–162. *see also* Same-sex marriage
Honduras, 174
Honorius III, Pope, 112
Human Opportunity Index, 133–134
Human trafficking, 59
Hummes, Cardinal Claudio, 72
Hungary, 142
Hurtado, Saint Alberto, 39

I

Iberian Peninsula, 46, 109, 136, 168, 169
Iceland, 124, 160
Iglesia y Dictadura (Church and Dictatorship), 81
Ignatius of Loylola, Saint, 37, 42, 107
"Il Duce" (Mussolini), 4
Il Giornale, 95
Immaculada Concepción School, 41
Immaculate Conception, 144
Immigrants
    to Argentina, 6–7
    Bolivian, in Argentina, 59
    in Europe, 186
    in North America, 5–6
Inca Empire, 167–168
India, 183, 190, 195

Infant mortality, poverty and, 124
Innocent II, Pope, 139
Innocent III, Pope, 111
Institute for the Works of Religion (Vatican Bank), 104
International Monetary Fund (IMF), 88, 184, 190
Interreligious cooperation, 116–117. *see also* Ecumenism
Iran, 154, 179
Iraq, 185
Ireland, 136, 160, 163
Irish Republican Army (IRA), 136
Iron Guard, 78–80
Islam, 112, 116, 136–137, 150
Italy
    fascism in, 3–4, 7
    Franciscan order in, 111
    Holy Roman Empire and, 109
    emigration from, 4–5, 7
    name of "Francis" in, 119
    Piedmont region, 3, 16, 129–130, 131, 133

J

Jaime, Juan José, 55
Jalics, Father Francisco, 80–83
Jansenism, 130, 131, 140
Japan, 68, 124, 185
Jesuit priests, kidnapping of, 83, 180
Jesuit Reductions, 173
Jesuits (Society of Jesus)
    Clement XIV and, 108
    Córdoba and, 45
    institutions of, 117
    overview, 37–38
    Pope Francis and, 40, 42, 43, 44, 46, 71
    power within the Catholic Church, 117
    Saint Ignatius of Loyola, 37, 39, 108
    suppression/expulsion of, 108, 173
Jesuit Seminary of Santiago de Chile, 76
Jews/Judaism, 137, 150
John Paul II, Pope
    Apostolic Constitution approved by, 100
    Calabresi and, 51
    Castro and, 177

conservatism, 94
death, 48, 93
Don Orione canonized by, 132
encyclicals issued by, 126–127, 149
Luján pilgrimage, 64
Pontifical Council for Interreligious
Dialogue, 150
Pope Francis and, 46, 47, 58, 80, 93
Soviet Empire and, 180, 193
succession to, 93, 95
John VI, King of Portugal, 169
John XXII, Pope, 149
John XXIII, Pope, 71–73
Judaism/Jews, 137, 150
Justice, Pope Francis on, 64–65
Justice and Peace Commission, 73–74
Justicialist movement, 70

K
Kazakhstan, 142
Kerygma, 59
Kiev, Ukraine, 146
King, Martin Luther Jr., 75
Kingdom of Samaria, 85
Kirchner, Cristina Fernández de, 67, 81,
91, 92, 99, 103, 179, 180
Kirchner, Néstor, 67, 90–91, 179
Kyrgyzstan, 142

L
Laboreum Exercens (On Human Work)
encyclical, 126
*La Comunidad Organizada (An
Organized Community)*, 79
"La Gente Venia del Sur" (Pigna), 33
Laghi, Pio, 52
La Nación, 123, 180
La Noche de los Bastones Largos (the
Night of the Long Batons), 78
La Opinión (newspaper), 33
Last Supper, 144
Latin, 73
Latin America. *see also* individual
country names
Aparecida Document, 97–99
Base Communities in, 74

Castro revolutionaries and, 176–177
Catholic Church's role in, 171–173
Chávism, 178–179
colonization and multiculturalism in,
167–169
corruption in, 174
drug trade and violence in, 174–175
economies of, 170–171
global role, 183
independence from European
colonization, 169–170
potential for new role of, 195
poverty in, 173–174
theological doctrine of, 75
Latin American Church
Aparecida Document, 97–99
relationship with government, 172
Second Vatican Council and, 74
Latin Church, 192
Latvia, 142
Law, Cardinal Bernard, 164
Leadership Conference of Women
Religious (LCWR), 118
Lebanon, 142
Lei Áurea (Golden Law), 170
Leo XIII, Pope, 125, 126
L'Espresso, 94
Liberation theology, 74–75, 76, 81
Libya, 179
Licinius I, Emperor, 135
Life expectancy, poverty and, 124
Literacy rate, 125
Lithuania, 142
"Litte Italy" neighborhoods, 5
Little Missionary Sisters of Charity, 132
Little Work of Divine Providence, 131–132
Liturgy, differences over, 144–145
Los 36 Billares, 79
L'Osservatore Romano, 192
Loyalty Day, 33
Luanda, Angola, 37
Luciferian Schism, 139
Luján Virgin image, 63
Luna Park, Buenos Aires, 151
Luther, Martin, 136, 139, 142, 147
Lutheran churches, 149
Lutherans, 143

M

Macedonia, 142
Madonna, 33
Magister, Sandro, 93–94
Manzoni, Alessandro, 24, 25
Margarita, Rosa, 36
Martinez, Manuel Perez, 75
Martín García Island, 32
Martini, Carlo Maria, 94
Martino, Cardinal Rafaello, 101
Marxism, 4, 74, 76, 126, 187, 193
Mary (mother of Jesus), 144, 148, 157–158
Mary Help of Christians, 130
Massa, Lorenzo, 19–21
Matthew, Gospel of, 127
Mayol, Luis Felipe, 9
May Revolution homily (1998), 86–87
Mazzarollo, María Dominga, 130
"Meeting culture" concept, 70
Mein Kampf (Hitler), 4
Meir, Golda, 52
Menem, Carlos Saúl, 68, 86
Mennonites, 143
Messi, Lionel, 103
Messori, Vittorio, 95
Methodist churches, 149
Methodists, 143
Metropolitan Cathedral, 32, 54–55, 86
Mexico, 170, 174
Michetti, Gabriela, 92
Middle East, St. Francis of Assisi's trips to, 112
Mignone, Emilio Fermín, 81
Milvian Bridge, Battle of, 135
Minas Gerais, Brazil, 96
Minjung theology, 75
Minor Prophets, 85
Moldavia, 142
Montenegro, 142
Montesquieu, 37
Montoneros, 78, 79, 80, 81
Moors, the, 136
Morales, Evo, 179
Mormons, 143
Mothers of the Plaza de Mayo, 29, 30–31
Mother Theresa, 52

Movement of Priests for the Third World, 52, 61, 67–68, 75, 76
Mugica, Carlos, 61
Müller, Gerhard, 164
Musante, Roberto, 36–37
Muslims, 112, 116, 136–137, 150
Mussolini, Benito, 3, 4
Mysticism, 44

N

Nardín, Leonardo, 40–41
National Gendarmerie, 61
National Liberation Army, 75
National Socialist state concept, 4
Nativity scene, Christmas tradition of, 112–113
Navy School of Mechanics, 29
Nazi Party, 4, 43, 44, 137
Neoliberalism, 86, 88
Netherlands, the, 136, 142
Nicaragua, 77, 174, 178
Niger, birth rate in, 184
Nile Delta, 112
Niño, Gustavo, 30
Nobel Peace Prize (1930), 148
Northern Ireland, 136
Northern Kingdom of Israel, 85, 86
Norway, 160
Novation (priest), 139
Nuestra Palabra y Propósitos (Our World and Purposes), 39, 69
Nuestra Señora de Caacupé Church, 62
Nuns, 118

O

Ognénovich, Emilio, 46
Oil industry, in Venezuela, 178, 179
Once Tragedy, 62
Onganía, Juan Carlos, 77
Opus Dei, 150
Orange-Nassau, Calvinist family of, 136
Order of Friars Conventional (O.F.M. Conv.), 118
Order of Friars Minor (O.F.M.), 118
Order of Friars Minor Capuchin (O.F.M. Cap), 118

Order of Saint Clare, 118
Organization Command, 79
Orione, Luigi (Don Orione), 16–17, 129, 131–132
Ortega, Daniel, 179
Orthodox Church. *See* Eastern Orthodox Church
Orthodox Church of Alexandria, 141
Orthodox Church of Antioch, 141
Orthodox Church of Constantinople, 141
Orthodox Church of Jerusalem, 141
Ottomon Turks, 136–137
Our Lady of Aparecida Basilica Church, 96–97
Our Lady's Immaculate Conception statue, 96

P

Padre Hurtado, Chile, 39, 76
Página 12, 80, 81, 82
Panama, 77
Papal Basilica of Santa Maria Maggiore, 164
Papal bulls, 168
Papal conclave, 67, 71, 72, 93, 94–95, 100–102
Papal Infallibility, 71
Paraguay, 77, 130, 173, 174
Paraiba River, 96
"Passive schism," "active schism" vs., 138
Pastor Aeternus, 71
"Pastoralists," 101
Patagonia, 130
Patriarch of Belgrade, 141
Patriarch of Bucharest, 141
Patriarch of Constantinople, 146
Patriarch of Kiev, 142
Patriarch of Moscow, 141, 142, 146
Patriarch of Sophia, 141
Patriarch of Tiblisi, 141
Patriarchy, differences on authority of, 145
Paul III, Pope, 37
Paul V, Pope, 54
Paul VI, Pope, 52, 126
Paul VI Audience Hall, 108
Peasant theology, 75

Pedophilia, 162–164
Peninsular War, 169
Pentacostalists, 143, 148
"The People Came from the South" (Pigna), 33
People's Liberation Army (China), 189
Pepe, Father, 60, 61
Pérez, Carlos Andrés, 178
Perón, Isabel, 67, 71, 80
Perón, Juan Domingo, 31–34, 32, 67, 69, 79, 80
Perón, María Eva Duarte de (Evita), 31, 34
Peronism, 31–34, 67–68, 69–71, 77, 79
Perpetual Virginity of Mary, doctrine of, 144
Peter (apostle), 145, 147
Peter, Saint, 140–141
Petrine texts, 145
Philippines, 75, 176
Photian Schism, 139
Piazza Ungheria, 47
Piedmont, Italy, 3, 16–17, 133
Pigna, Felipe, 33
Pilgrimages
    to Aparecida, Brazil, 96–97
    to Franciscan sanctuary, 112
    to Luján, 63
    of Saint Francis of Assisi to the East, 112, 116
Piñon, Francisco ("Cacho"), 79
Pius X, Pope, 71
Pius XI, Pope, 63, 71, 126, 131
Pius XII, Pope, 71, 131
Pizarro, Francisco, 168
Plaza de Mayo, 32, 33, 34, 69
Poland, 142
Polish Orthodox Church, 141, 142
Politics. *see also* Peronism
    Chávism, 178–179
    Communism, 68–69
    Cuban, 175–177
    Iron Guard, 78–80
    Kirchners-Francis relationship, 90–92
    liberation theology, 74–75
    Peronism, 67–68, 69–71, 77, 79
    Yorio and Jalics kidnapping case, 80–83
    youth involvement in (1960s), 77–78

Pontecurone, Italy, 16, 131
Ponte de San Giovanni, Battle of, 109
Pontifical Commission for Latin
    America, 81
Pontifical Council for Interreligious
    Dialogue, 150
Pontifical Council for Promoting
    Christian Unity, 149
"Poor Clares" order of Franciscans, 118
Pope
    in hierarchical structure, 192
    infallibility and authority of, 144,
        147, 149
    role of, East-West Schism and, 139
Pope Francis: His Life in His Own Words
    (Rubin/Ambrogetti), 82, 83
Populorum Progressio (Development of
    Peoples) encyclical, 126
Portacomaro, Italy, 3, 7
Portiroli, Tatiana, 62
Portugal, 86, 167, 168
Potreros, 21
Poverty
    access to education and, 125
    Aparecida Document on, 98
    Base Communities, 74
    in Chile, 76–77
    Church's role in overcoming causes
        and effects of, 125–127
    defined, 123–124
    during economic recession, 1998-
        2002, 88
    Francis' first experience with, 123
    Francis' inspirations for working with,
        129–132
    Francis' position on material and
        spiritual, 127–129
    liberation theology and, 74–76
    life expectancy/infant mortality and,
        124
    name of Pope Francis and, 114–115
    prevalence in Latin America, 173–174
    Saint Francis of Assisi's theology and,
        75–76
    Second Vatican Council and, 72–73, 74
    spiritual, 127, 128
    winning the war against, 133–134

Pozzoli, Father Enrique, 36
Presbyterians, 143
The Priest Lorenzo (film), 22
Priests/priesthood
    celibacy, 145, 147, 157
    commitment to, 156–157
    Leadership Conference of Women
        Religious (LCWR), 118
    Protestant-Catholic differences on,
        147–148
    women's role in, 157–158
    Principessa Mafalda (ship), 7, 8–15
Pro Eligendo Pontifice, 48
Protestantism/Protestants, 136, 142–143,
    147–148, 150
Protestant Reformation, 136, 139–140
Provincial of Argentina's Society of Jesus, 42
Public Consistory, 47
Puerto Rico, 175, 176
Purgatory, 144

Q
Quarracino, Antonio (cardinal), 47, 49
Querandies tribe, 54
Quiroga, Estela, 23–24

R
Radio del Estado (Radio Nacional), 23
"Rassa Nostrana" (Costa), 57
Ratzinger, Joseph, 80, 94, 95, 193. see also
    Benedict XVI, Pope
The Ratzinger Report (Messori), 95
Reagan, Ronald, 193
"Red Front," 79
Reformed Christians, 143
Reformed churches, 149
Rega, José López, 80
Regular Franciscans, 118
Religious conflict, 135–137
Religious vocation, 156–157
Rerum Novarum (Of New Things)
    encyclical, 126, 127
Restrepo, Camilo Torres, 75
Ricci, Mateo, 79
Roman Catholic Church. See Catholic
    Church

Roman Curia, 192

Roman Empire, 4, 145, 193. *see also* Holy Roman Empire

Romania, 142

Romanian Orthodox Church, 141

Romero, Oscar, 75

Romero, Walter, 79

Roosevelt, Teddy, 189

Rossi, Ángel, 45–46

Rothenfels Castle, 44

Rousseff, Dilma, 103

Rubin, Sergio, 82

Russian Orthodox Church, 141, 187–188

Russia/Russian Federation, 142, 183, 184, 186–187, 195

S

Sacrament of Ordination, 147

Sacrament of Reconciliation, 35

Sacraments, 144–145

Saint Bartholomew's Day Massacre of 1572, 136

Saint Damian Chapel, 109

Saint Peter's Basilica, 48

Saints, originating in Piedmont, Italy region, 16–17. *see also* individual names of saints

Salesian Chapel of San Antonio de Padua, 19, 20

Salesian Order, 16, 37, 130, 131

Salesian mission, Angola, 37

Salvation, Protestant-Catholic differences on, 147

Samaria, Kingdom of, 85

Same-sex marriage, 92, 160–162, 179

San Antonio de Padua Chapel. See Chapel of San Antonio de Padua

Sanctuary of Saint Cayetano, 64

Sandri, Cardinal Leonardo, 81

Sanguinetti, Julio María, 68

San José Church, 42

Sankt Georgen Jesuit community, Frankfurt, Germany, 43

San Lorenzo, 22

San Lorenzo de Almagro soccer team, 20–22, 25–26

San Martin, José de, 172

San Pablo parish, Buenos Aires, 29

San Patricio Church, 91

San Remo, Italy, 132

San Roberto Belarmino, 47

Santa Cruz Church, Buenos Aires, 29, 30, 31

Santiago, Chile, 39

Santo porteño, 64

São Vicente, 10

Scandinavia, 142, 143

Scherer, Cardinal Odilo, 101

Schism, concept of, 138

Schism of the Three Chapters, 139

Schisms within Christian Church, 138–140

Schmalkaldic War (1546-1547), 136

School of Theology at Colegio Maximo de San Jose, 41

Science, 155–156

Scola, Angelo, 101

Scotland, 142, 148

Scriptures, authority in, 147

Second Council of Lyons, 139

Second Vatican Council, 52, 71, 72–74, 149

Secretariat for Non-Christians, 150

Secular Franciscans, 118

Sede Vacante (Vacant Seat), 100

Segni, Ricardo, 151

Segundo, Juan Luis, 75

Seminary of Villa Barilari, 42

September 11th terrorist attacks, 96

Serbia, 142

Serbian Orthodox Church, 141

Sievernich, Michael, 44

Sigampa, Fabriciano, 92

Silva, Luiz Inácio Lula da, 68

Singapore, 124

Sistine Chapel, 48, 49, 72, 101

Sívori, Francesco, 36

Sivori, Regina María, 16, 19

Skorka, Rabbi Abraham, 98, 150–151

Slavery, 132, 168–169, 170

Slums, 47, 58–61

Sobre el Cielo y la Tierra (On Heaven and Earth), 127

Soccer team (Lorenzo de Almagro), 20–22, 25–26

Socialism, 70, 176, 178–179

Society of Jesus (Jesuits). See Jesuits
(Society of Jesus)
Society of St. Francis de Sales, 16
Society's Educational Networks, 117
Söderblom, Nathan, 148
Sola fide (by faith alone), 147
Sola scriptura (by scripture alone)
concept, 147
Solicitudo Rei Socialis (Concern for the
Social Order) encyclical, 126–127
Somalo, Cardinal Camarlengo Eduardo
Martínez, 48
Sons of Divine Providence, 17
South Africa, 75
South Sudan, 125
Soviet Union, 141–142, 177, 187
Spain, 86, 111, 160, 167, 169
Spanish-American War, 175–176
Spiritual poverty, 127, 128
St. Francis of Assisi, A Biography
(Englebert), 108
Stockholm International Peace Research
Institute (SIPRI), 184
Stratfor, 187
Sultan of Damascus, 112
Sultan of Egypt, 112
Sweden, 160
Swedish Lutheran Church, 148
Swiss Church, 140
Switzerland, 142
Syria, 112, 142, 179

T
Tauran, Jean Louis, 107
Technology, 155–156
Te Deum ceremony, 151
Te Deum message (1998), 86–87
Te Deum message (2000), 89
Te Deum message (2003), 90
Thatcher, Margaret, 103, 193
Third World Priests. See Movement of
Priests for the Third World
Thirty Years' War (1614-1648), 136
Titular Bishop of the Diocese of Auca in
the Buenos Aires Cathedral, 46–47
Tobin, Joseph, 118

Tornielli, Andrea, 95
Transparency International, 174
Treaty of Tordesillas, 168
Treaty of Versailles, 4
Trimarco, Susana, 59
Tupí-Guaraní ethnic group, 173
Turkemenistan, 142
Twelve Prophets, 85
Twenty-First Century Socialism, 178–179

U
Uganda, 142
Ukraine, 142, 146
Ukrainian Autocephalous Orthodox
Church, 142
Ukrainian Greek Catholic Church, 146
Ukrainian Orthodox Church, 142
Unemployment rate, 87–88
Unión Cívica Radical Party, 88
Union of Brest, 146
Unitatis Redintegratio Decree on
Ecumenism, 149
United Nations Department of Economic
and Social Affairs, 124
United Nations Economic Commission
for Latin America and the Caribbean
(CEPAL), 174
United Nations Office on Crime and
Drugs, 175
United Nations' Population Division, 124
United States
birth rate in, 184
Cuba and, 175, 176
economic success in, 115
free trade treaties of, 97
global role, 184–185, 191
in new world order, 195
same-sex marriage in, 160
Universidad Alcalá de Henares, 42
Universidad de Buenos Aires, 77
Universidad de El Salvador, 38
Universidad del Salvador, 44, 77, 78, 79
Universidad Nacional de la Matanza, 162
University National Concentration, 79
University of Berlin, 43–44
University system, in Argentina, 44–45

Urbi et Orbi blessing, 102
Uruguay, 68, 160, 179
    Salesian Order in, 130
Utrecth Schism, 140
Ut Unum Sint (That They May Be One)
    encyclical, 149
Uzbekistan, 142

V
Vargas, Getulio, 68
Vasallo, Rosa Margherita, 3, 4–8
Vatican Bank, 104, 194
Vatican chief of state, 146
Venezuela, 77, 97, 174, 178, 179
Veni Creator Spiritus, 48
Verbitsky, Horacio, 81, 82, 83
Verón, María de los Ángeles, 59
Versailles, Treaty of, 4
Vicaria Episcopal para la Pastoral en
    Villas de Emergencia, 58
Victor Emmanuel III, King, 4
Videla, Jorge Rafael, 52
Villa 1-11-14, Buenos Aires, 58, 61–62, 81
Villa 21-21, Buenos Aires, 60
Villa 21-24, Buenos Aires, 60, 61
Villaflor, Azucena, 31
Villas miserias, 175
Virgin Mary, 63, 144, 148
Voltaire, 37

W
Walesa, Lech, 193
War, 132–133
Wars of the Three Kingdoms, 136
Weber, Andrew Lloyd, 33
Week of Prayer for Christian Unity, 148
Western Schism (1378-1417), 139
Women
    Mary Help of Christians (Salesian
        Order), 130
    in Pope Francis' life, 23–25
    role in society and in the church,
        157–158
    sacraments and, 147
    Salesian Order of, 130
    St. Clare of Assisi and, 118

World Bank, 124, 133–134, 189
World Council of Churches, 148
World Population Prospect 2010 report,
    124
World War I, 186
World War II, 137, 186, 187
World Youth Day, 103

Y
Yorio, Father Orlando, 80–83

Z
Zanetti, Javier "Pupi," 103
Zechariah, 85
Zorzín, Victor, 45